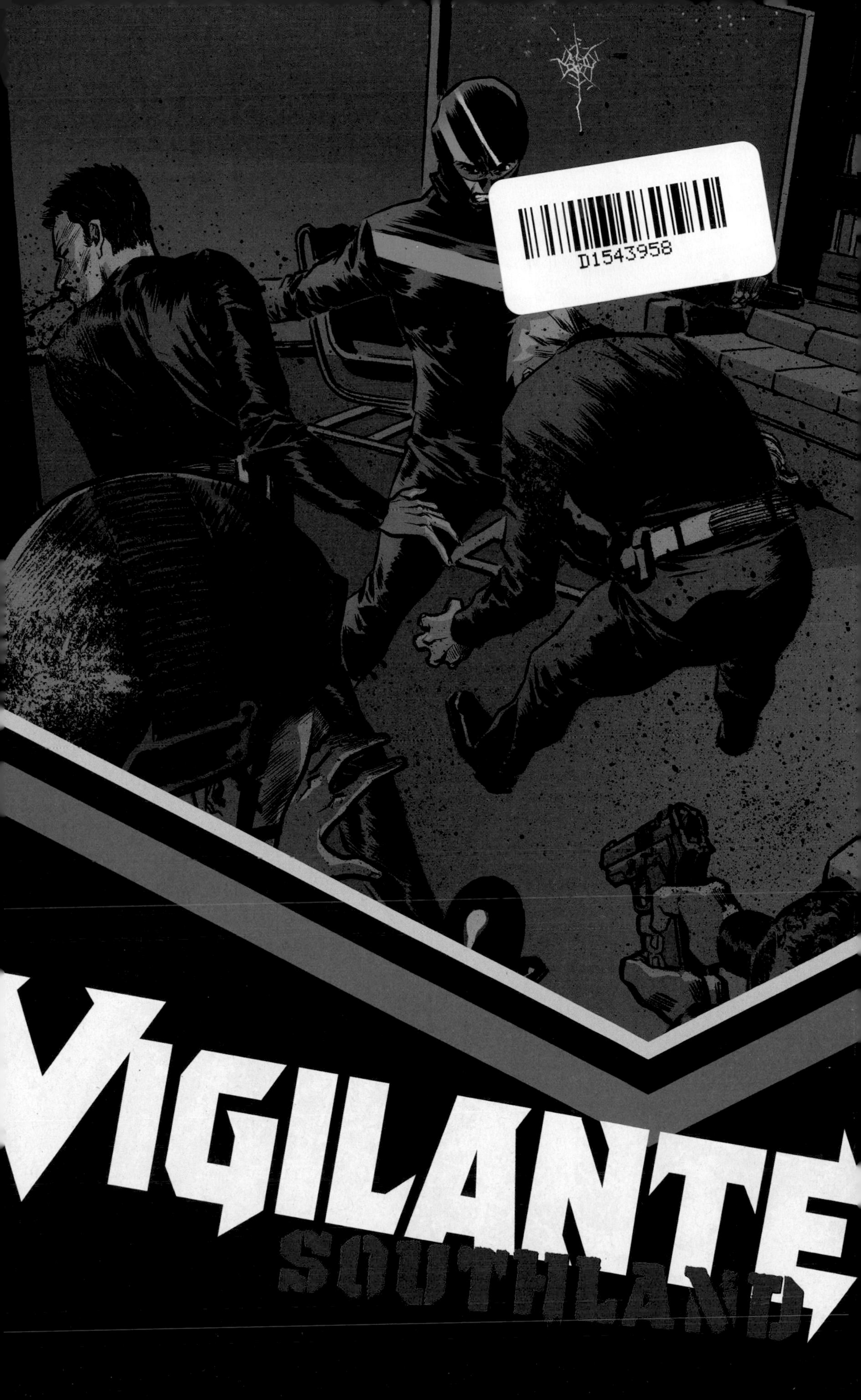
VIGILANTE
SOUTHLAND

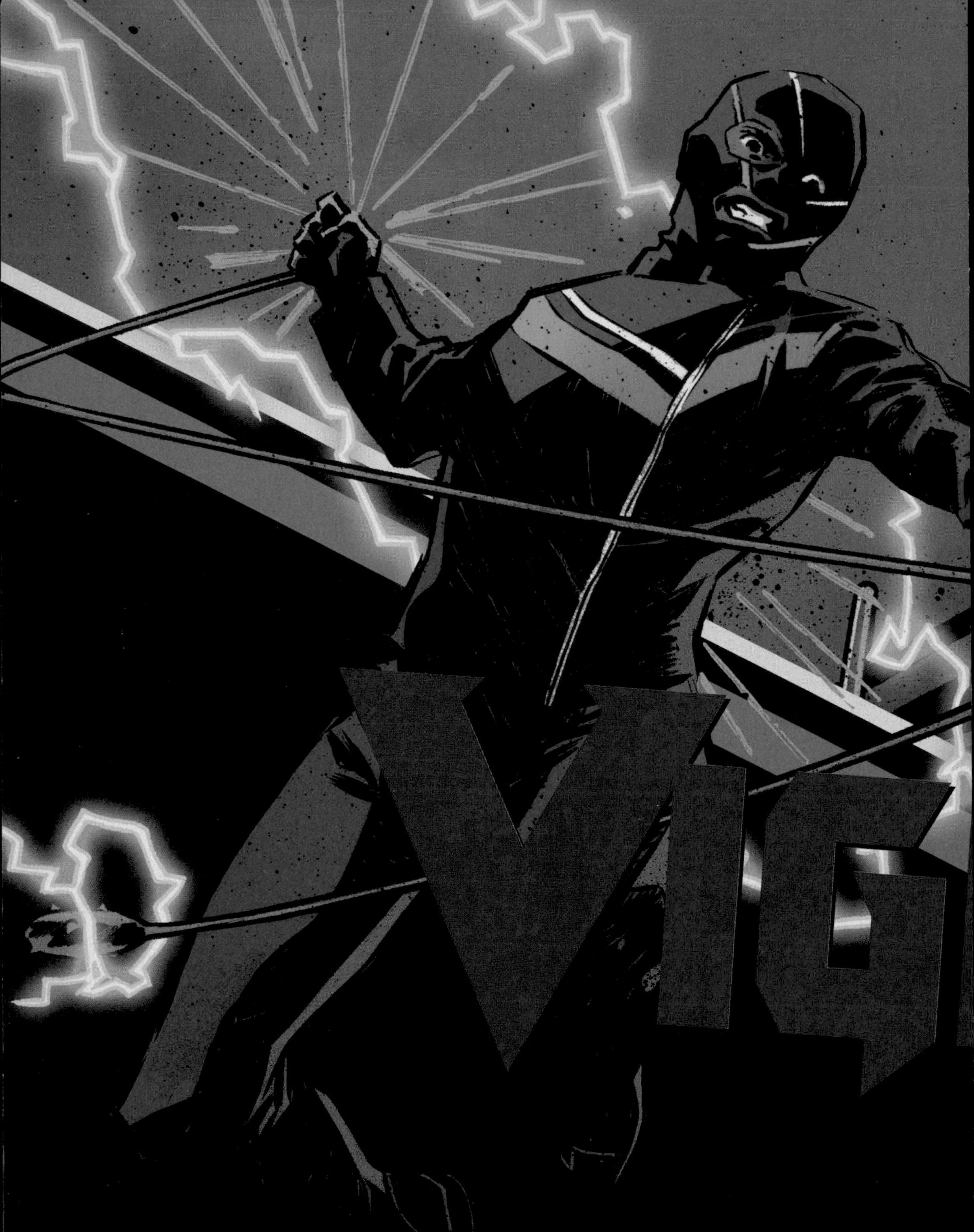
VIG

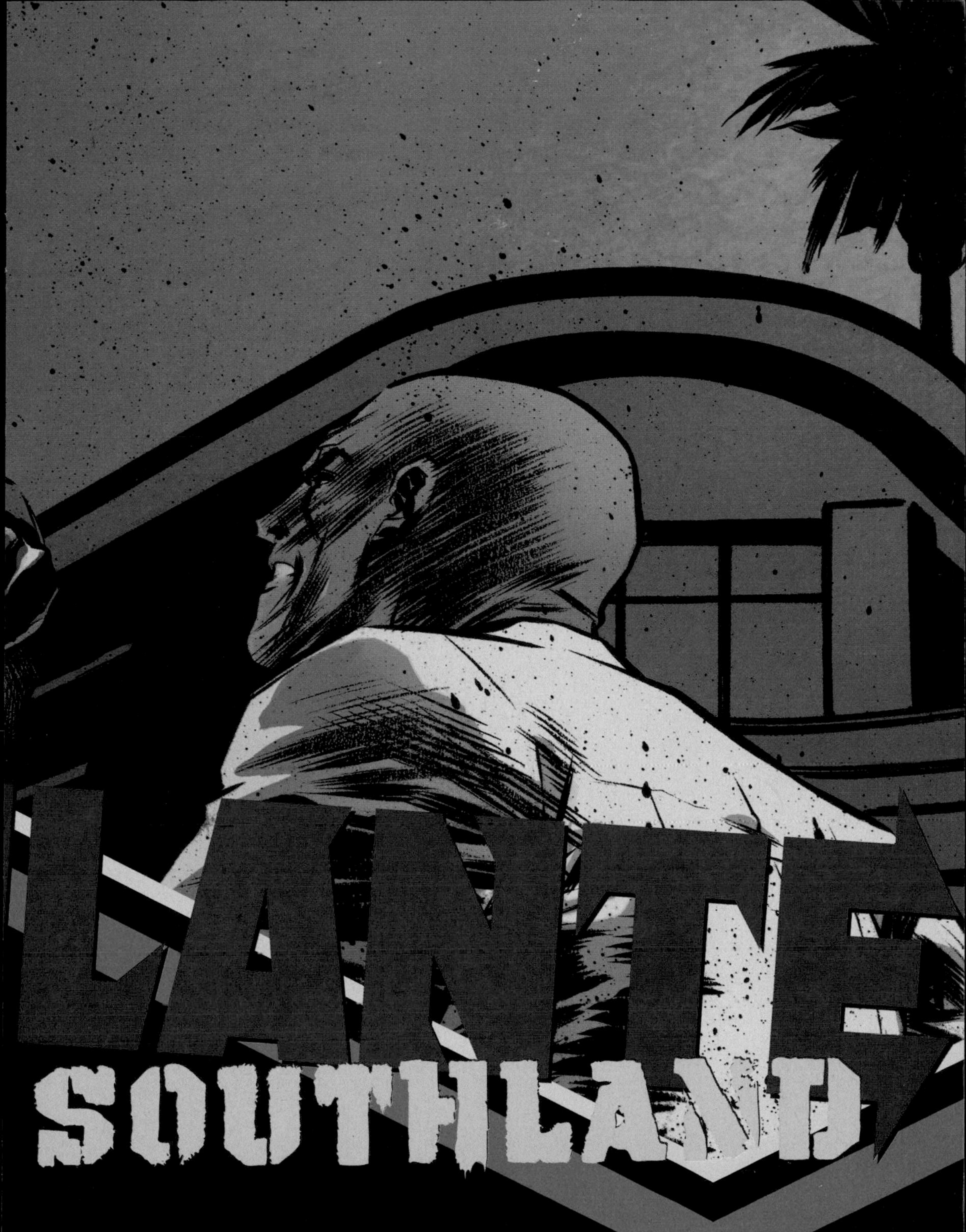
LANTE
SOUTHLAND

GARY PHILLIPS
WRITER

ELENA CASAGRANDE
ARTIST

MORITAT
ADDITIONAL ART

GIULIA BRUSCO
COLORIST

TODD KLEIN
LETTERER

MITCH GERADS
COVER ARTIST

JAMIE S. RICH *Editor – Original Series*
JEB WOODARD *Group Editor – Collected Editions*
ROBIN WILDMAN *Editor – Collected Edition*
STEVE COOK *Design Director – Books*
CURTIS KING JR. *Publication Design*
BOB HARRAS *Senior VP – Editor-in-Chief, DC Comics*
PAT McCALLUM *Executive Editor, DC Comics*

DIANE NELSON *President*
DAN DiDIO *Publisher*
JIM LEE *Publisher*
GEOFF JOHNS *President & Chief Creative Officer*
AMIT DESAI *Executive VP – Business & Marketing Strategy, Direct to Consumer & Global Franchise Management*
SAM ADES *Senior VP & General Manager, Digital Services*
BOBBIE CHASE *VP & Executive Editor, Young Reader & Talent Development*

MARK CHIARELLO *Senior VP – Art, Design & Collected Editions*
JOHN CUNNINGHAM *Senior VP – Sales & Trade Marketing*
ANNE DePIES *Senior VP – Business Strategy, Finance & Administration*
DON FALLETTI *VP – Manufacturing Operations*
LAWRENCE GANEM *VP – Editorial Administration & Talent Relations*
ALISON GILL *Senior VP – Manufacturing & Operations*
HANK KANALZ *Senior VP – Editorial Strategy & Administration*
JAY KOGAN *VP – Legal Affairs*
JACK MAHAN *VP – Business Affairs*
NICK J. NAPOLITANO *VP – Manufacturing Administration*
EDDIE SCANNELL *VP – Consumer Marketing*
COURTNEY SIMMONS *Senior VP – Publicity & Communications*
JIM (SKI) SOKOLOWSKI *VP – Comic Book Specialty Sales & Trade Marketing*
NANCY SPEARS *VP – Mass, Book, Digital Sales & Trade Marketing*
MICHELE R. WELLS *VP – Content Strategy*

VIGILANTE: SOUTHLAND

Published by DC Comics. Compilation, VIGILANTE: SOUTHLAND 4-6 and all new material Copyright © 2018 DC Comics. All Rights Reserved.

Originally published in single magazine form in VIGILANTE: SOUTHLAND 1-3. Copyright © 2016, 2017 DC Comics. All Rights Reserved. All characters, their distinctive likenesses and related elements featured in this publication are trademarks of DC Comics. The stories, characters and incidents featured in this publication are entirely fictional. DC Comics does not read or accept unsolicited submissions of ideas, stories or artwork.

DC Comics, 2900 West Alameda Ave., Burbank, CA 91505
Printed by Vanguard Graphics, LLC, Ithaca, NY, USA. 12/29/17. First Printing.
ISBN: 978-1-4012-6873-2

Library of Congress Cataloging-in-Publication Data is available.

FSC
www.fsc.org

MIX
Paper from
responsible sources
FSC® C016956

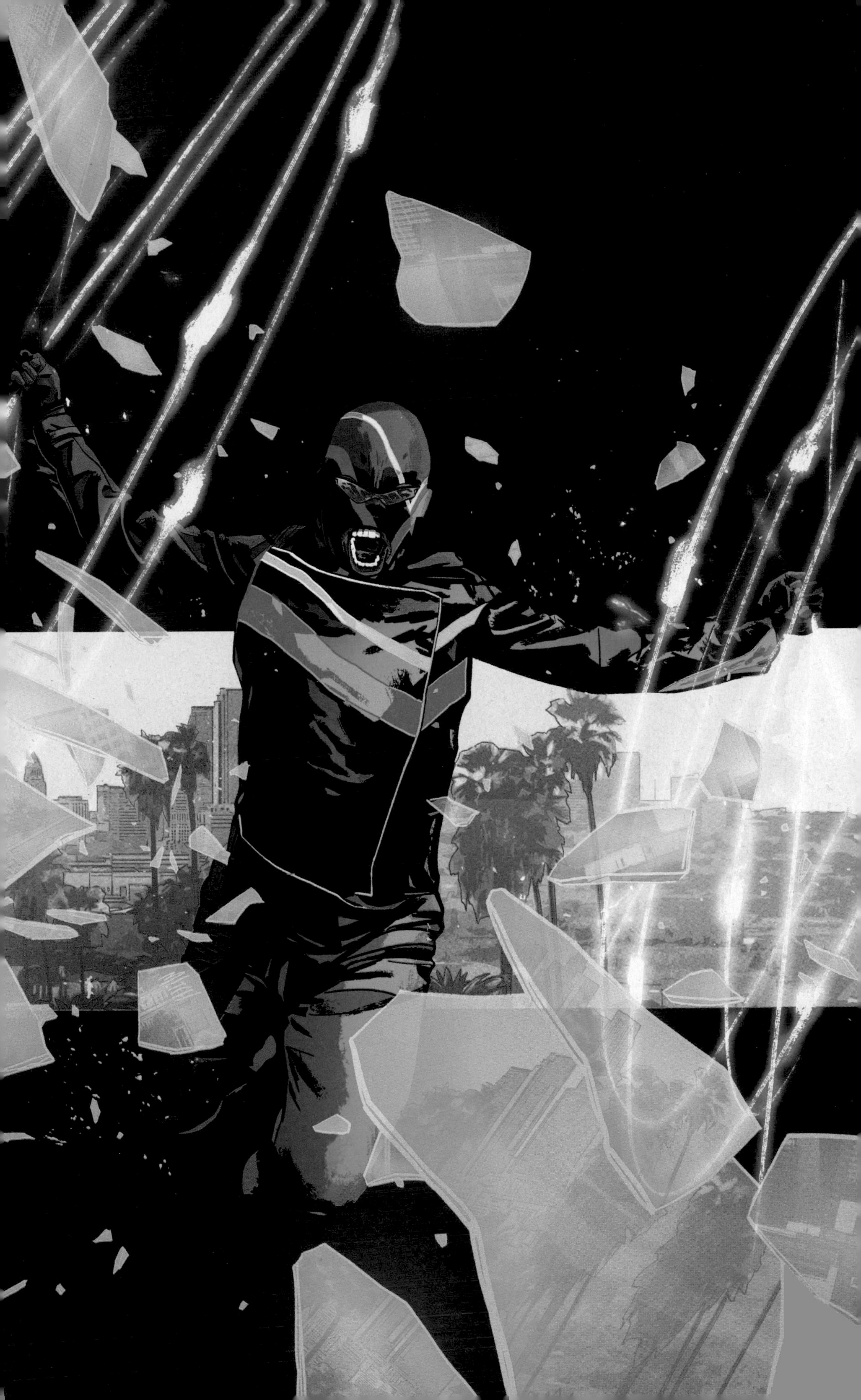

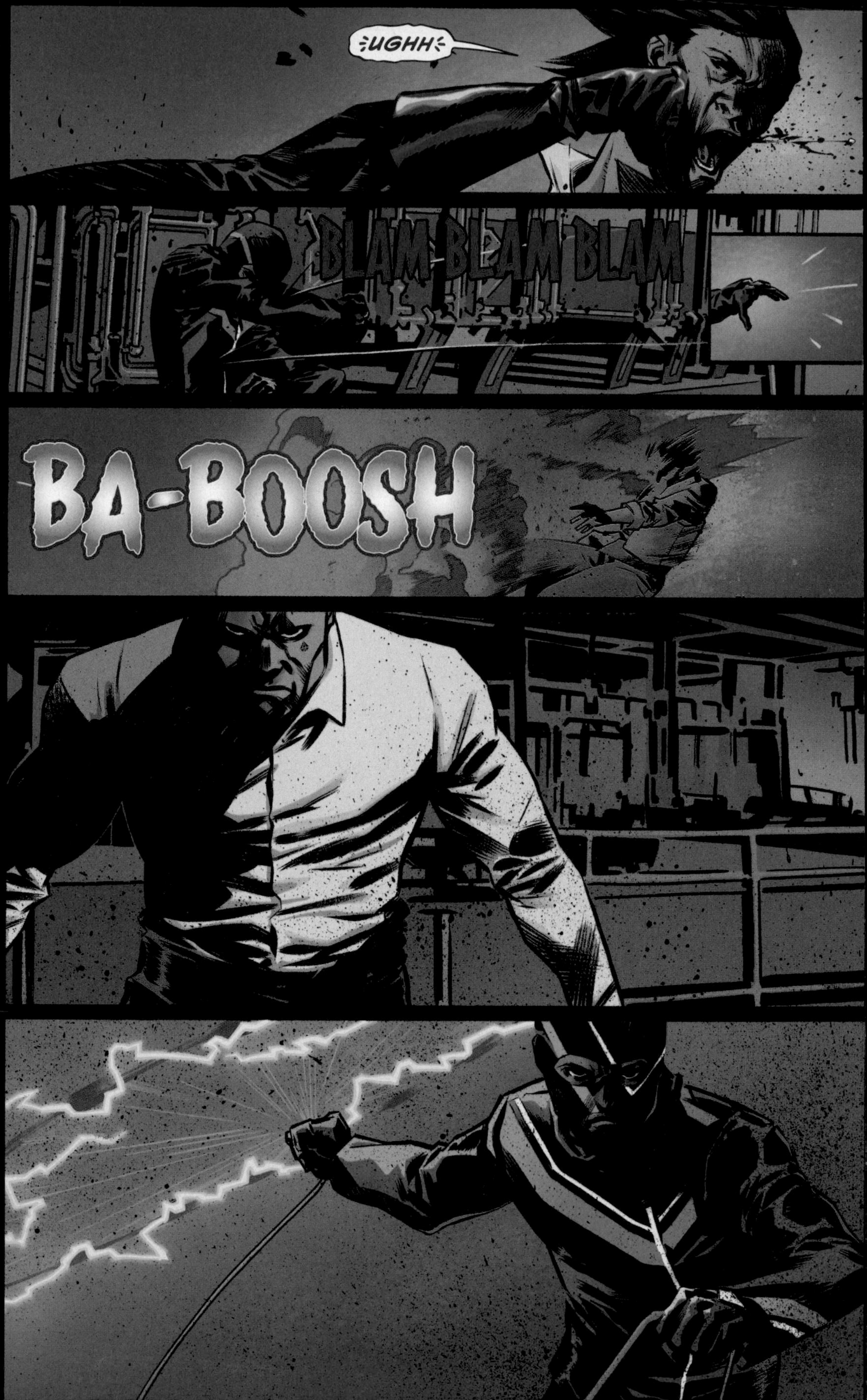
UGHH
BLAM BLAM BLAM
BA-BOOSH

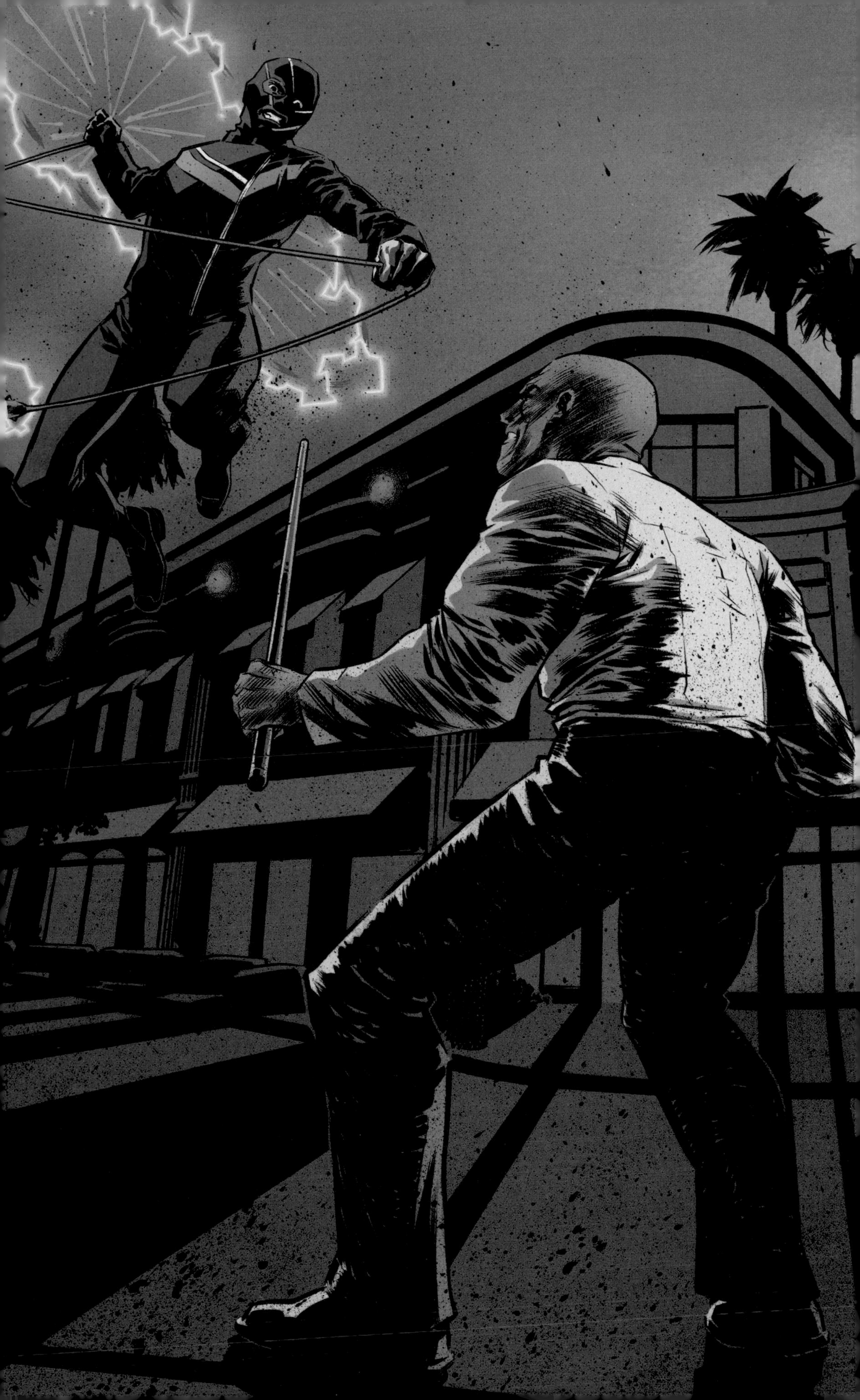

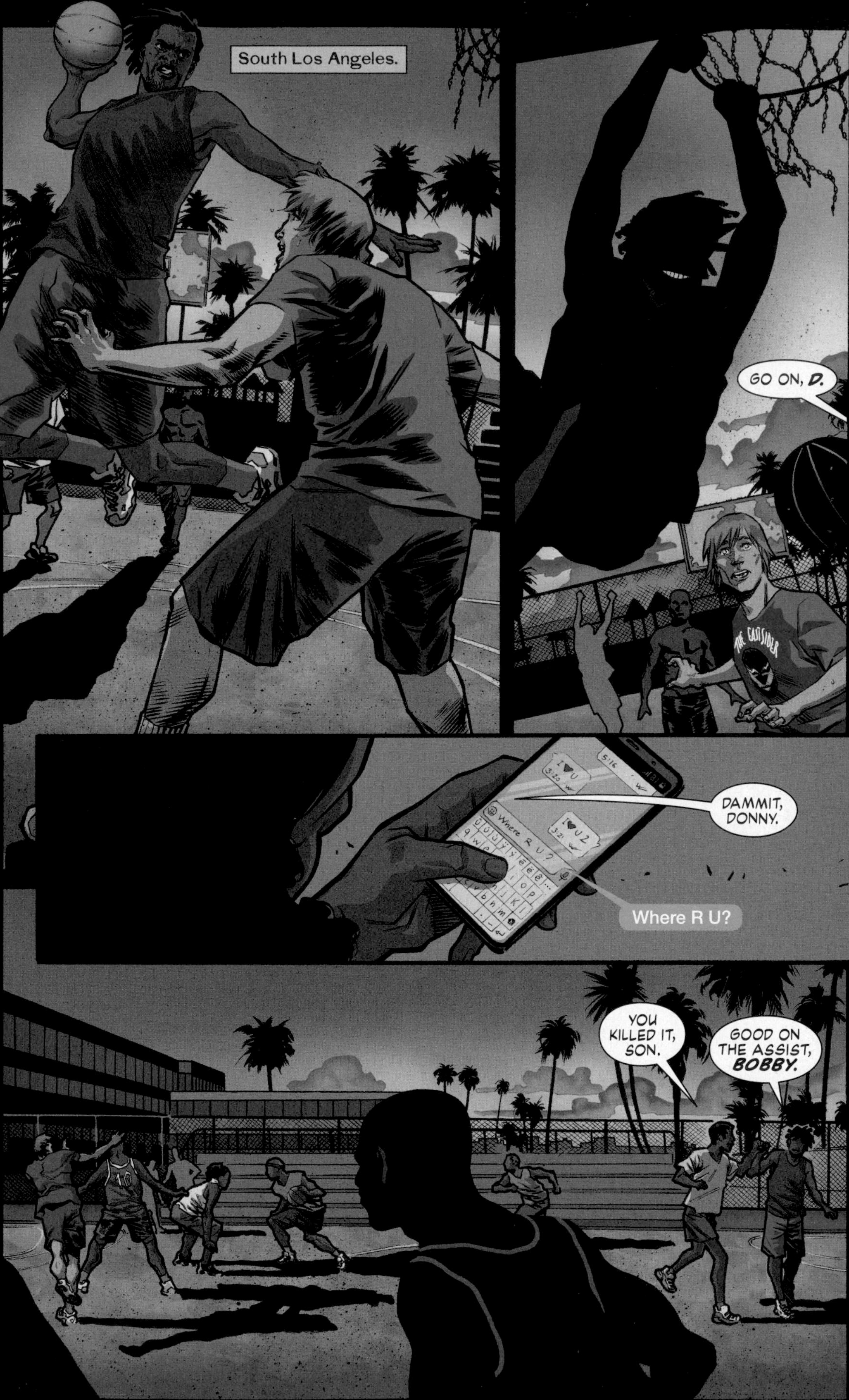
South Los Angeles.
GO ON, D.
DAMMIT, DONNY.
Where R U?
YOU KILLED IT, SON.
GOOD ON THE ASSIST, BOBBY.

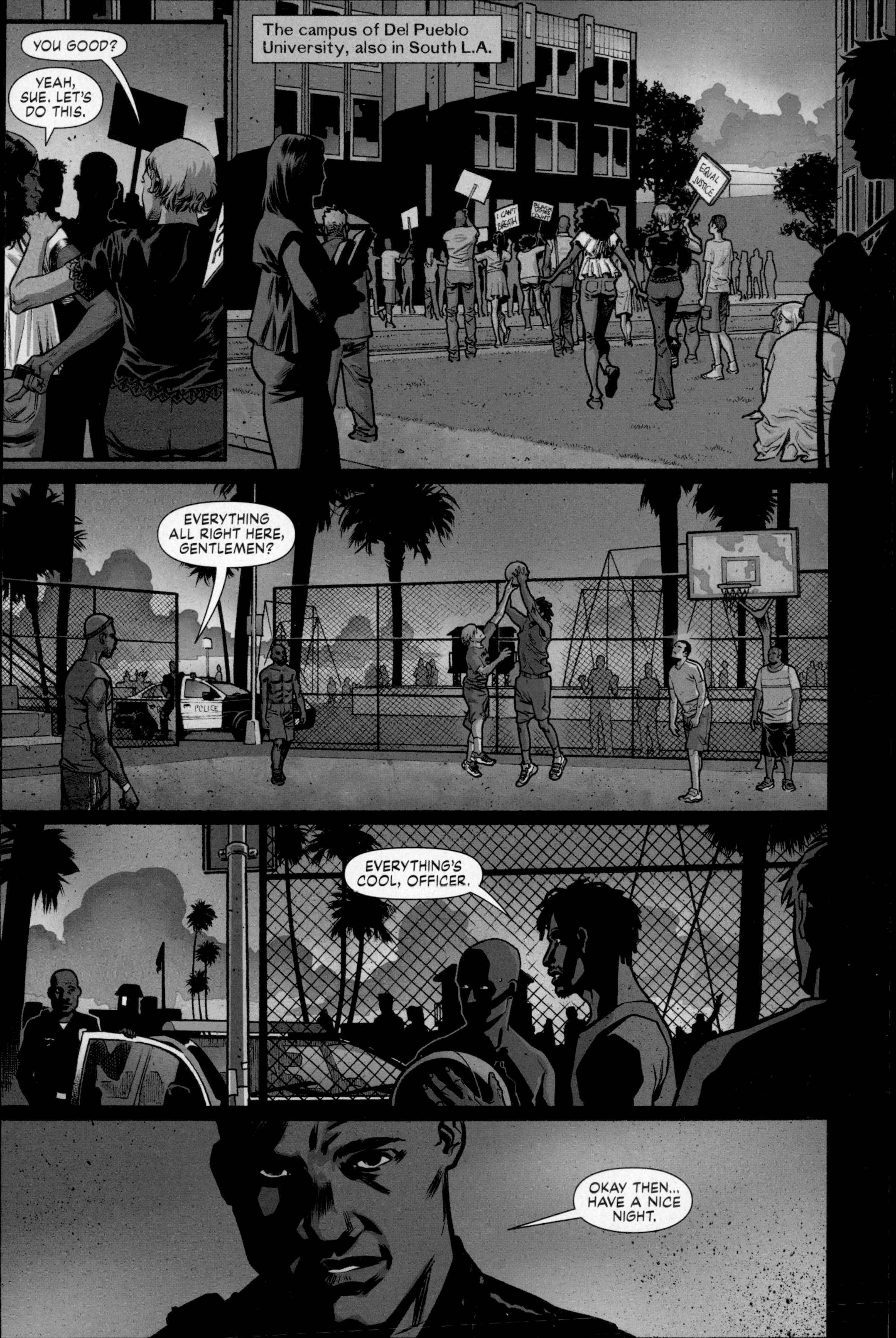
YOU GOOD?
YEAH, SUE. LET'S DO THIS.
The campus of Del Pueblo University, also in South L.A.
I CAN'T BREATH
BLACK LIVES COUNT
EQUAL JUSTICE
EVERYTHING ALL RIGHT HERE, GENTLEMEN?
POLICE
EVERYTHING'S COOL, OFFICER.
OKAY THEN... HAVE A NICE NIGHT.

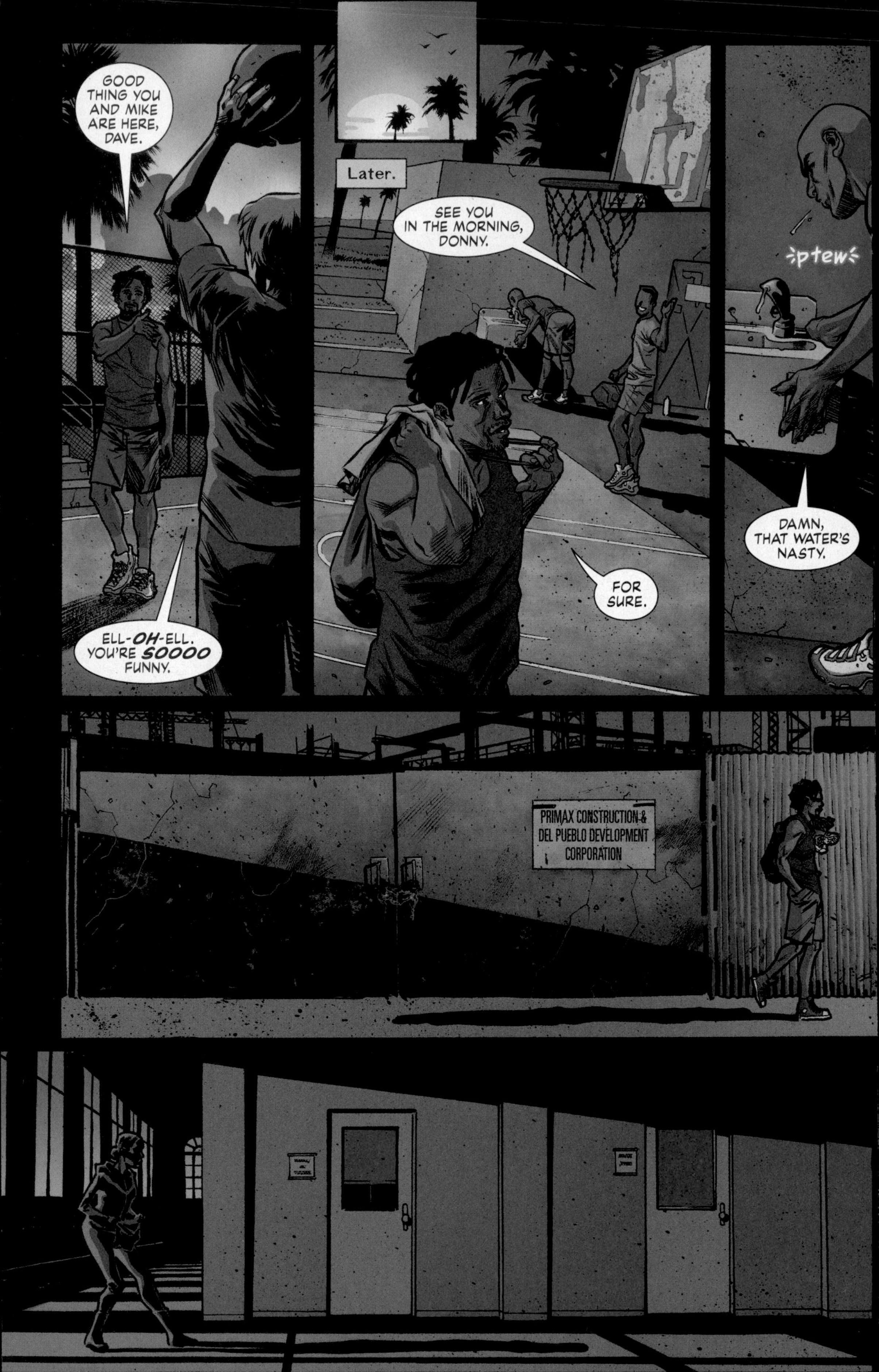
GOOD THING YOU AND MIKE ARE HERE, DAVE.
ELL-OH-ELL. YOU'RE SOOOO FUNNY.
Later.
SEE YOU IN THE MORNING, DONNY.
FOR SURE.
ptew
DAMN, THAT WATER'S NASTY.
PRIMAX CONSTRUCTION & DEL PUEBLO DEVELOPMENT CORPORATION

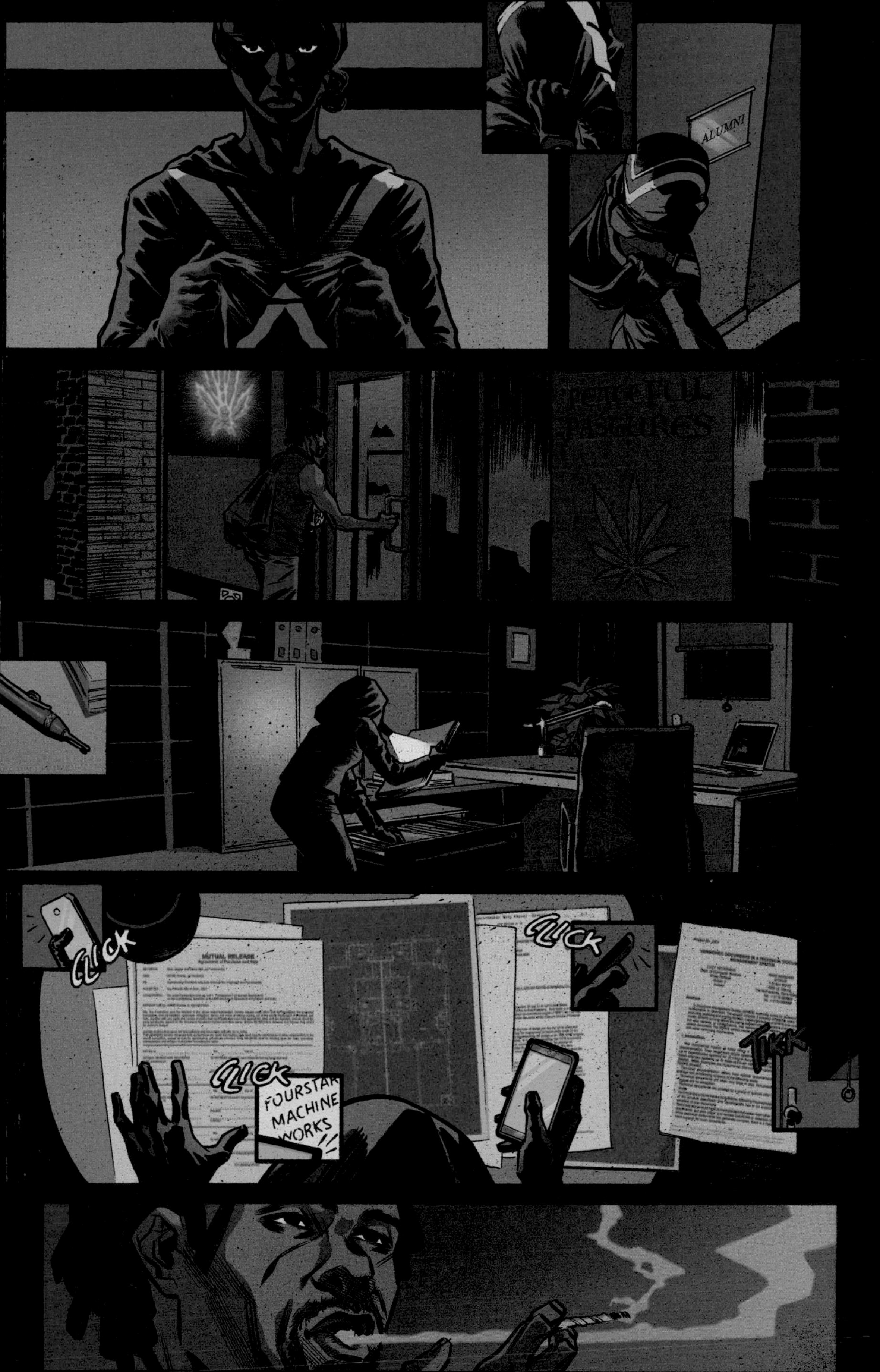
ALUMNI
PEACEFUL PASTURES
CLICK
MUTUAL RELEASE
CLICK
CLICK
FOURSTAR MACHINE WORKS
TIKK

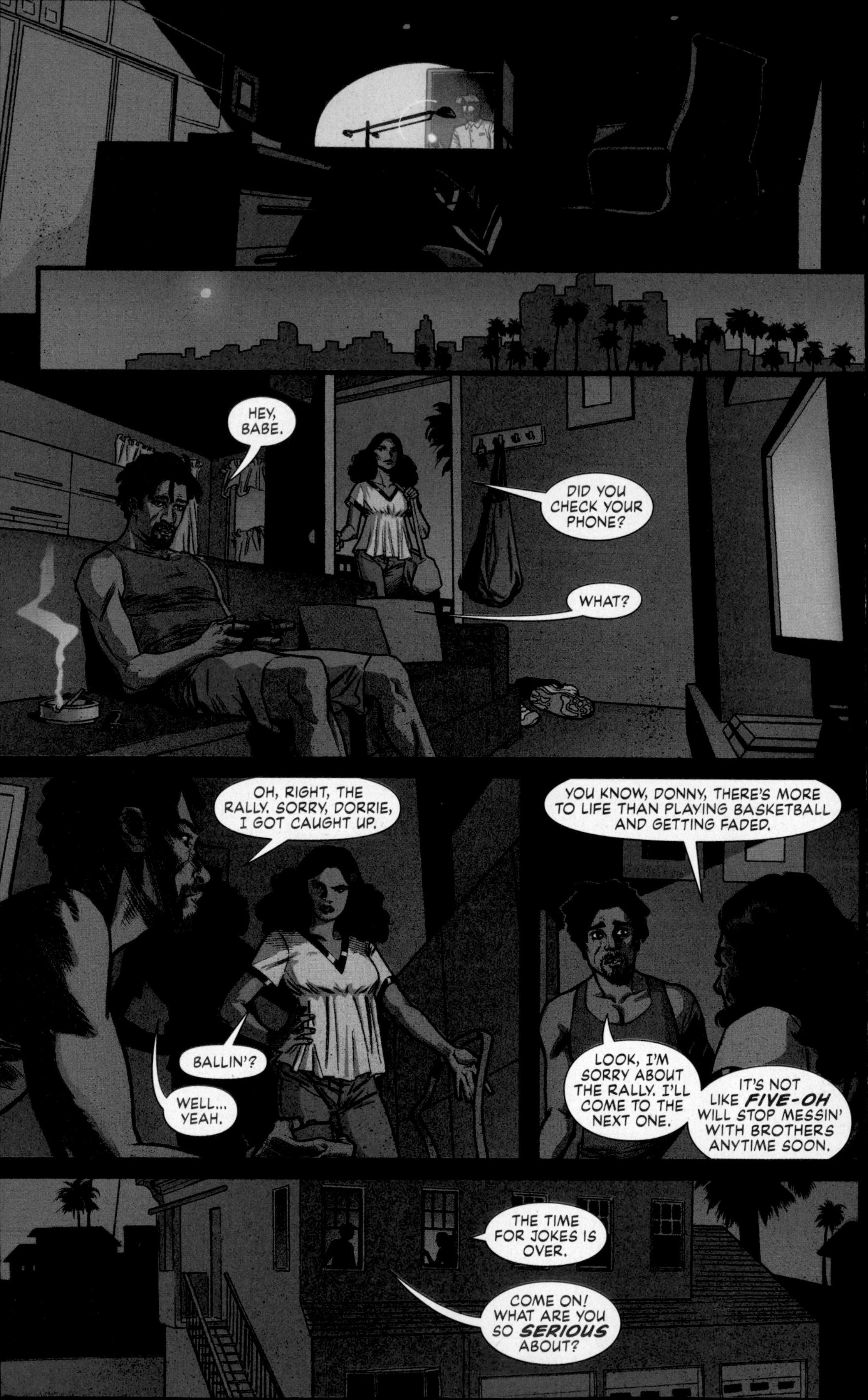
HEY, BABE.
DID YOU CHECK YOUR PHONE?
WHAT?
OH, RIGHT, THE RALLY. SORRY, DORRIE, I GOT CAUGHT UP.
BALLIN'?
WELL... YEAH.
YOU KNOW, DONNY, THERE'S MORE TO LIFE THAN PLAYING BASKETBALL AND GETTING FADED.
LOOK, I'M SORRY ABOUT THE RALLY. I'LL COME TO THE NEXT ONE.
IT'S NOT LIKE *FIVE-OH* WILL STOP MESSIN' WITH BROTHERS ANYTIME SOON.
THE TIME FOR JOKES IS OVER.
COME ON! WHAT ARE YOU SO *SERIOUS* ABOUT?

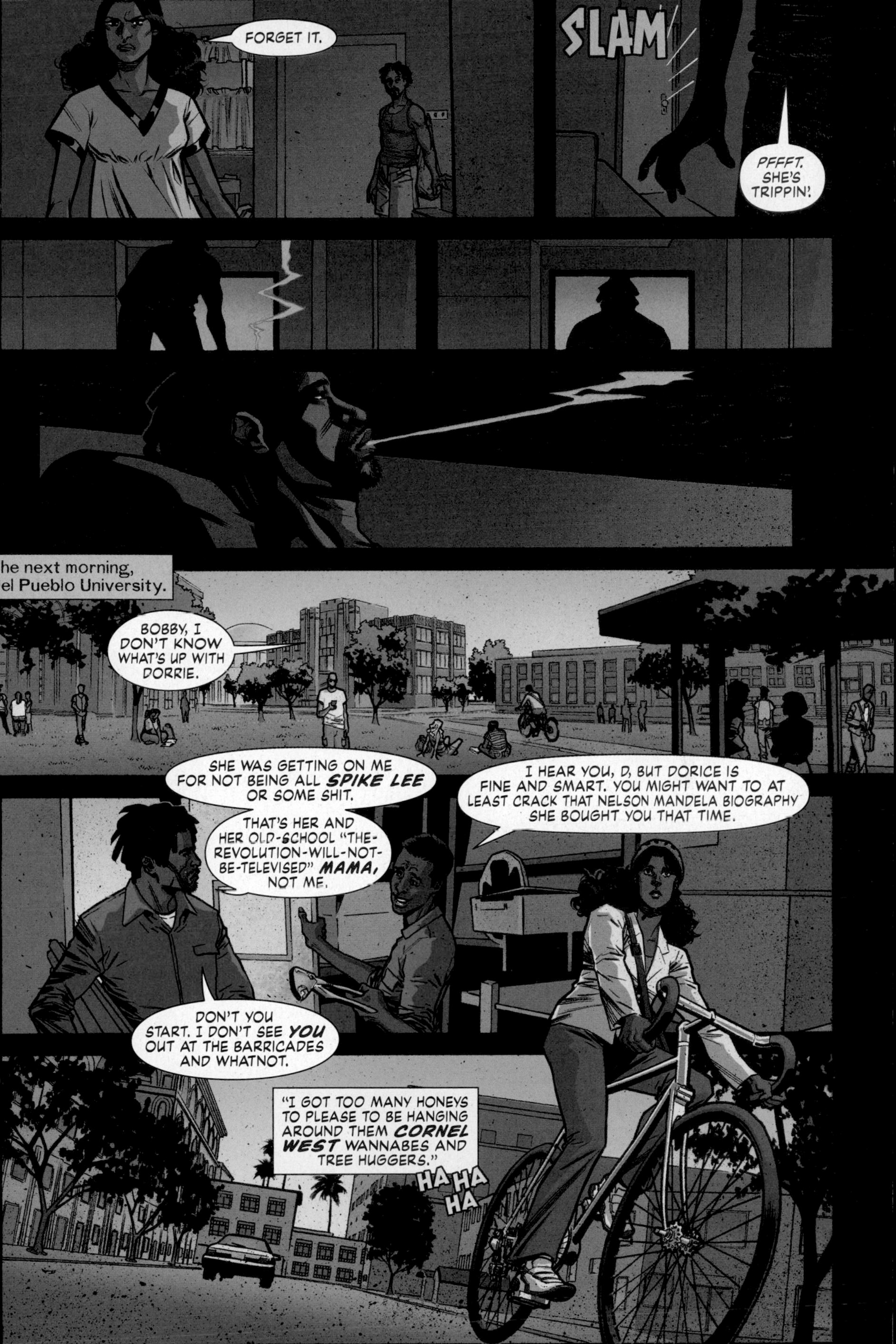
FORGET IT.
SLAM
PFFFT. SHE'S TRIPPIN'.
he next morning,
el Pueblo University.
BOBBY, I DON'T KNOW WHAT'S UP WITH DORRIE.
SHE WAS GETTING ON ME FOR NOT BEING ALL SPIKE LEE OR SOME SHIT.
THAT'S HER AND HER OLD-SCHOOL "THE-REVOLUTION-WILL-NOT-BE-TELEVISED" MAMA, NOT ME.
I HEAR YOU, D, BUT DORICE IS FINE AND SMART. YOU MIGHT WANT TO AT LEAST CRACK THAT NELSON MANDELA BIOGRAPHY SHE BOUGHT YOU THAT TIME.
DON'T YOU START. I DON'T SEE YOU OUT AT THE BARRICADES AND WHATNOT.
"I GOT TOO MANY HONEYS TO PLEASE TO BE HANGING AROUND THEM CORNEL WEST WANNABES AND TREE HUGGERS."
HA HA HA

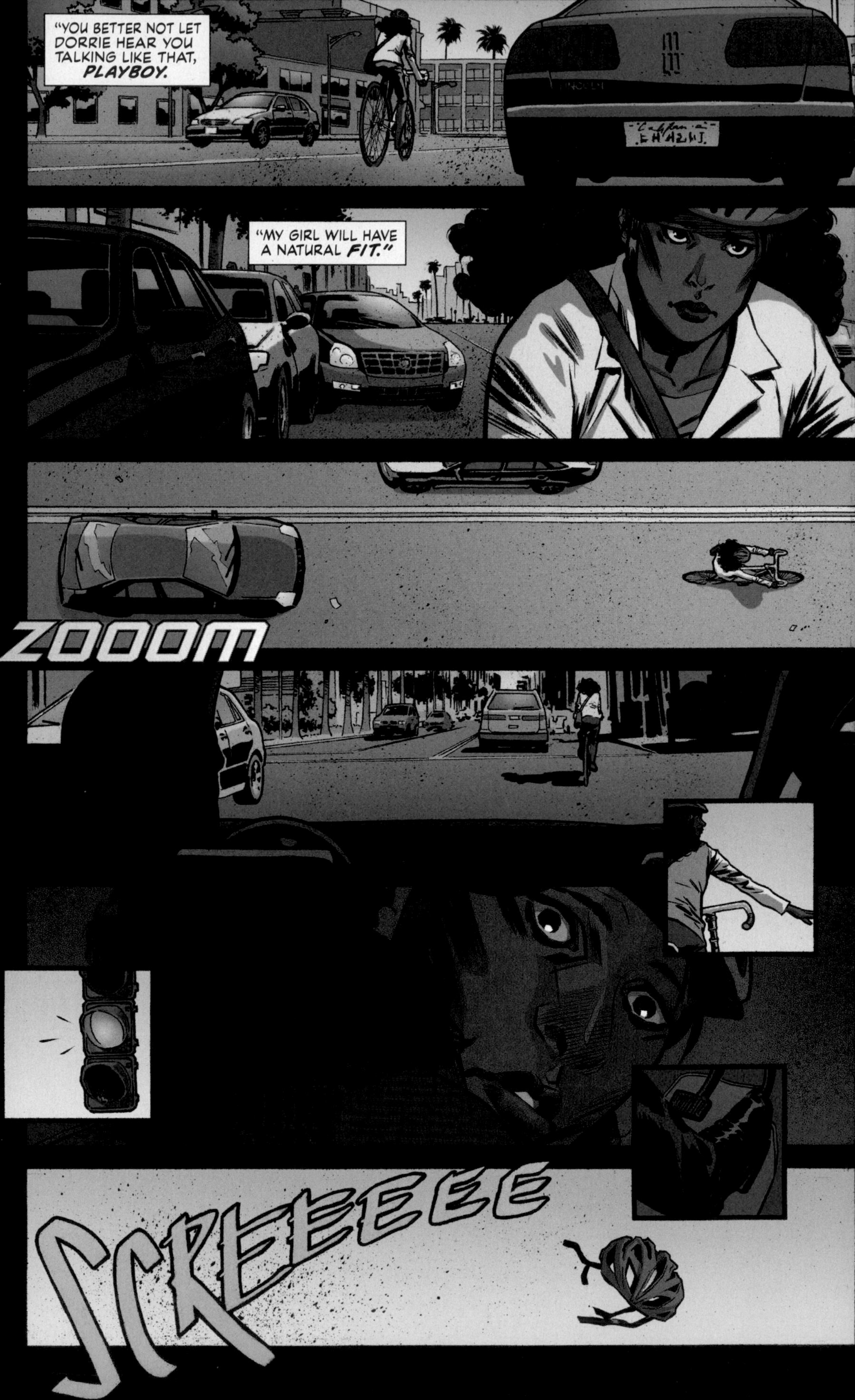
"YOU BETTER NOT LET DORRIE HEAR YOU TALKING LIKE THAT, PLAYBOY.
"MY GIRL WILL HAVE A NATURAL FIT."
ZOOOM
SCREEEEE

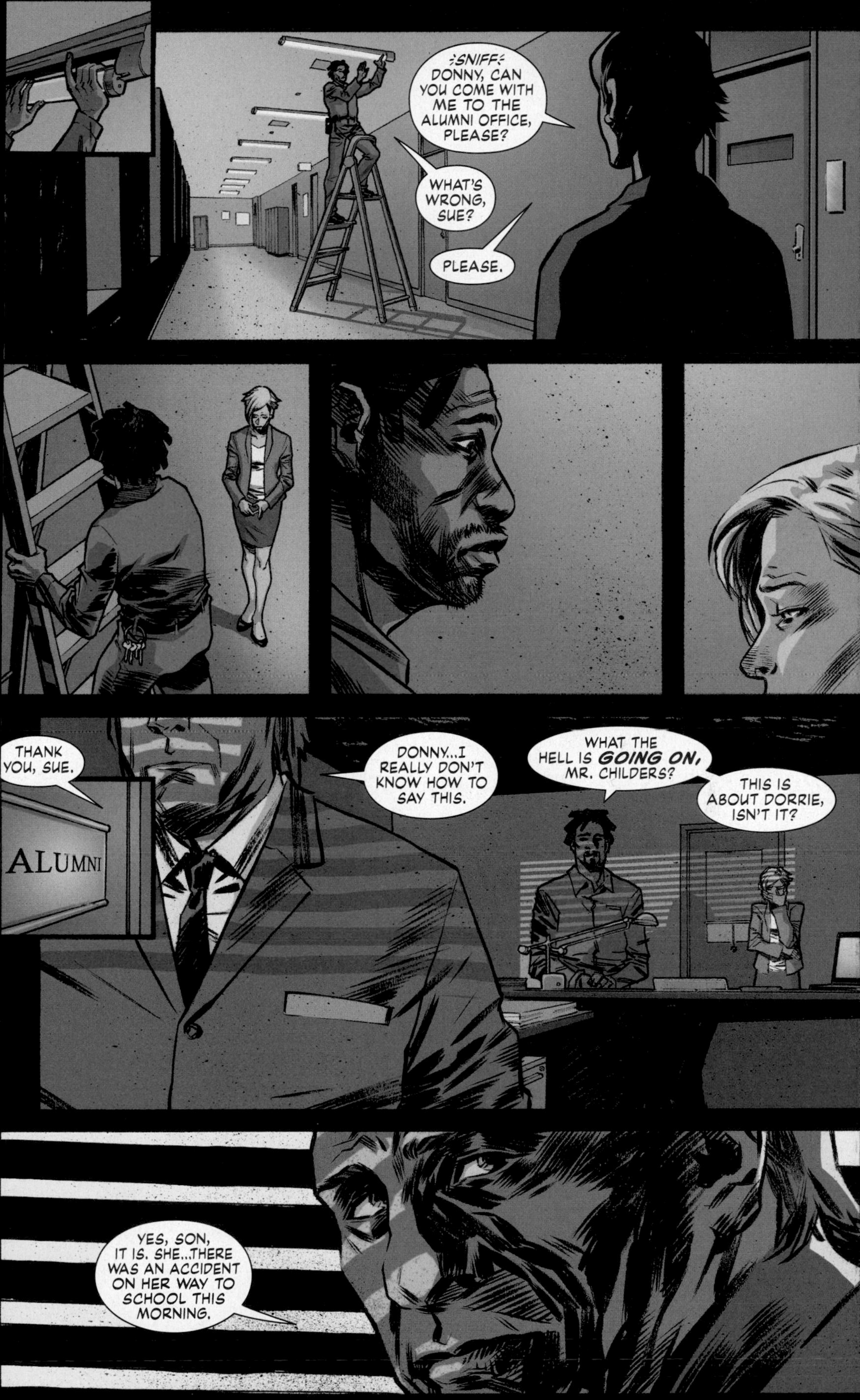

:SNIFF: DONNY, CAN YOU COME WITH ME TO THE ALUMNI OFFICE, PLEASE?
WHAT'S WRONG, SUE?
PLEASE.
THANK YOU, SUE.
ALUMNI
DONNY...I REALLY DON'T KNOW HOW TO SAY THIS.
WHAT THE HELL IS GOING ON, MR. CHILDERS?
THIS IS ABOUT DORRIE, ISN'T IT?
YES, SON, IT IS. SHE...THERE WAS AN ACCIDENT ON HER WAY TO SCHOOL THIS MORNING.

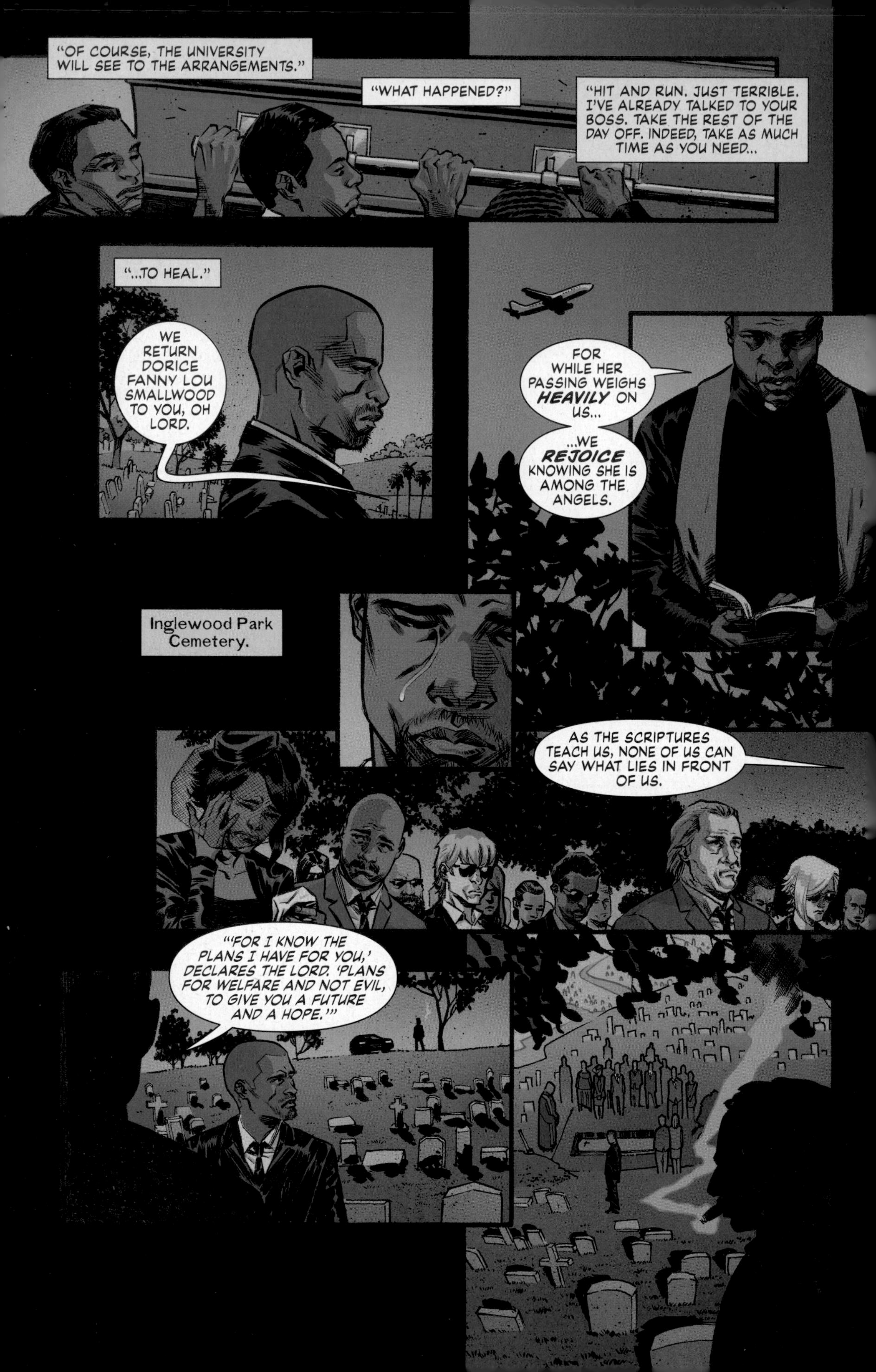
"OF COURSE, THE UNIVERSITY WILL SEE TO THE ARRANGEMENTS."
"WHAT HAPPENED?"
"HIT AND RUN. JUST TERRIBLE. I'VE ALREADY TALKED TO YOUR BOSS. TAKE THE REST OF THE DAY OFF. INDEED, TAKE AS MUCH TIME AS YOU NEED...
"...TO HEAL."
WE RETURN DORICE FANNY LOU SMALLWOOD TO YOU, OH LORD.
FOR WHILE HER PASSING WEIGHS HEAVILY ON US...
...WE REJOICE KNOWING SHE IS AMONG THE ANGELS.
Inglewood Park Cemetery.
AS THE SCRIPTURES TEACH US, NONE OF US CAN SAY WHAT LIES IN FRONT OF US.
"'FOR I KNOW THE PLANS I HAVE FOR YOU,' DECLARES THE LORD. 'PLANS FOR WELFARE AND NOT EVIL, TO GIVE YOU A FUTURE AND A HOPE.'"

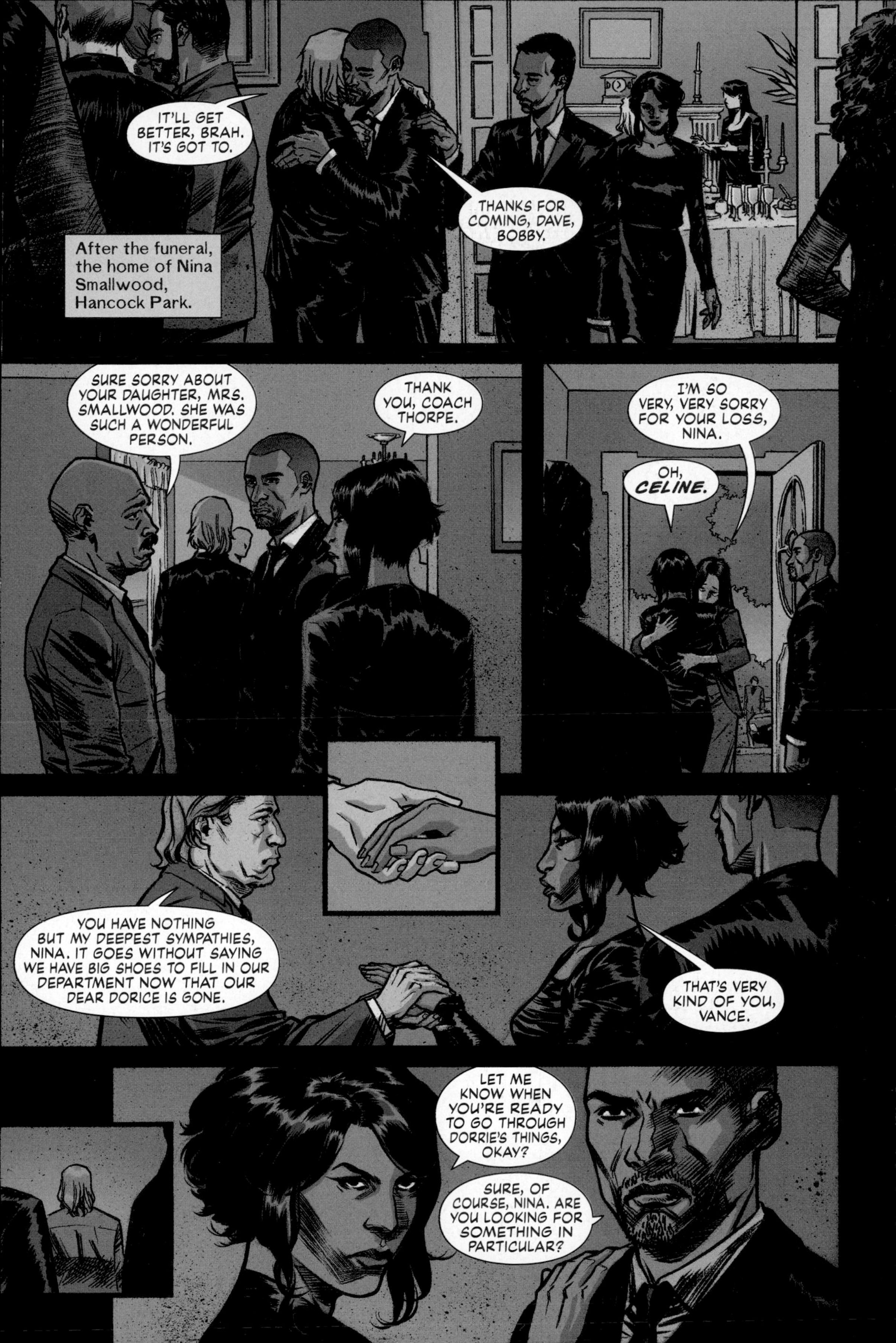
IT'LL GET BETTER, BRAH. IT'S GOT TO.
THANKS FOR COMING, DAVE, BOBBY.
After the funeral, the home of Nina Smallwood, Hancock Park.
SURE SORRY ABOUT YOUR DAUGHTER, MRS. SMALLWOOD. SHE WAS SUCH A WONDERFUL PERSON.
THANK YOU, COACH THORPE.
I'M SO VERY, VERY SORRY FOR YOUR LOSS, NINA.
OH, CELINE.
YOU HAVE NOTHING BUT MY DEEPEST SYMPATHIES, NINA. IT GOES WITHOUT SAYING WE HAVE BIG SHOES TO FILL IN OUR DEPARTMENT NOW THAT OUR DEAR DORICE IS GONE.
THAT'S VERY KIND OF YOU, VANCE.
LET ME KNOW WHEN YOU'RE READY TO GO THROUGH DORRIE'S THINGS, OKAY?
SURE, OF COURSE, NINA. ARE YOU LOOKING FOR SOMETHING IN PARTICULAR?

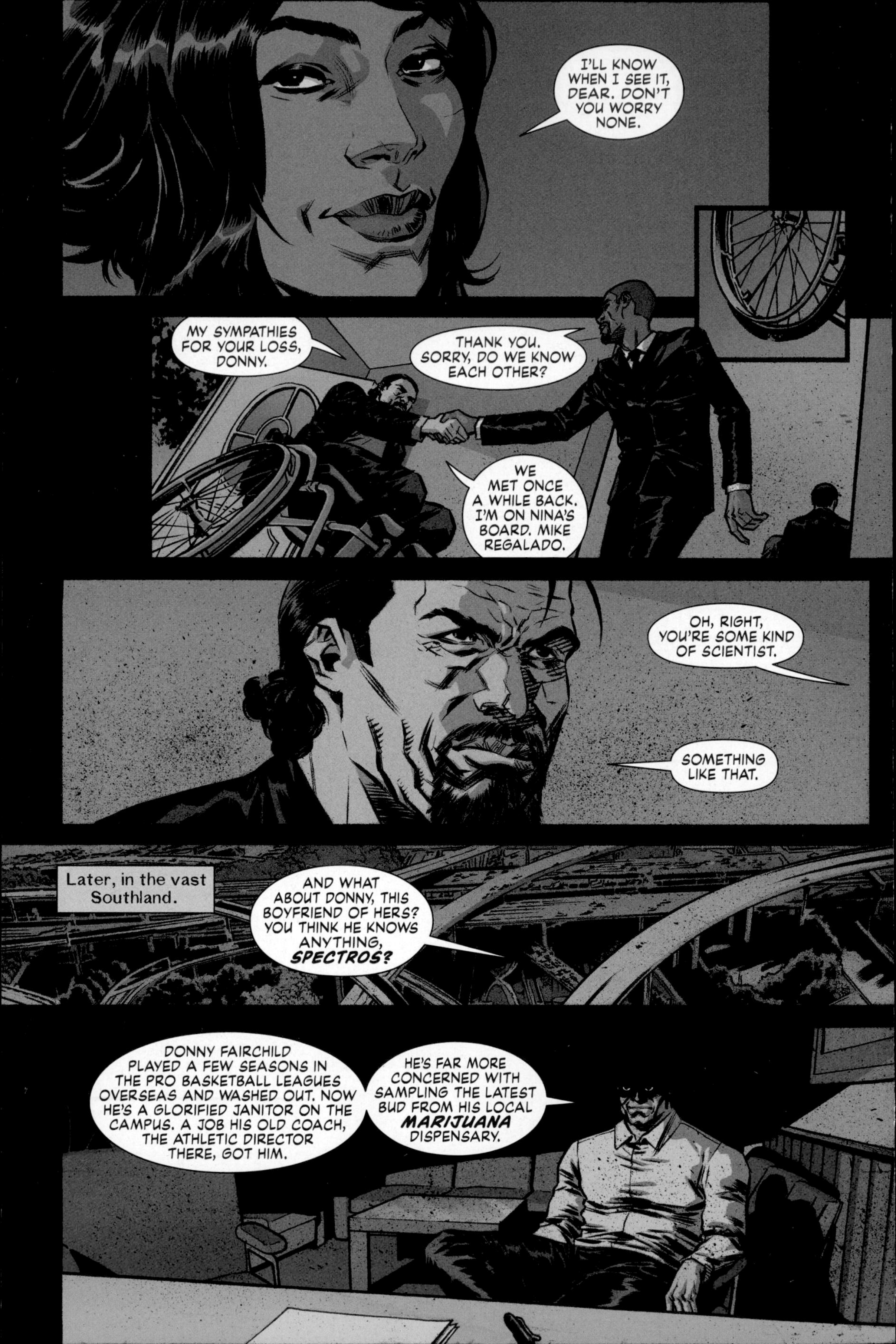
I'LL KNOW WHEN I SEE IT, DEAR. DON'T YOU WORRY NONE.
MY SYMPATHIES FOR YOUR LOSS, DONNY.
THANK YOU. SORRY, DO WE KNOW EACH OTHER?
WE MET ONCE A WHILE BACK. I'M ON NINA'S BOARD. MIKE REGALADO.
OH, RIGHT, YOU'RE SOME KIND OF SCIENTIST.
SOMETHING LIKE THAT.
Later, in the vast Southland.
AND WHAT ABOUT DONNY, THIS BOYFRIEND OF HERS? YOU THINK HE KNOWS ANYTHING, SPECTROS?
DONNY FAIRCHILD PLAYED A FEW SEASONS IN THE PRO BASKETBALL LEAGUES OVERSEAS AND WASHED OUT. NOW HE'S A GLORIFIED JANITOR ON THE CAMPUS. A JOB HIS OLD COACH, THE ATHLETIC DIRECTOR THERE, GOT HIM.
HE'S FAR MORE CONCERNED WITH SAMPLING THE LATEST BUD FROM HIS LOCAL MARIJUANA DISPENSARY.

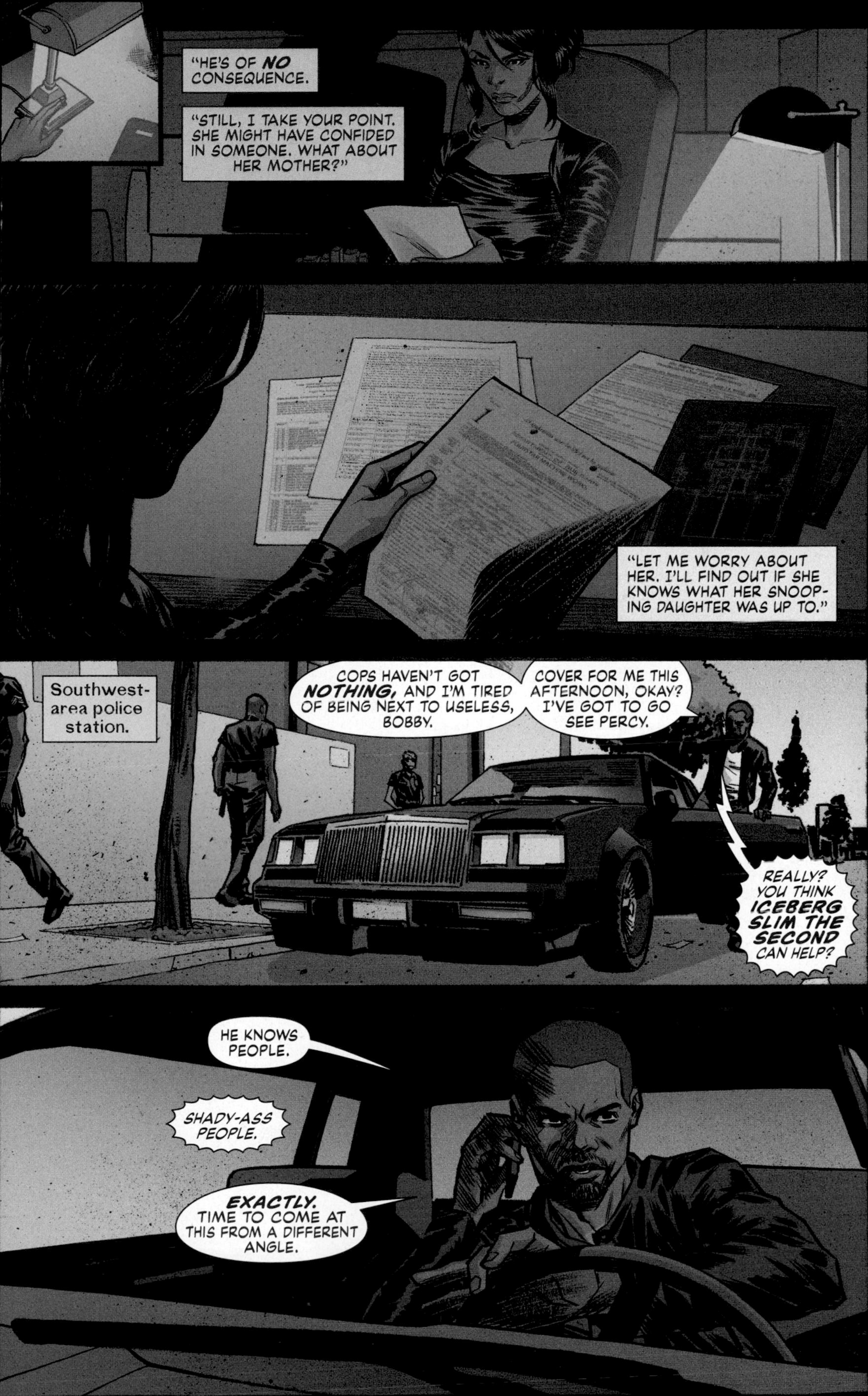

"HE'S OF NO CONSEQUENCE.
"STILL, I TAKE YOUR POINT. SHE MIGHT HAVE CONFIDED IN SOMEONE. WHAT ABOUT HER MOTHER?"
"LET ME WORRY ABOUT HER. I'LL FIND OUT IF SHE KNOWS WHAT HER SNOOPING DAUGHTER WAS UP TO."
Southwest-area police station.
COPS HAVEN'T GOT NOTHING, AND I'M TIRED OF BEING NEXT TO USELESS, BOBBY.
COVER FOR ME THIS AFTERNOON, OKAY? I'VE GOT TO GO SEE PERCY.
REALLY? YOU THINK ICEBERG SLIM THE SECOND CAN HELP?
HE KNOWS PEOPLE.
SHADY-ASS PEOPLE.
EXACTLY. TIME TO COME AT THIS FROM A DIFFERENT ANGLE.

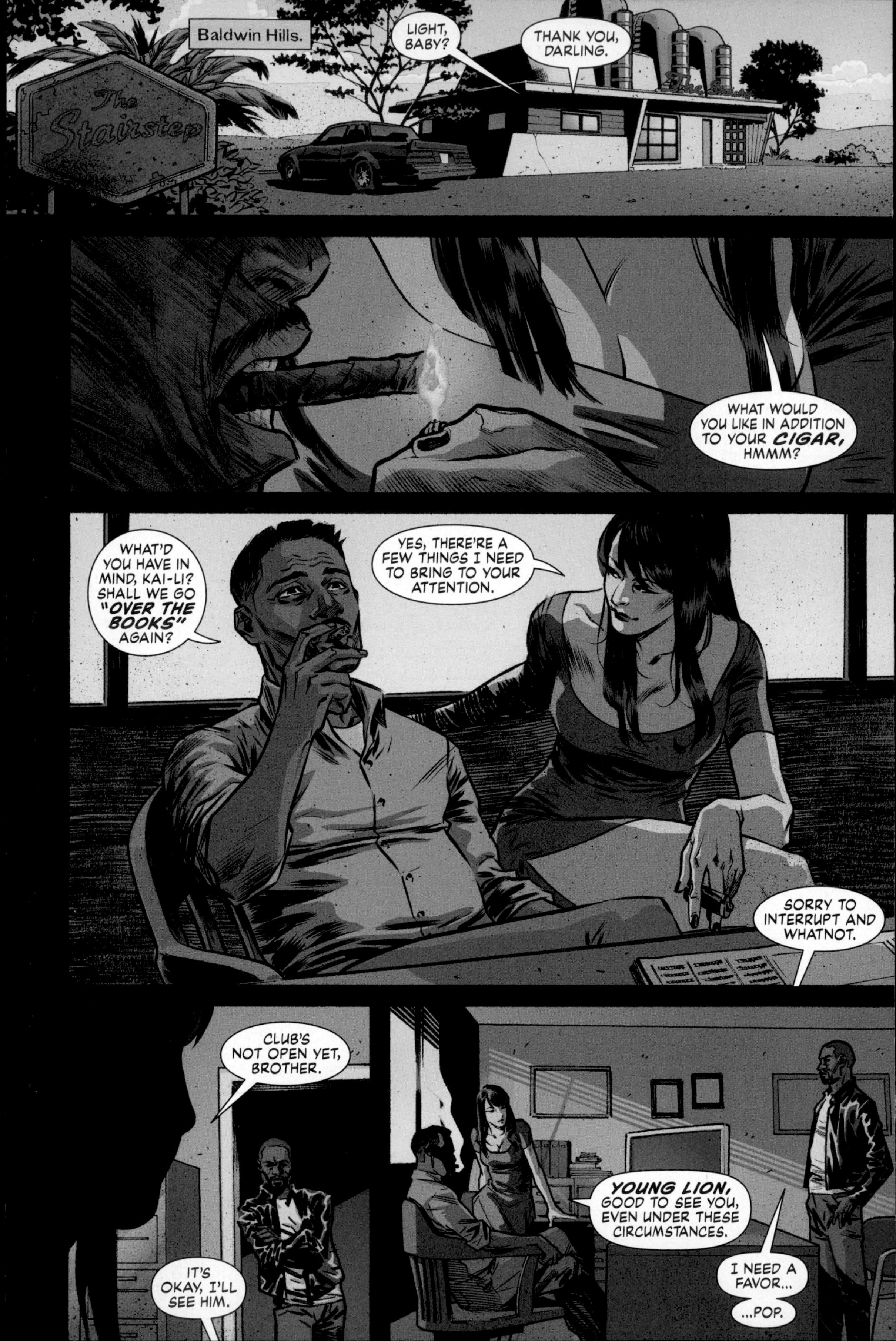
Baldwin Hills.
The Stairstep
LIGHT, BABY?
THANK YOU, DARLING.
WHAT WOULD YOU LIKE IN ADDITION TO YOUR CIGAR, HMMM?
WHAT'D YOU HAVE IN MIND, KAI-LI? SHALL WE GO "OVER THE BOOKS" AGAIN?
YES, THERE'RE A FEW THINGS I NEED TO BRING TO YOUR ATTENTION.
SORRY TO INTERRUPT AND WHATNOT.
CLUB'S NOT OPEN YET, BROTHER.
IT'S OKAY, I'LL SEE HIM.
YOUNG LION, GOOD TO SEE YOU, EVEN UNDER THESE CIRCUMSTANCES.
I NEED A FAVOR...
...POP.

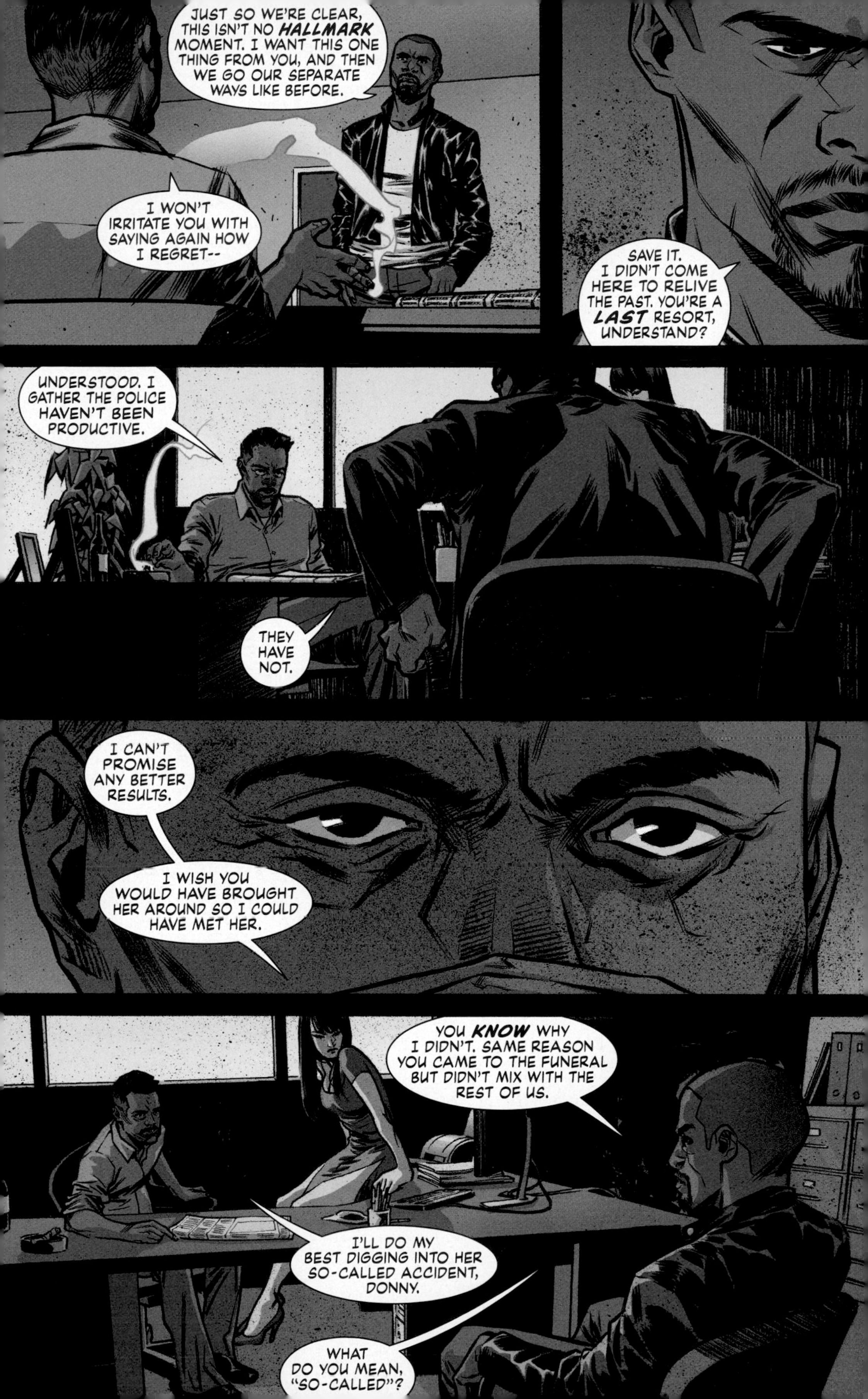
JUST SO WE'RE CLEAR, THIS ISN'T NO HALLMARK MOMENT. I WANT THIS ONE THING FROM YOU, AND THEN WE GO OUR SEPARATE WAYS LIKE BEFORE.
I WON'T IRRITATE YOU WITH SAYING AGAIN HOW I REGRET--
SAVE IT. I DIDN'T COME HERE TO RELIVE THE PAST. YOU'RE A LAST RESORT, UNDERSTAND?
UNDERSTOOD. I GATHER THE POLICE HAVEN'T BEEN PRODUCTIVE.
THEY HAVE NOT.
I CAN'T PROMISE ANY BETTER RESULTS.
I WISH YOU WOULD HAVE BROUGHT HER AROUND SO I COULD HAVE MET HER.
YOU KNOW WHY I DIDN'T. SAME REASON YOU CAME TO THE FUNERAL BUT DIDN'T MIX WITH THE REST OF US.
I'LL DO MY BEST DIGGING INTO HER SO-CALLED ACCIDENT, DONNY.
WHAT DO YOU MEAN, "SO-CALLED"?

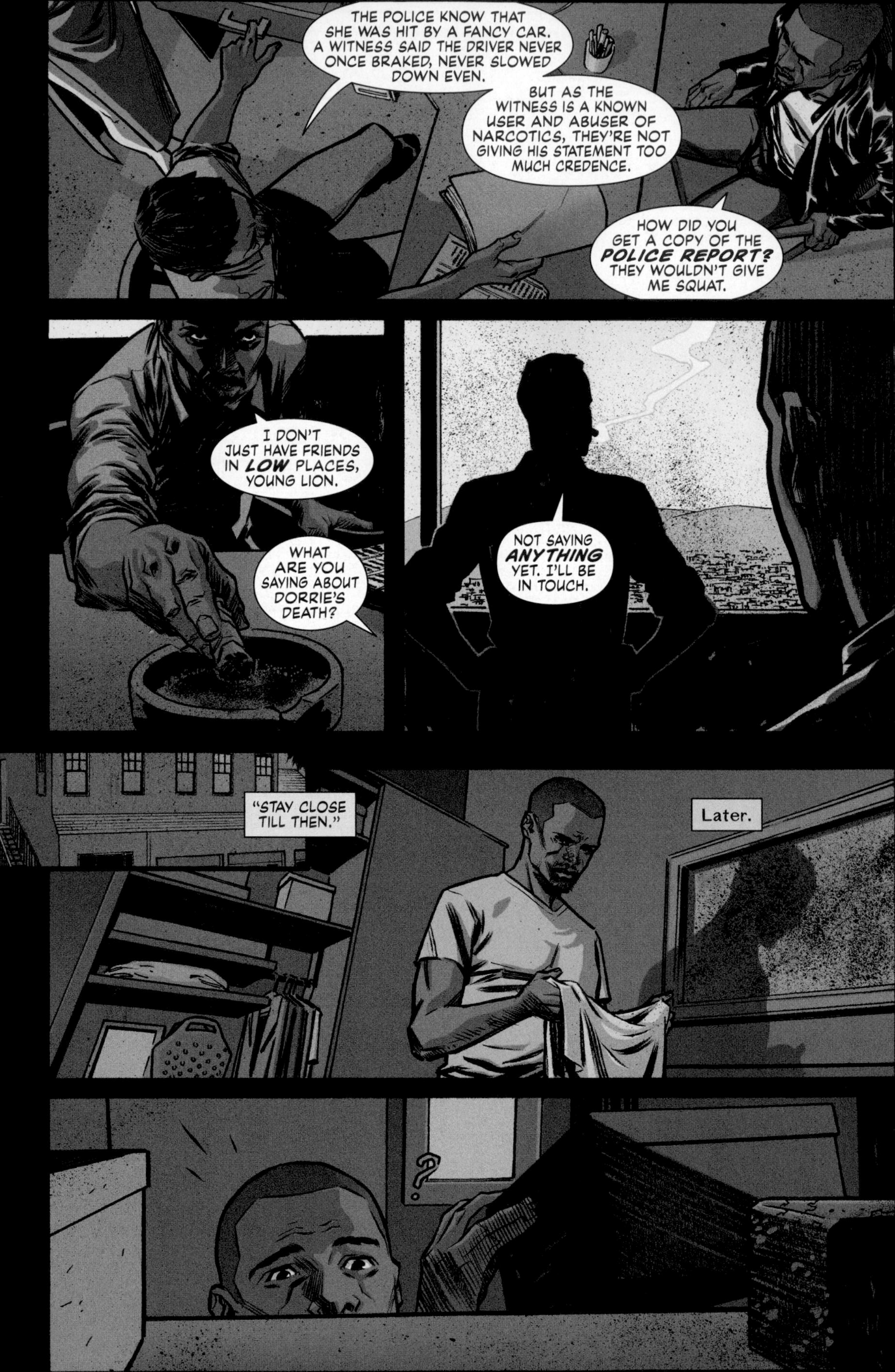
THE POLICE KNOW THAT SHE WAS HIT BY A FANCY CAR. A WITNESS SAID THE DRIVER NEVER ONCE BRAKED, NEVER SLOWED DOWN EVEN.
BUT AS THE WITNESS IS A KNOWN USER AND ABUSER OF NARCOTICS, THEY'RE NOT GIVING HIS STATEMENT TOO MUCH CREDENCE.
HOW DID YOU GET A COPY OF THE POLICE REPORT? THEY WOULDN'T GIVE ME SQUAT.
I DON'T JUST HAVE FRIENDS IN LOW PLACES, YOUNG LION.
WHAT ARE YOU SAYING ABOUT DORRIE'S DEATH?
NOT SAYING ANYTHING YET. I'LL BE IN TOUCH.
"STAY CLOSE TILL THEN."
Later.

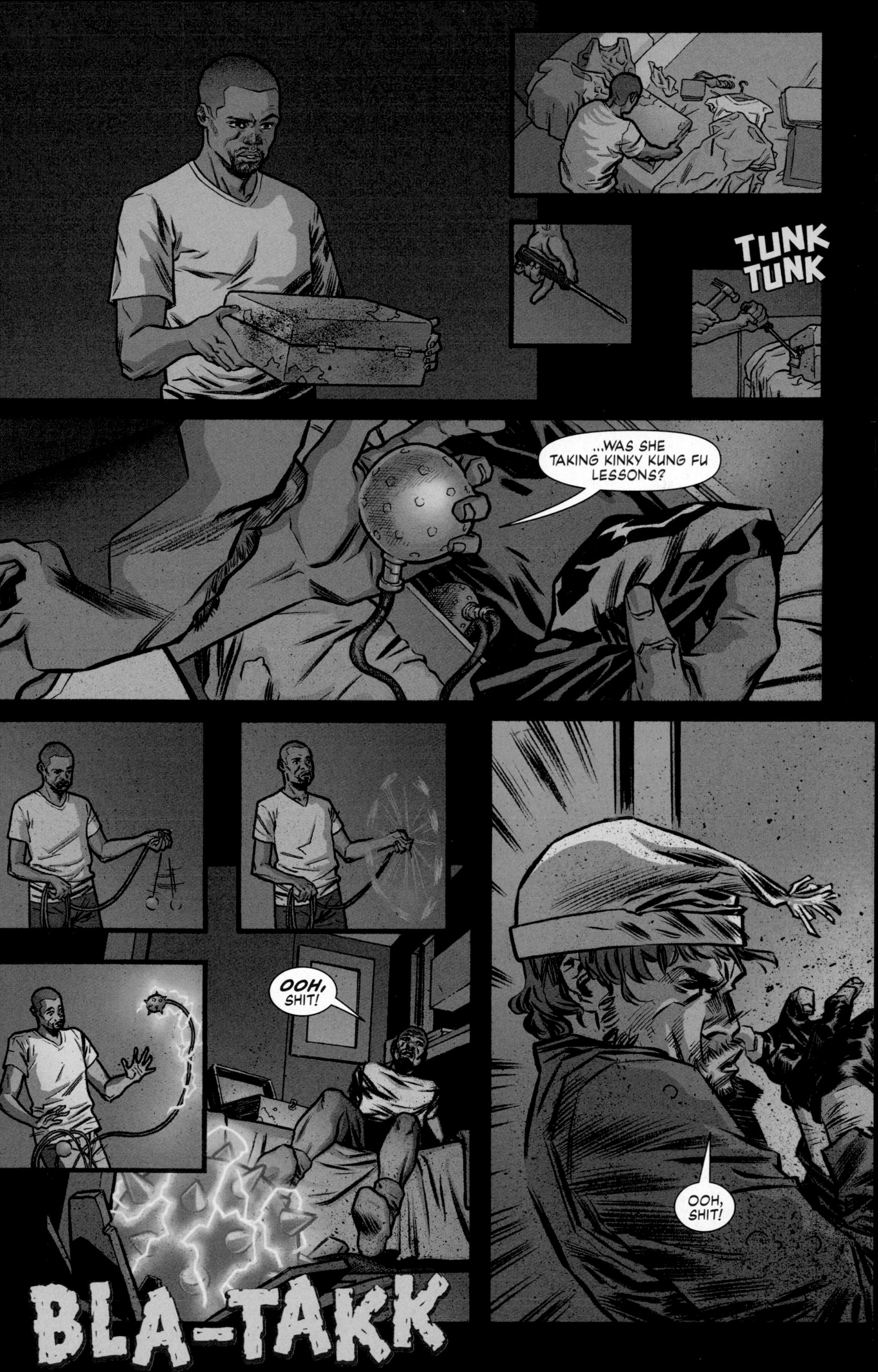
TUNK
TUNK
...WAS SHE TAKING KINKY KUNG FU LESSONS?
OOH, SHIT!
OOH, SHIT!
BLA-TAKK

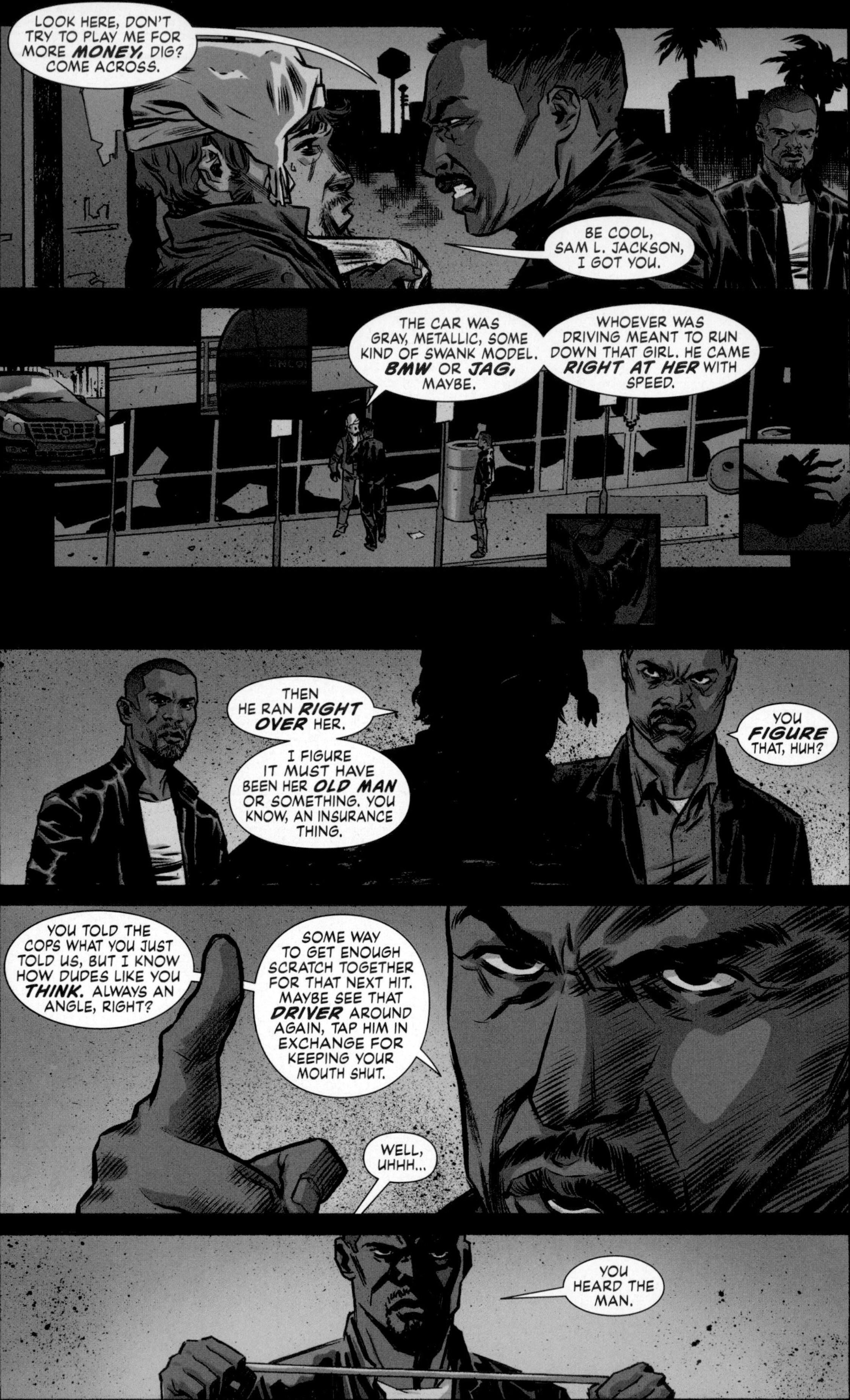

LOOK HERE, DON'T TRY TO PLAY ME FOR MORE MONEY, DIG? COME ACROSS.
BE COOL, SAM L. JACKSON, I GOT YOU.
THE CAR WAS GRAY, METALLIC, SOME KIND OF SWANK MODEL. BMW OR JAG, MAYBE.
WHOEVER WAS DRIVING MEANT TO RUN DOWN THAT GIRL. HE CAME RIGHT AT HER WITH SPEED.
THEN HE RAN RIGHT OVER HER.
I FIGURE IT MUST HAVE BEEN HER OLD MAN OR SOMETHING. YOU KNOW, AN INSURANCE THING.
YOU FIGURE THAT, HUH?
YOU TOLD THE COPS WHAT YOU JUST TOLD US, BUT I KNOW HOW DUDES LIKE YOU THINK. ALWAYS AN ANGLE, RIGHT?
SOME WAY TO GET ENOUGH SCRATCH TOGETHER FOR THAT NEXT HIT. MAYBE SEE THAT DRIVER AROUND AGAIN, TAP HIM IN EXCHANGE FOR KEEPING YOUR MOUTH SHUT.
WELL, UHHH...
YOU HEARD THE MAN.

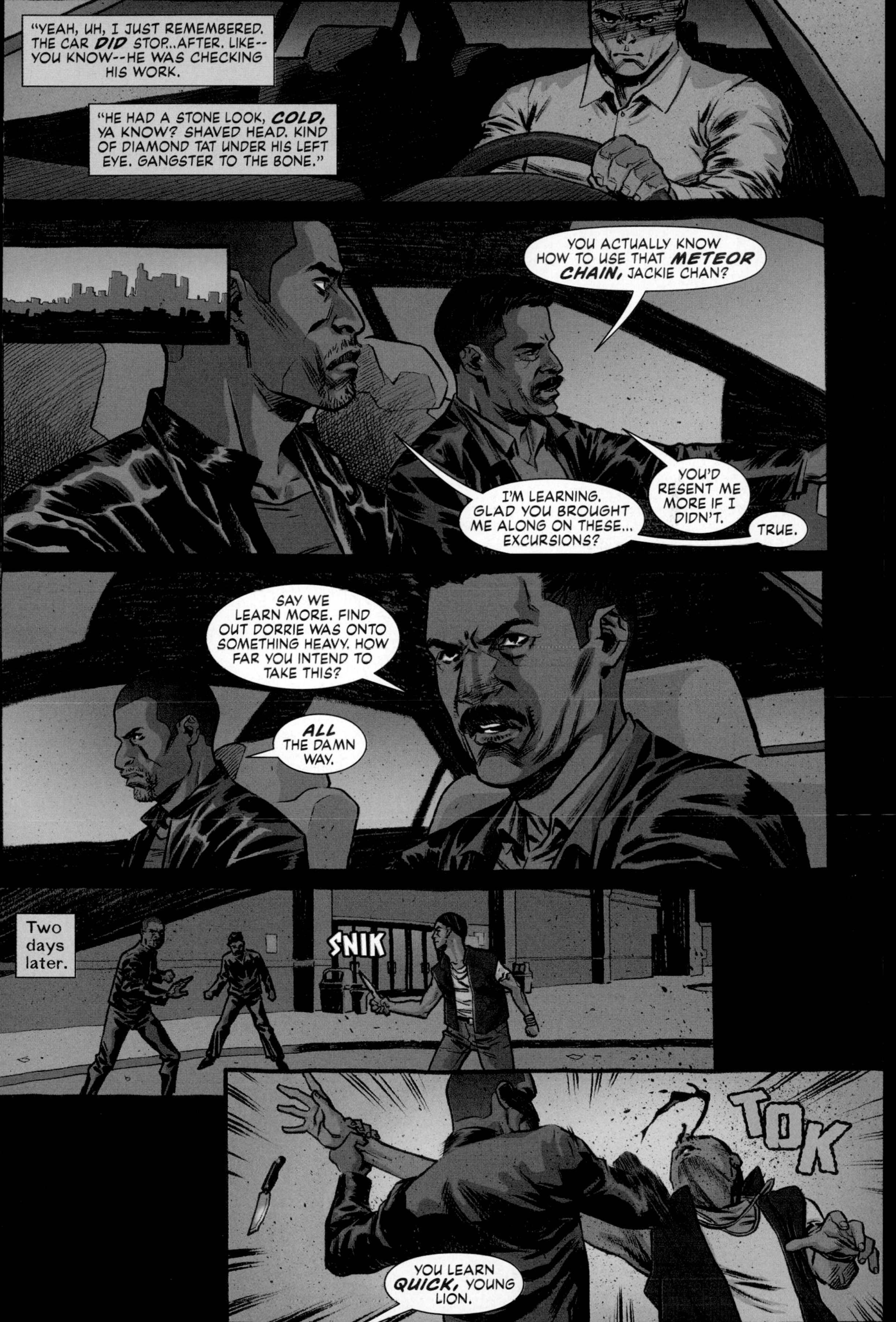
"YEAH, UH, I JUST REMEMBERED. THE CAR DID STOP...AFTER. LIKE--YOU KNOW--HE WAS CHECKING HIS WORK.
"HE HAD A STONE LOOK, COLD, YA KNOW? SHAVED HEAD. KIND OF DIAMOND TAT UNDER HIS LEFT EYE. GANGSTER TO THE BONE."
YOU ACTUALLY KNOW HOW TO USE THAT METEOR CHAIN, JACKIE CHAN?
I'M LEARNING. GLAD YOU BROUGHT ME ALONG ON THESE... EXCURSIONS?
YOU'D RESENT ME MORE IF I DIDN'T.
TRUE.
SAY WE LEARN MORE. FIND OUT DORRIE WAS ONTO SOMETHING HEAVY. HOW FAR YOU INTEND TO TAKE THIS?
ALL THE DAMN WAY.
Two days later.
SNIK
TOK
YOU LEARN QUICK, YOUNG LION.

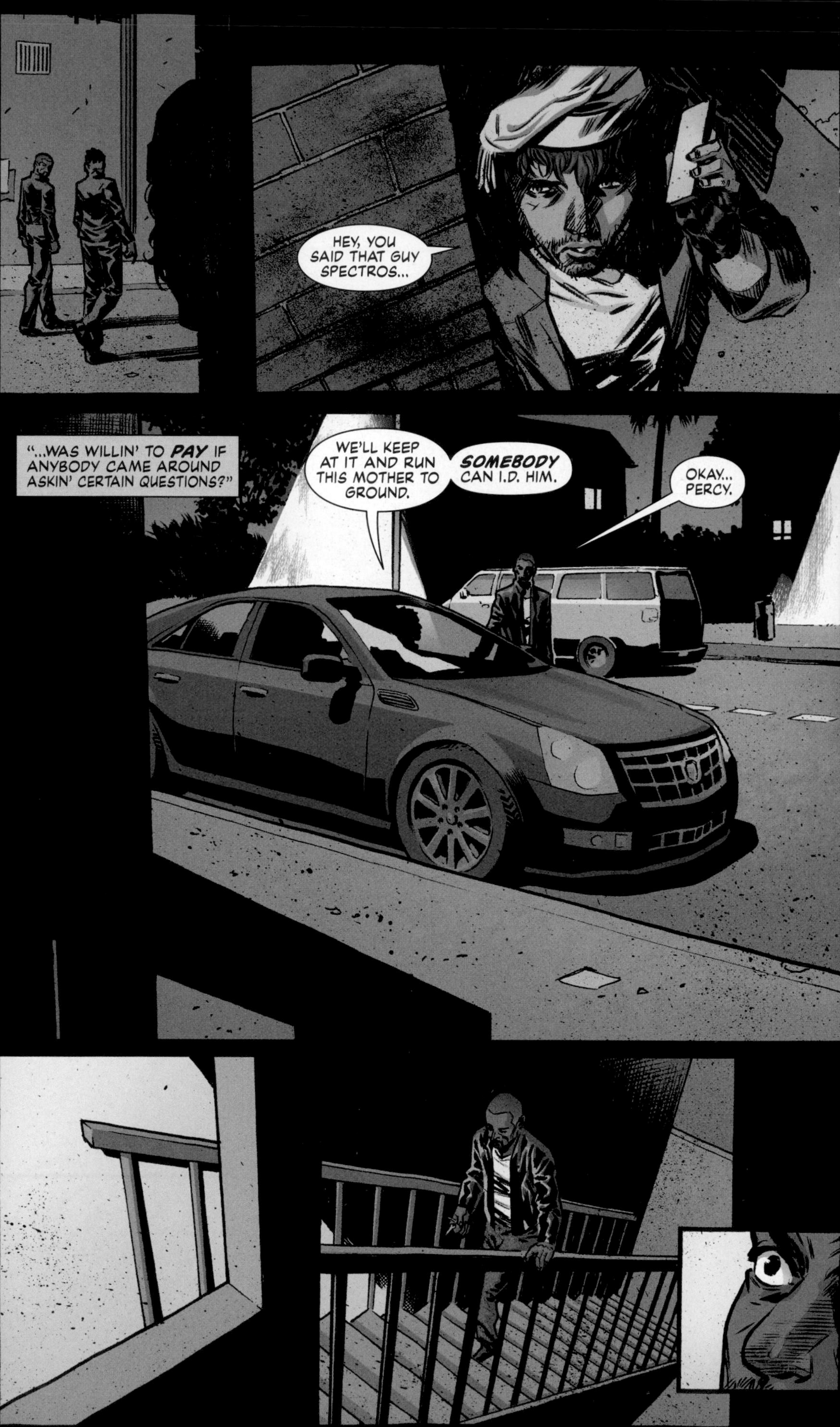
HEY, YOU SAID THAT GUY SPECTROS...
"...WAS WILLIN' TO PAY IF ANYBODY CAME AROUND ASKIN' CERTAIN QUESTIONS?"
WE'LL KEEP AT IT AND RUN THIS MOTHER TO GROUND.
SOMEBODY CAN I.D. HIM.
OKAY... PERCY.

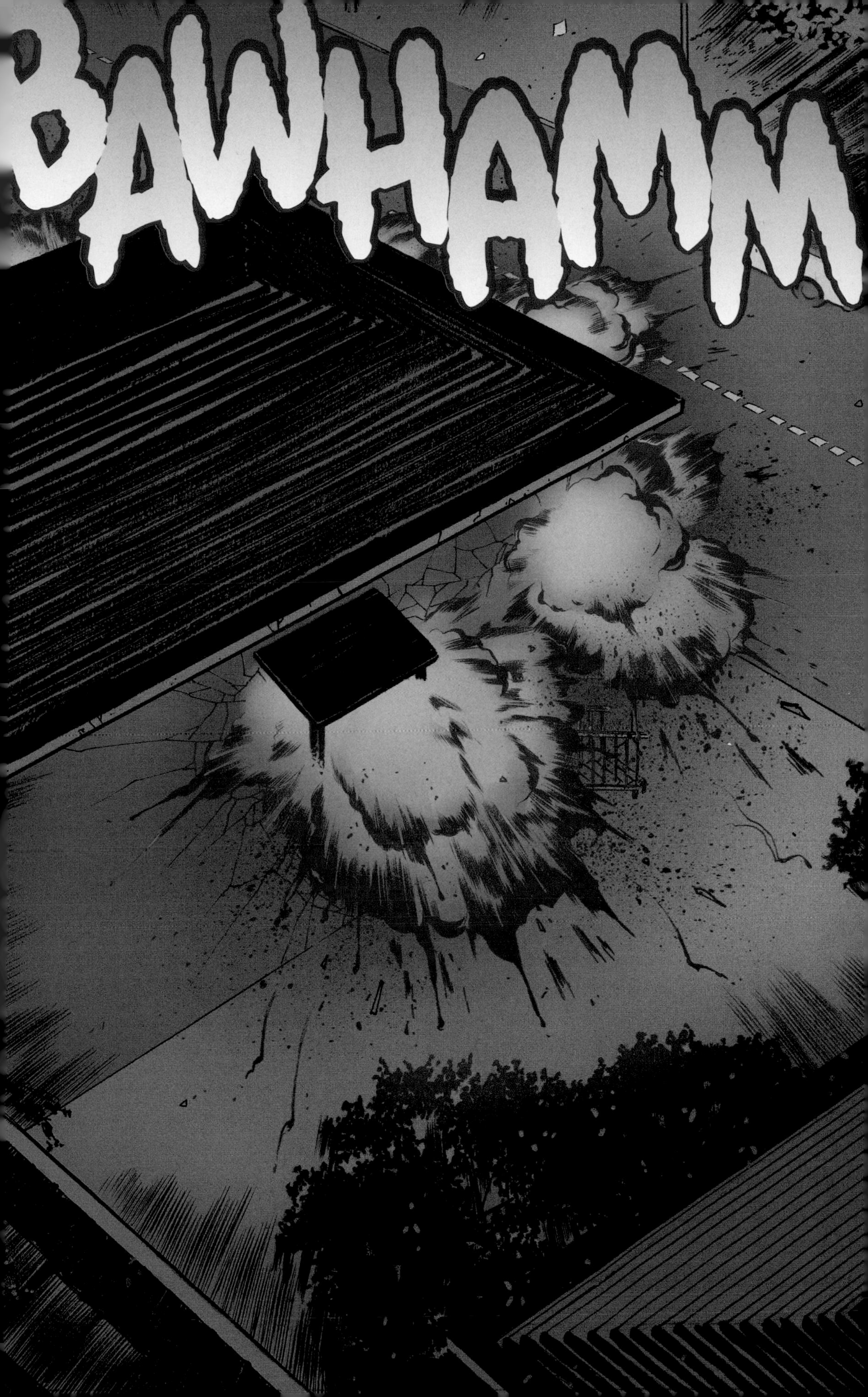
BAWHAMM

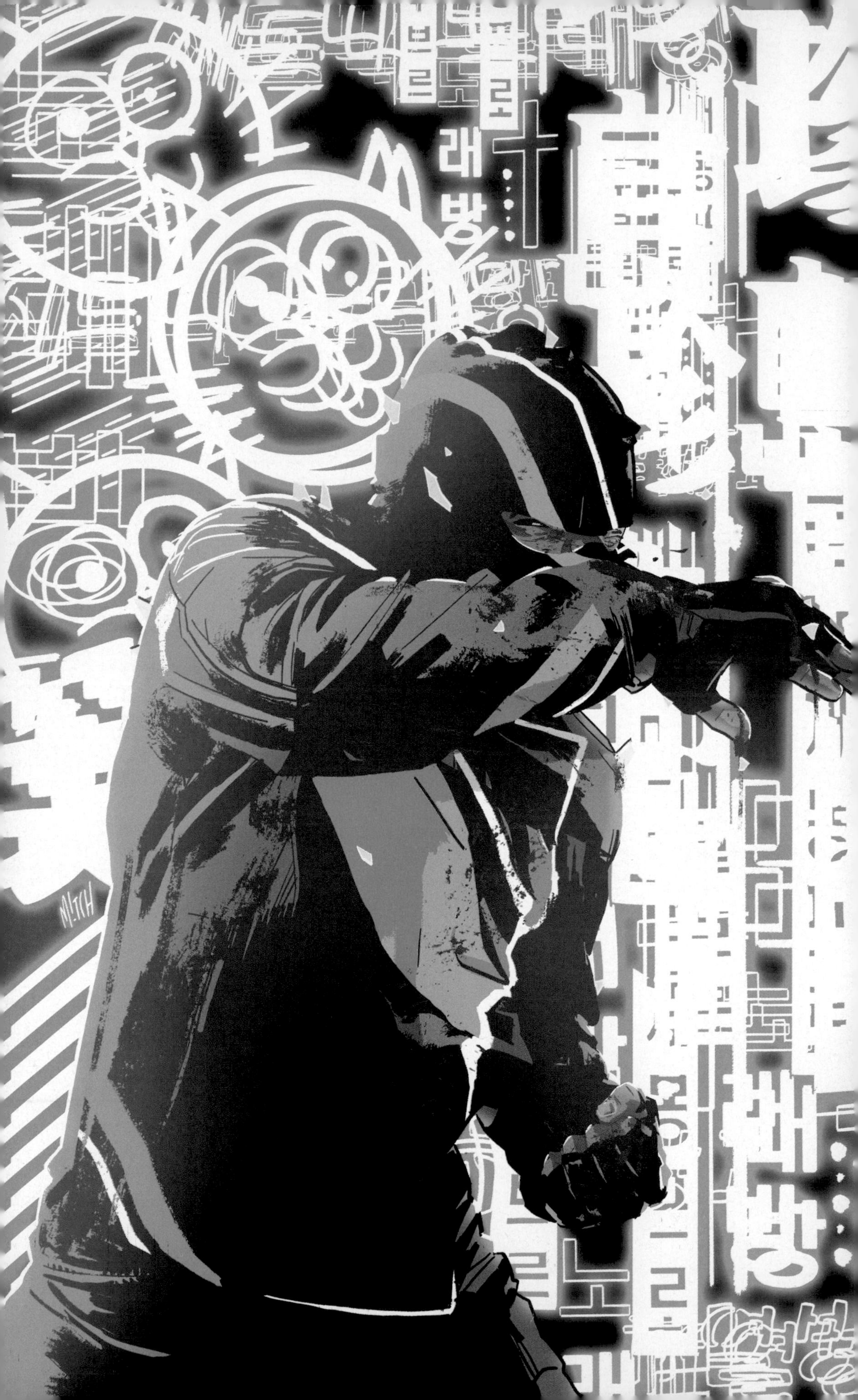

래
방

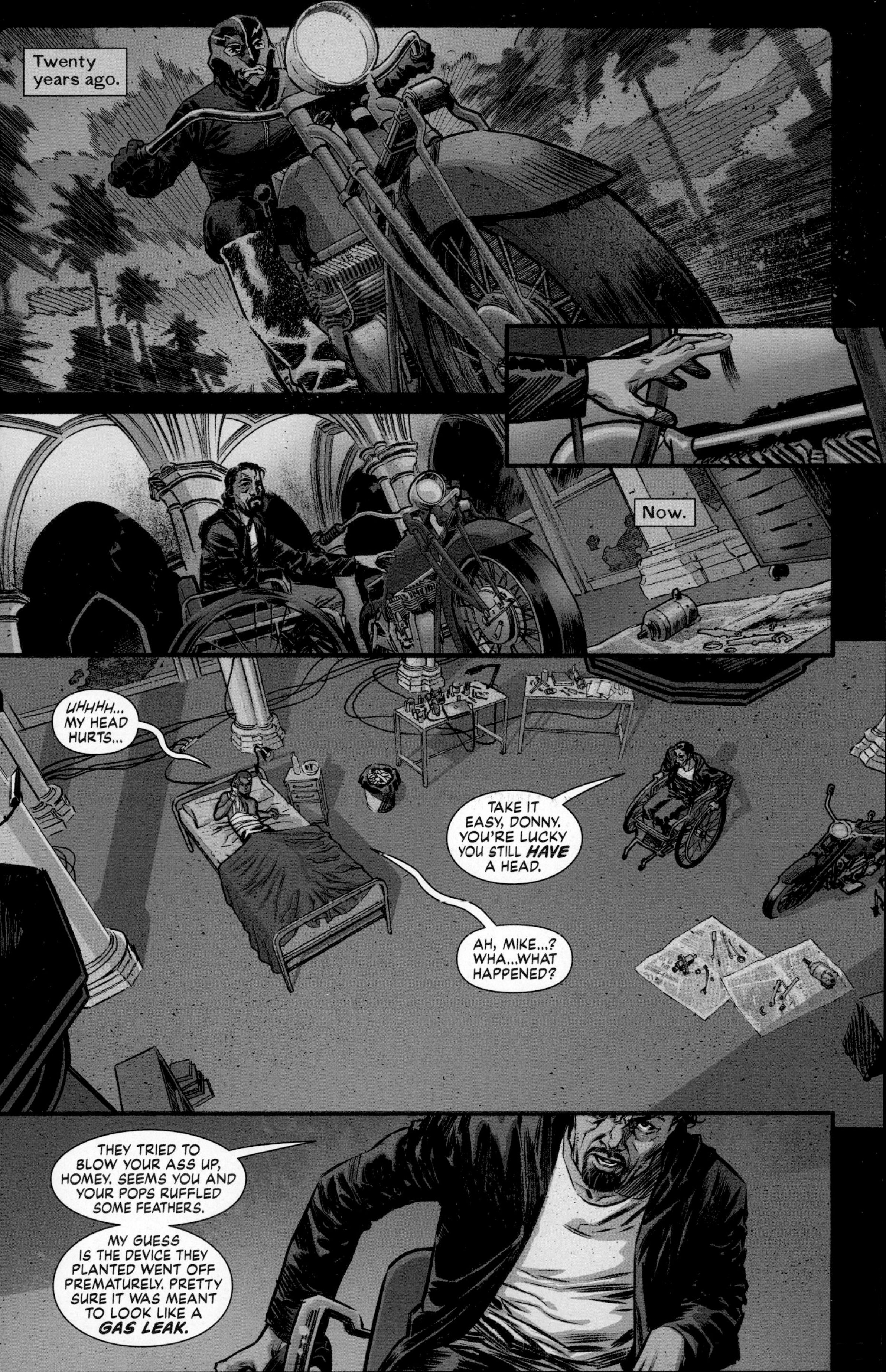

Twenty years ago.
Now.
UHHHH... MY HEAD HURTS...
TAKE IT EASY, DONNY. YOU'RE LUCKY YOU STILL HAVE A HEAD.
AH, MIKE...? WHA...WHAT HAPPENED?
THEY TRIED TO BLOW YOUR ASS UP, HOMEY. SEEMS YOU AND YOUR POPS RUFFLED SOME FEATHERS.
MY GUESS IS THE DEVICE THEY PLANTED WENT OFF PREMATURELY. PRETTY SURE IT WAS MEANT TO LOOK LIKE A GAS LEAK.

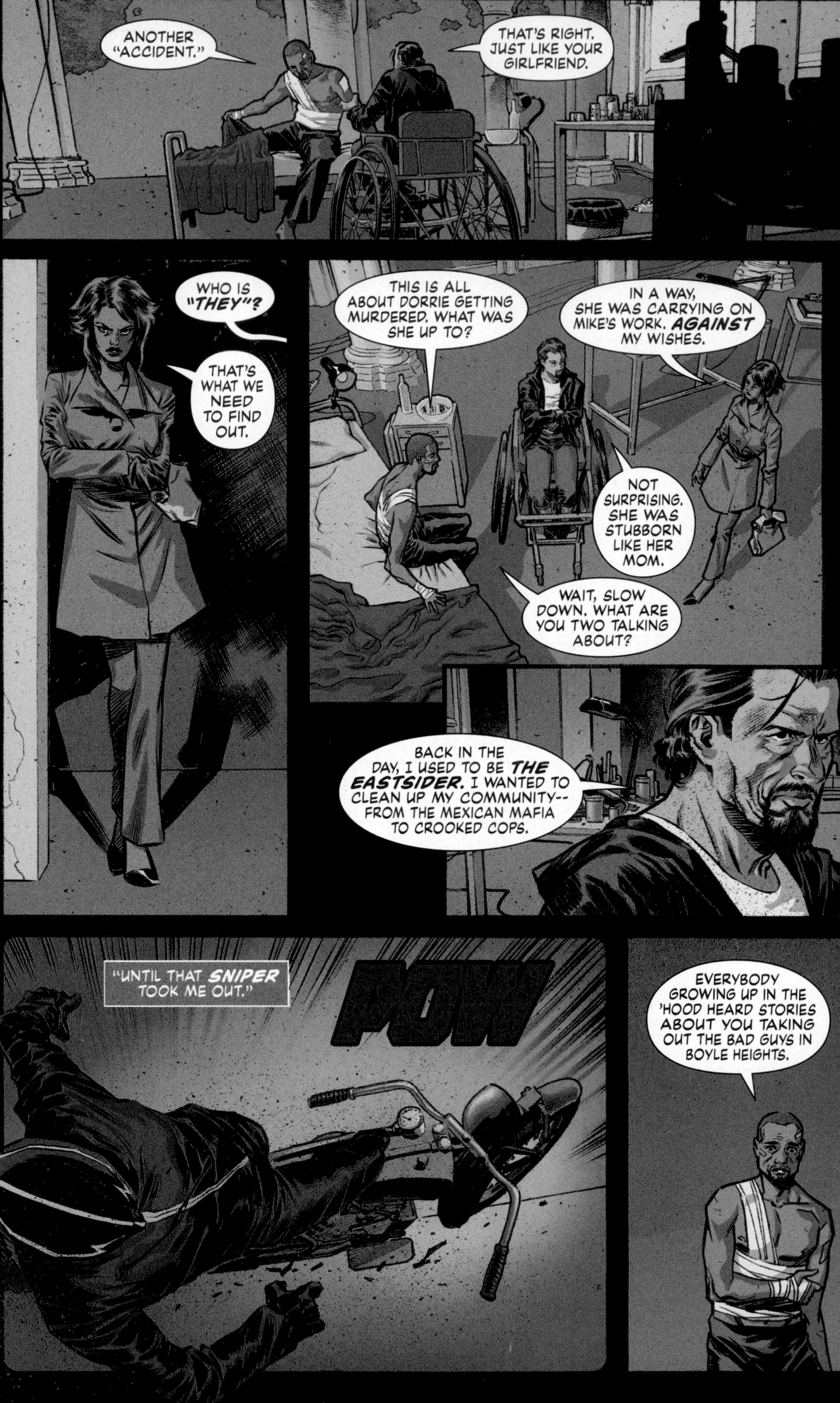
ANOTHER "ACCIDENT."
THAT'S RIGHT. JUST LIKE YOUR GIRLFRIEND.
WHO IS "THEY"?
THAT'S WHAT WE NEED TO FIND OUT.
THIS IS ALL ABOUT DORRIE GETTING MURDERED. WHAT WAS SHE UP TO?
IN A WAY, SHE WAS CARRYING ON MIKE'S WORK. AGAINST MY WISHES.
NOT SURPRISING. SHE WAS STUBBORN LIKE HER MOM.
WAIT, SLOW DOWN. WHAT ARE YOU TWO TALKING ABOUT?
BACK IN THE DAY, I USED TO BE THE EASTSIDER. I WANTED TO CLEAN UP MY COMMUNITY-- FROM THE MEXICAN MAFIA TO CROOKED COPS.
"UNTIL THAT SNIPER TOOK ME OUT."
POW
EVERYBODY GROWING UP IN THE 'HOOD HEARD STORIES ABOUT YOU TAKING OUT THE BAD GUYS IN BOYLE HEIGHTS.

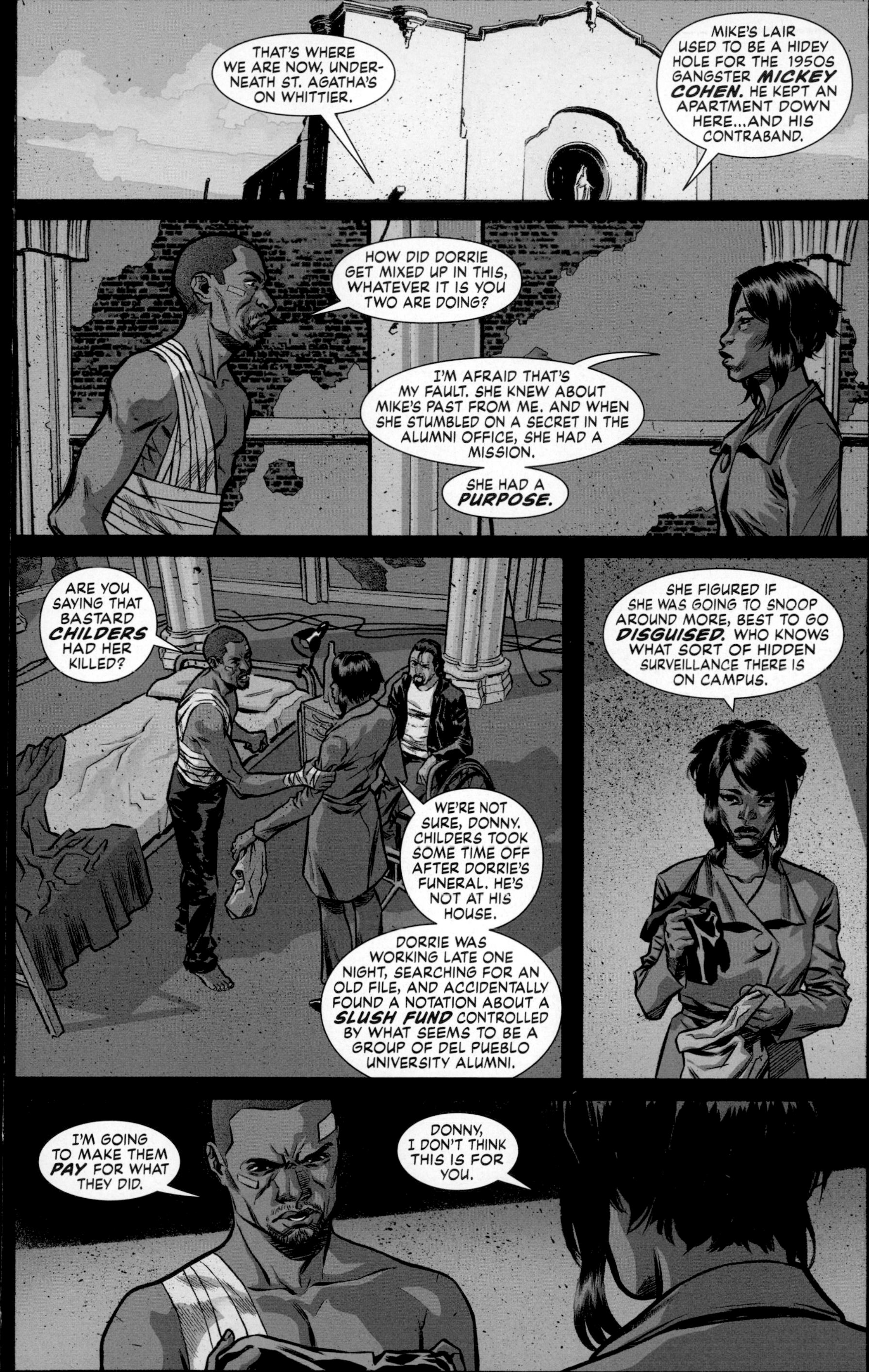
THAT'S WHERE WE ARE NOW, UNDERNEATH ST. AGATHA'S ON WHITTIER.
MIKE'S LAIR USED TO BE A HIDEY HOLE FOR THE 1950s GANGSTER MICKEY COHEN. HE KEPT AN APARTMENT DOWN HERE...AND HIS CONTRABAND.
HOW DID DORRIE GET MIXED UP IN THIS, WHATEVER IT IS YOU TWO ARE DOING?
I'M AFRAID THAT'S MY FAULT. SHE KNEW ABOUT MIKE'S PAST FROM ME. AND WHEN SHE STUMBLED ON A SECRET IN THE ALUMNI OFFICE, SHE HAD A MISSION.
SHE HAD A PURPOSE.
ARE YOU SAYING THAT BASTARD CHILDERS HAD HER KILLED?
WE'RE NOT SURE, DONNY. CHILDERS TOOK SOME TIME OFF AFTER DORRIE'S FUNERAL. HE'S NOT AT HIS HOUSE.
DORRIE WAS WORKING LATE ONE NIGHT, SEARCHING FOR AN OLD FILE, AND ACCIDENTALLY FOUND A NOTATION ABOUT A SLUSH FUND CONTROLLED BY WHAT SEEMS TO BE A GROUP OF DEL PUEBLO UNIVERSITY ALUMNI.
SHE FIGURED IF SHE WAS GOING TO SNOOP AROUND MORE, BEST TO GO DISGUISED. WHO KNOWS WHAT SORT OF HIDDEN SURVEILLANCE THERE IS ON CAMPUS.
I'M GOING TO MAKE THEM PAY FOR WHAT THEY DID.
DONNY, I DON'T THINK THIS IS FOR YOU.

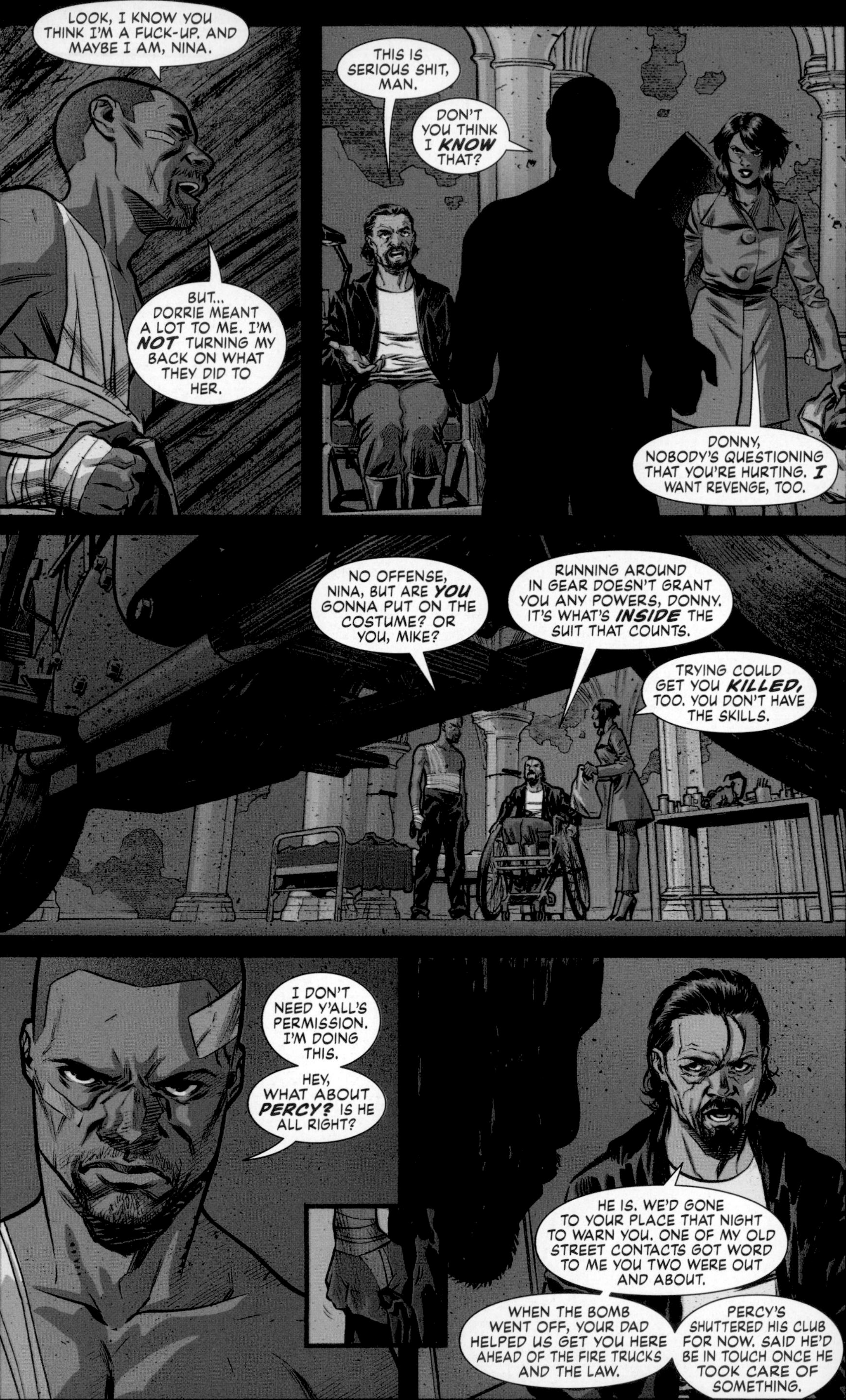
LOOK, I KNOW YOU THINK I'M A FUCK-UP. AND MAYBE I AM, NINA.
BUT... DORRIE MEANT A LOT TO ME. I'M **NOT** TURNING MY BACK ON WHAT THEY DID TO HER.
THIS IS SERIOUS SHIT, MAN.
DON'T YOU THINK I **KNOW** THAT?
DONNY, NOBODY'S QUESTIONING THAT YOU'RE HURTING. **I** WANT REVENGE, TOO.
NO OFFENSE, NINA, BUT ARE **YOU** GONNA PUT ON THE COSTUME? OR YOU, MIKE?
RUNNING AROUND IN GEAR DOESN'T GRANT YOU ANY POWERS, DONNY. IT'S WHAT'S **INSIDE** THE SUIT THAT COUNTS.
TRYING COULD GET YOU **KILLED,** TOO. YOU DON'T HAVE THE SKILLS.
I DON'T NEED Y'ALL'S PERMISSION. I'M DOING THIS.
HEY, WHAT ABOUT **PERCY?** IS HE ALL RIGHT?
HE IS. WE'D GONE TO YOUR PLACE THAT NIGHT TO WARN YOU. ONE OF MY OLD STREET CONTACTS GOT WORD TO ME YOU TWO WERE OUT AND ABOUT.
WHEN THE BOMB WENT OFF, YOUR DAD HELPED US GET YOU HERE AHEAD OF THE FIRE TRUCKS AND THE LAW.
PERCY'S SHUTTERED HIS CLUB FOR NOW. SAID HE'D BE IN TOUCH ONCE HE TOOK CARE OF SOMETHING.

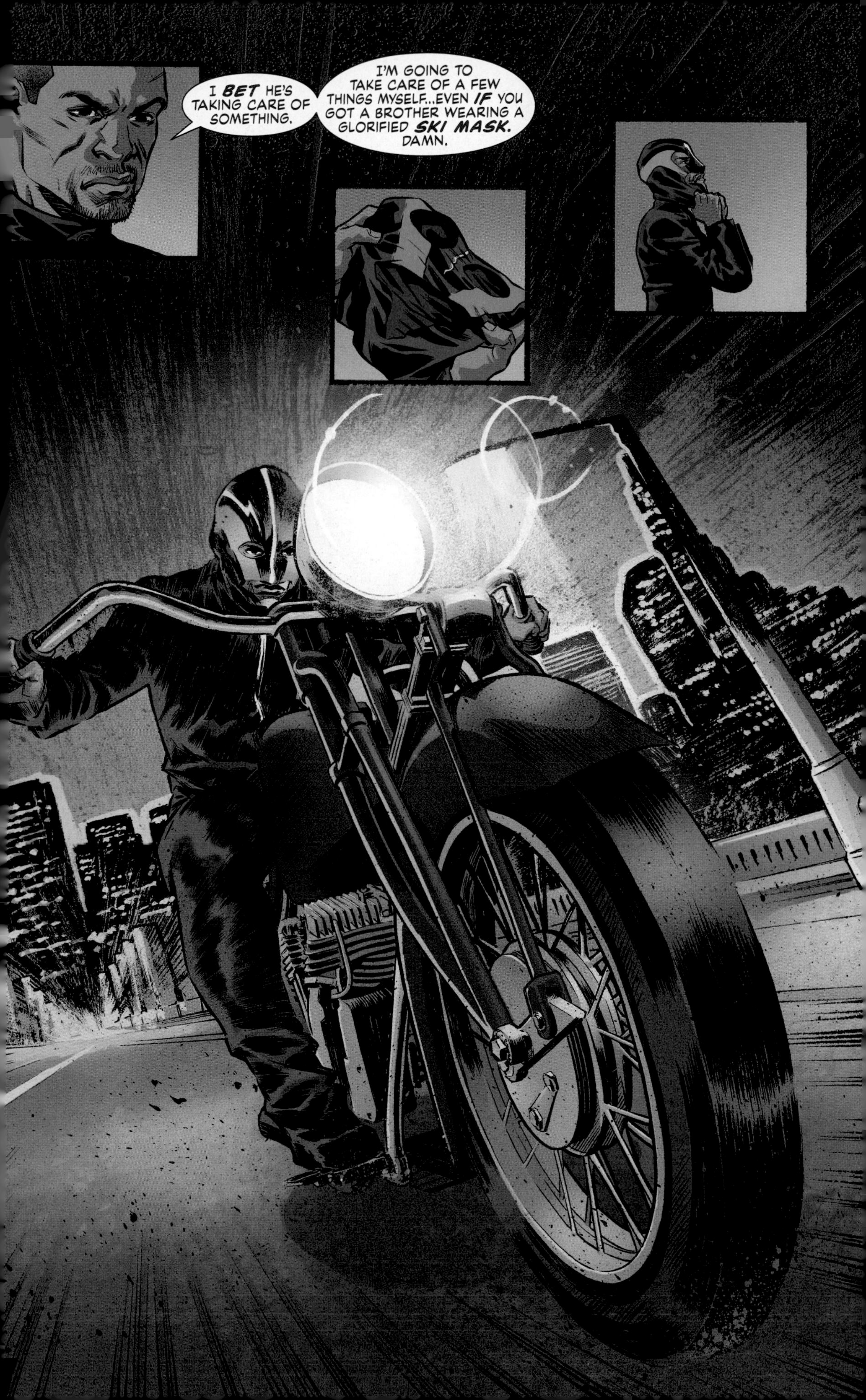
I BET HE'S TAKING CARE OF SOMETHING.
I'M GOING TO TAKE CARE OF A FEW THINGS MYSELF...EVEN IF YOU GOT A BROTHER WEARING A GLORIFIED SKI MASK. DAMN.

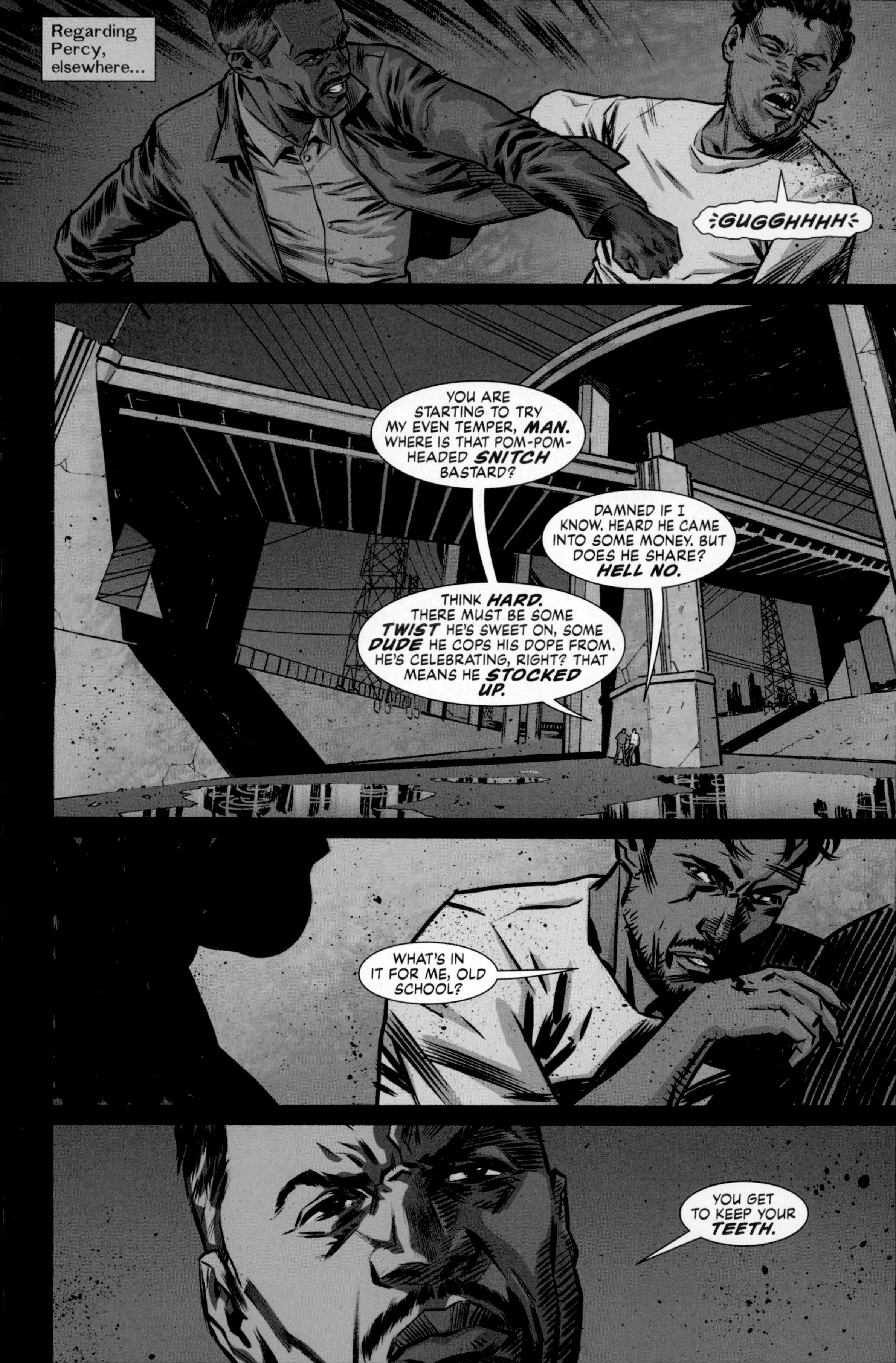
Regarding Percy, elsewhere...
GUGGHHHH
YOU ARE STARTING TO TRY MY EVEN TEMPER, MAN. WHERE IS THAT POM-POM-HEADED SNITCH BASTARD?
DAMNED IF I KNOW. HEARD HE CAME INTO SOME MONEY. BUT DOES HE SHARE? HELL NO.
THINK HARD. THERE MUST BE SOME TWIST HE'S SWEET ON, SOME DUDE HE COPS HIS DOPE FROM. HE'S CELEBRATING, RIGHT? THAT MEANS HE STOCKED UP.
WHAT'S IN IT FOR ME, OLD SCHOOL?
YOU GET TO KEEP YOUR TEETH.

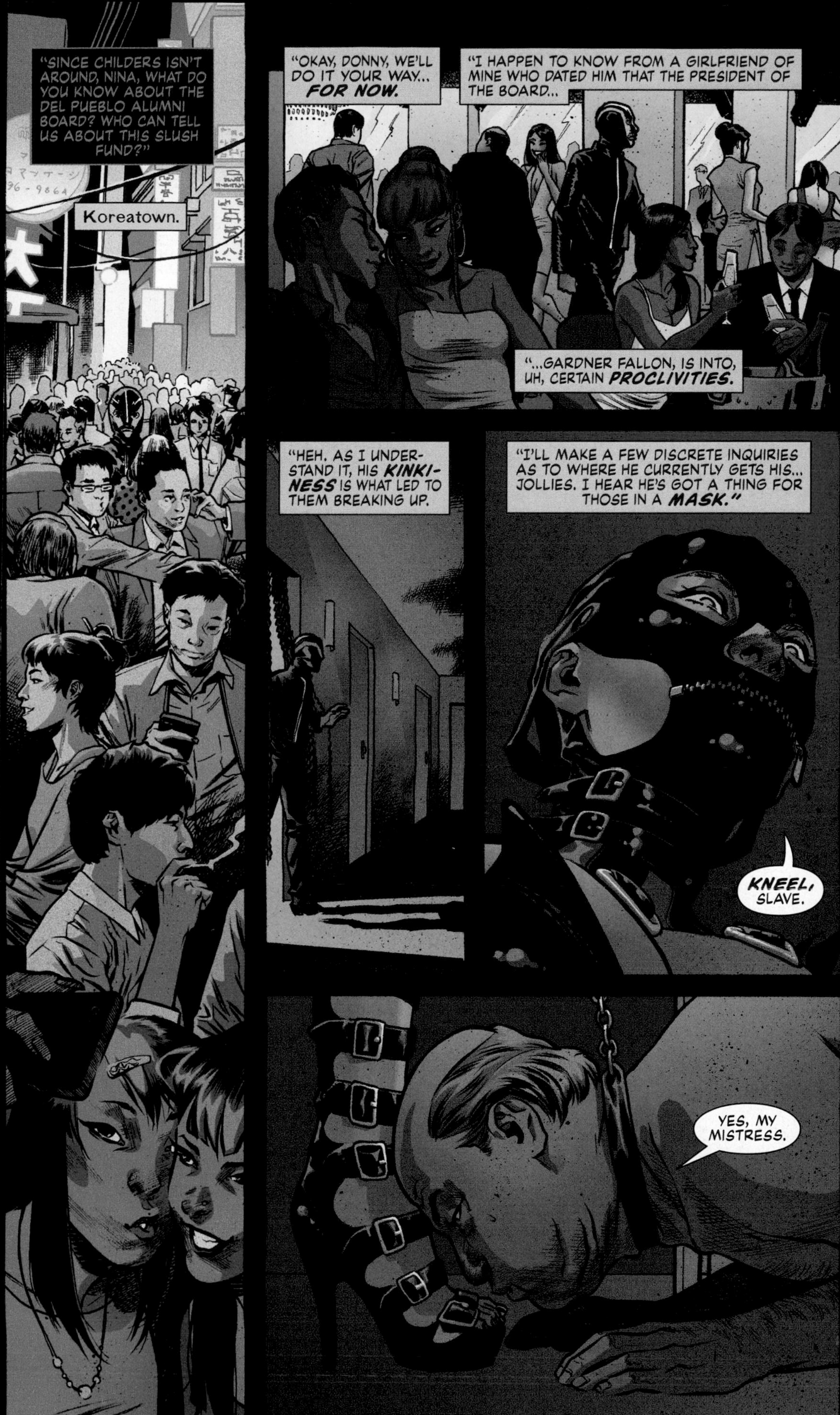
"SINCE CHILDERS ISN'T AROUND, NINA, WHAT DO YOU KNOW ABOUT THE DEL PUEBLO ALUMNI BOARD? WHO CAN TELL US ABOUT THIS SLUSH FUND?"
Koreatown.
"OKAY, DONNY, WE'LL DO IT YOUR WAY... FOR NOW.
"I HAPPEN TO KNOW FROM A GIRLFRIEND OF MINE WHO DATED HIM THAT THE PRESIDENT OF THE BOARD...
"...GARDNER FALLON, IS INTO, UH, CERTAIN PROCLIVITIES.
"HEH. AS I UNDERSTAND IT, HIS KINKINESS IS WHAT LED TO THEM BREAKING UP.
"I'LL MAKE A FEW DISCRETE INQUIRIES AS TO WHERE HE CURRENTLY GETS HIS... JOLLIES. I HEAR HE'S GOT A THING FOR THOSE IN A MASK."
KNEEL, SLAVE.
YES, MY MISTRESS.

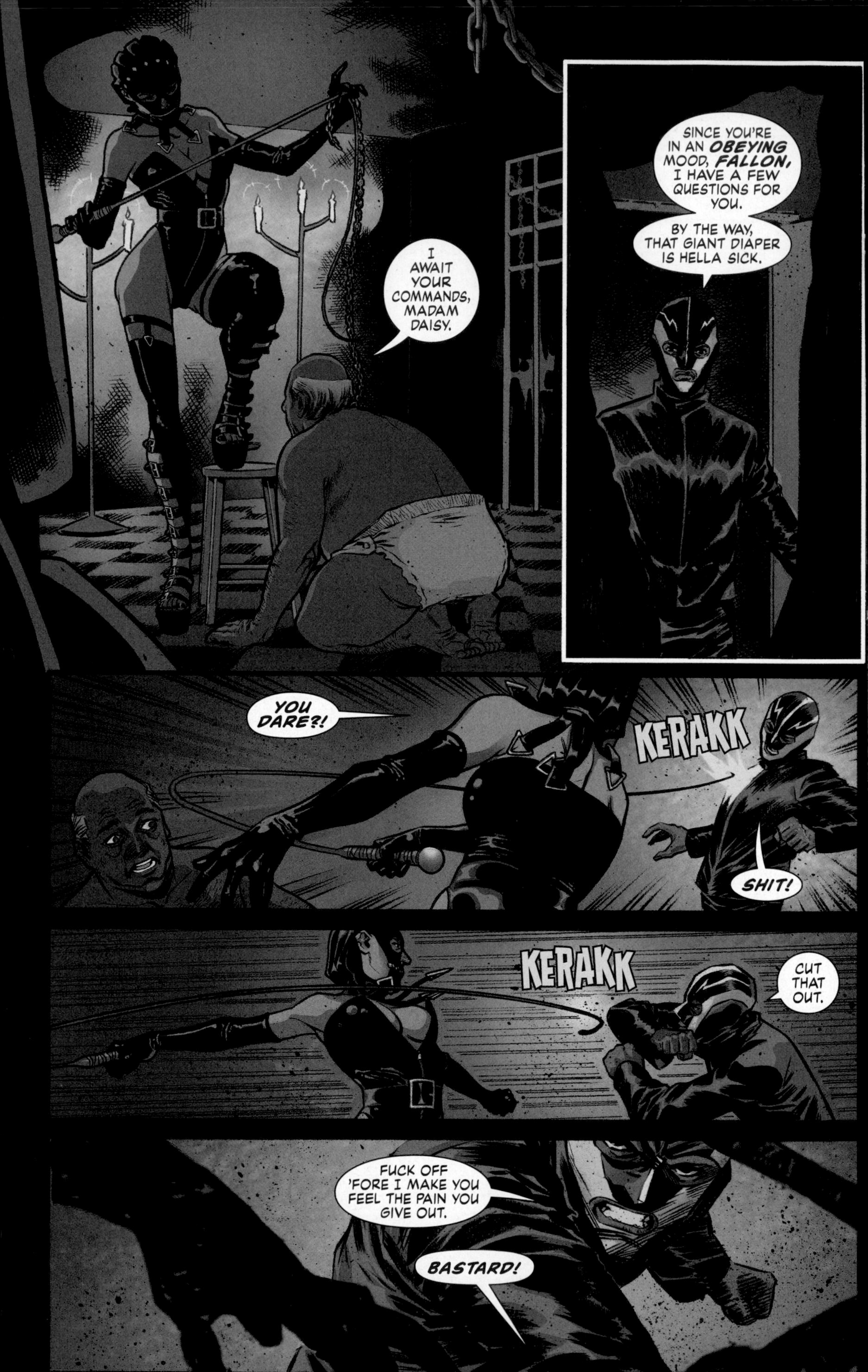

I AWAIT YOUR COMMANDS, MADAM DAISY.
SINCE YOU'RE IN AN OBEYING MOOD, FALLON, I HAVE A FEW QUESTIONS FOR YOU.
BY THE WAY, THAT GIANT DIAPER IS HELLA SICK.
YOU DARE?!
KERAKK
SHIT!
KERAKK
CUT THAT OUT.
FUCK OFF 'FORE I MAKE YOU FEEL THE PAIN YOU GIVE OUT.
BASTARD!

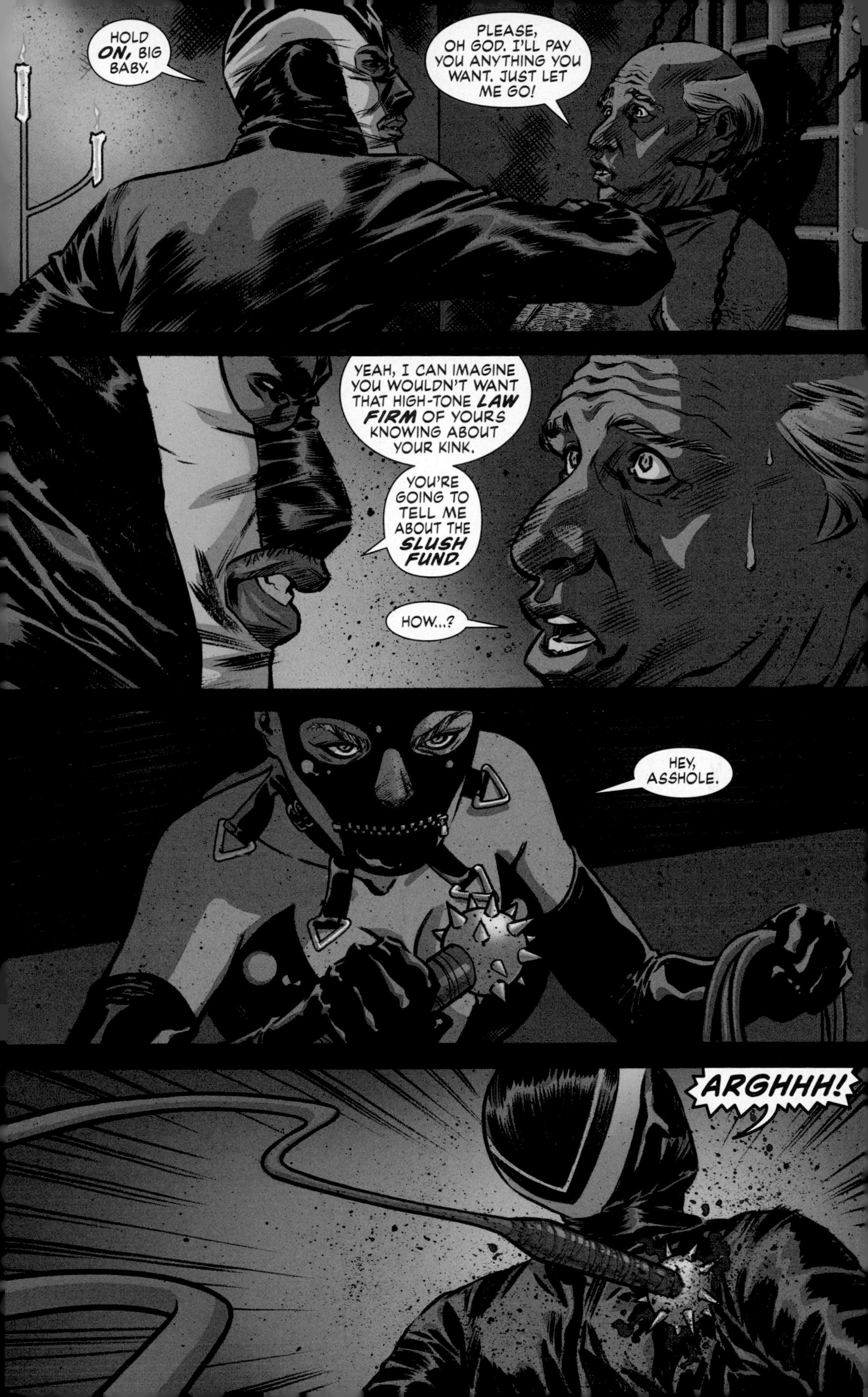
HOLD ON, BIG BABY.
PLEASE, OH GOD. I'LL PAY YOU ANYTHING YOU WANT. JUST LET ME GO!
YEAH, I CAN IMAGINE YOU WOULDN'T WANT THAT HIGH-TONE LAW FIRM OF YOURS KNOWING ABOUT YOUR KINK.
YOU'RE GOING TO TELL ME ABOUT THE SLUSH FUND.
HOW...?
HEY, ASSHOLE.
ARGHHH!

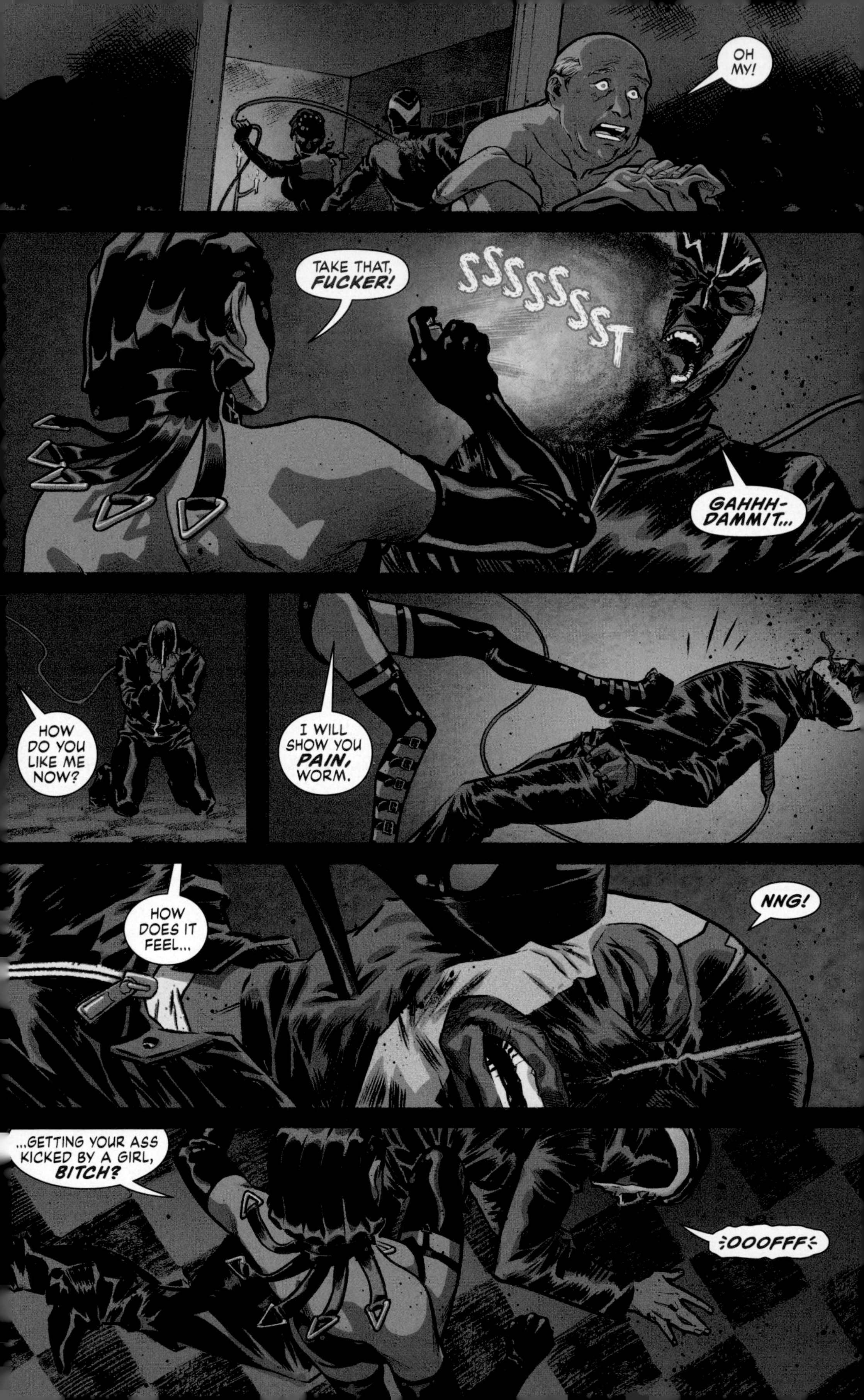
OH MY!
TAKE THAT, FUCKER!
SSSSSSST
GAHHH-DAMMIT...
HOW DO YOU LIKE ME NOW?
I WILL SHOW YOU PAIN, WORM.
HOW DOES IT FEEL...
NNG!
...GETTING YOUR ASS KICKED BY A GIRL, BITCH?
OOOFFF

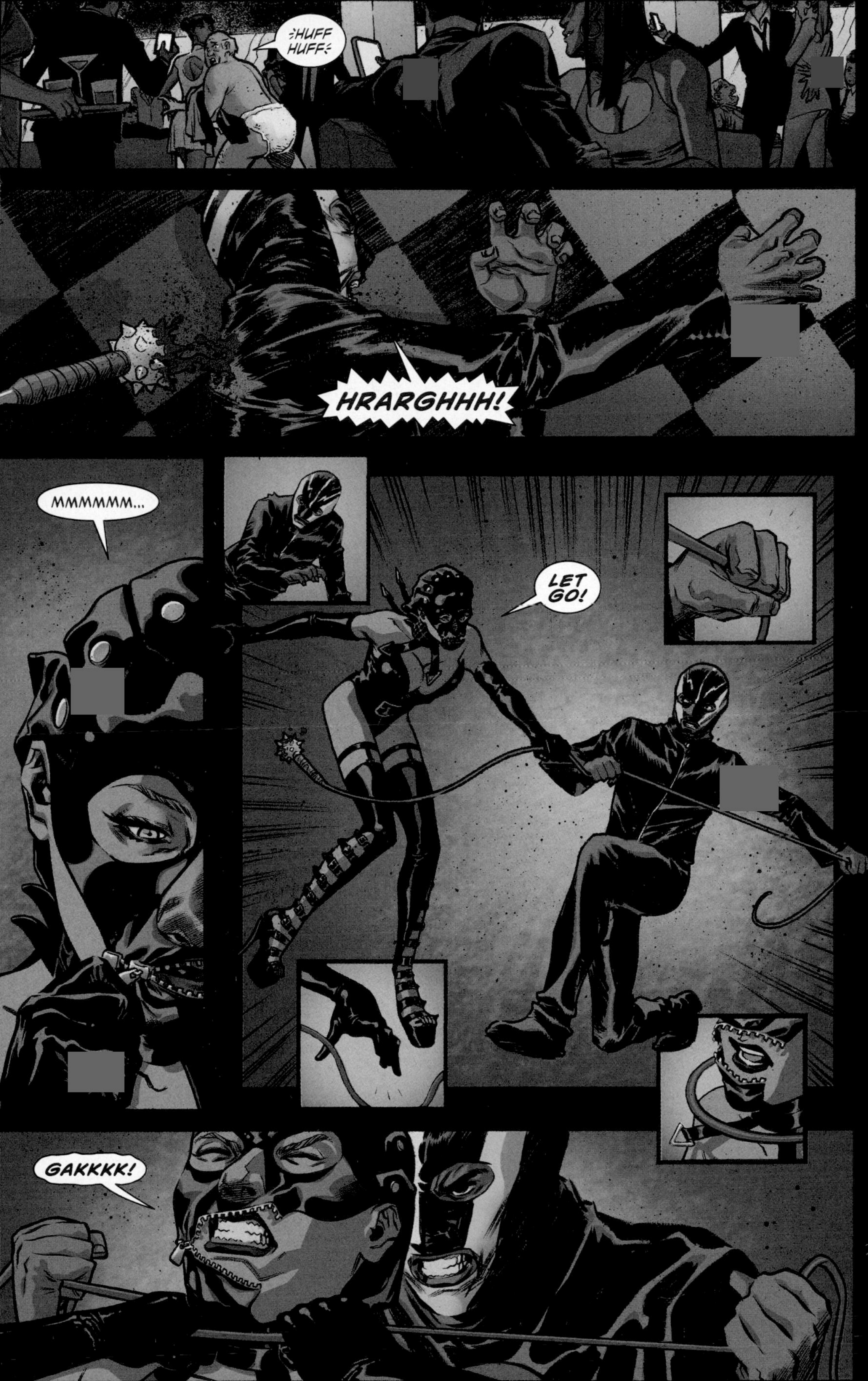
HUFF HUFF
HRARGHHH!
MMMMMM...
LET GO!
GAKKKK!

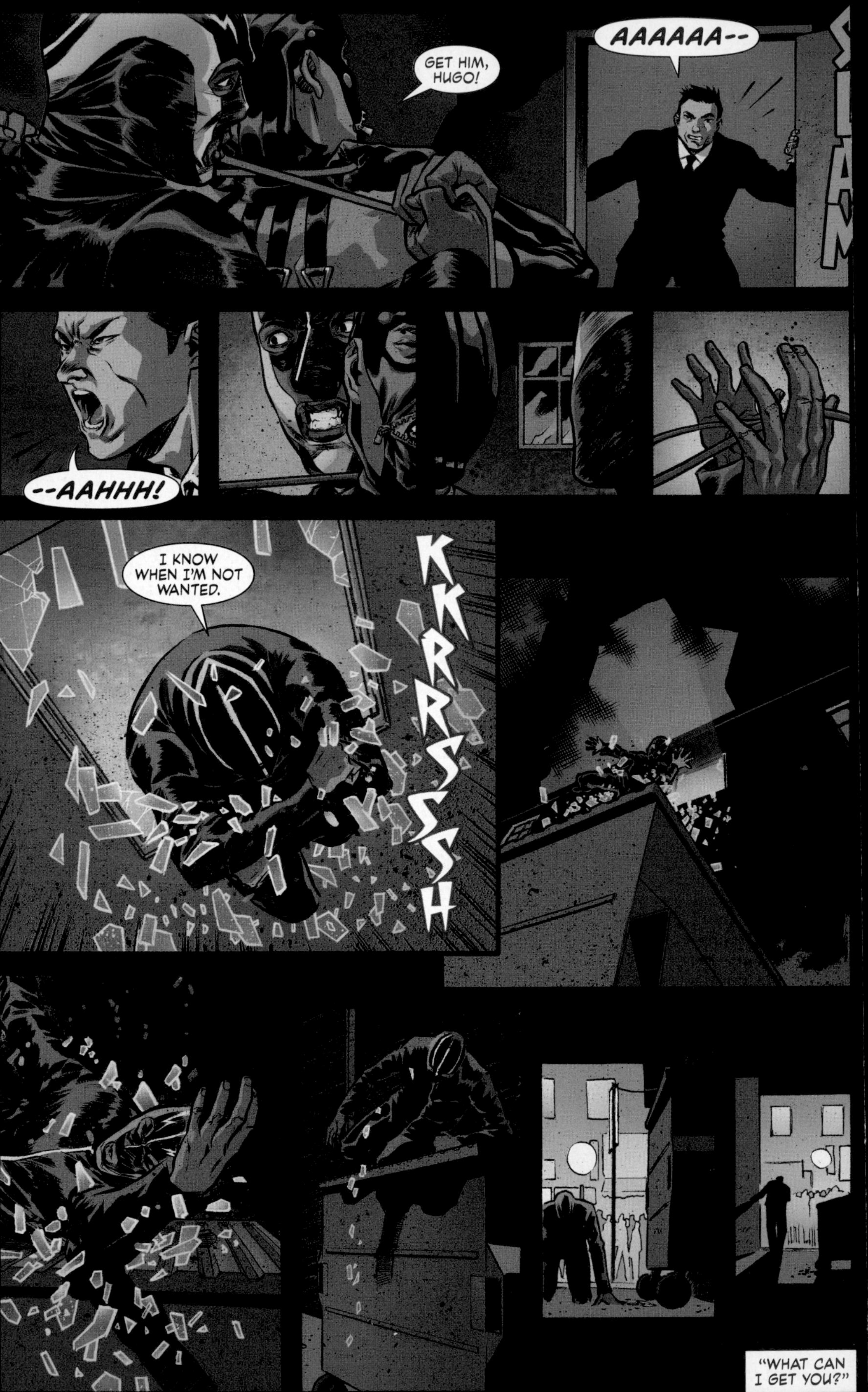
GET HIM, HUGO!
AAAAAA--
--AAHHH!
I KNOW WHEN I'M NOT WANTED.
KKRRSSSH
"WHAT CAN I GET YOU?"

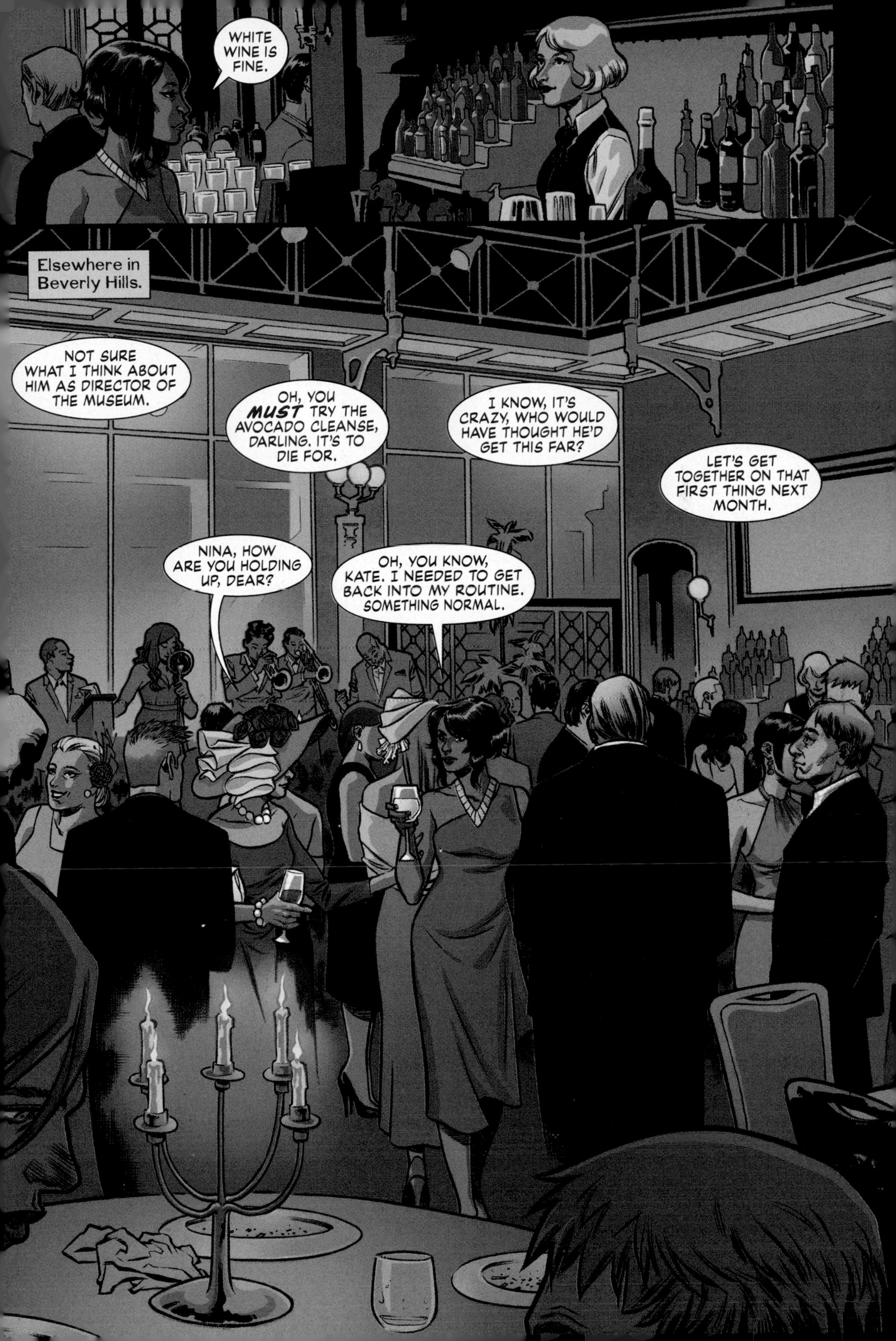
WHITE WINE IS FINE.
Elsewhere in Beverly Hills.
NOT SURE WHAT I THINK ABOUT HIM AS DIRECTOR OF THE MUSEUM.
OH, YOU MUST TRY THE AVOCADO CLEANSE, DARLING. IT'S TO DIE FOR.
I KNOW, IT'S CRAZY, WHO WOULD HAVE THOUGHT HE'D GET THIS FAR?
LET'S GET TOGETHER ON THAT FIRST THING NEXT MONTH.
NINA, HOW ARE YOU HOLDING UP, DEAR?
OH, YOU KNOW, KATE. I NEEDED TO GET BACK INTO MY ROUTINE. SOMETHING NORMAL.

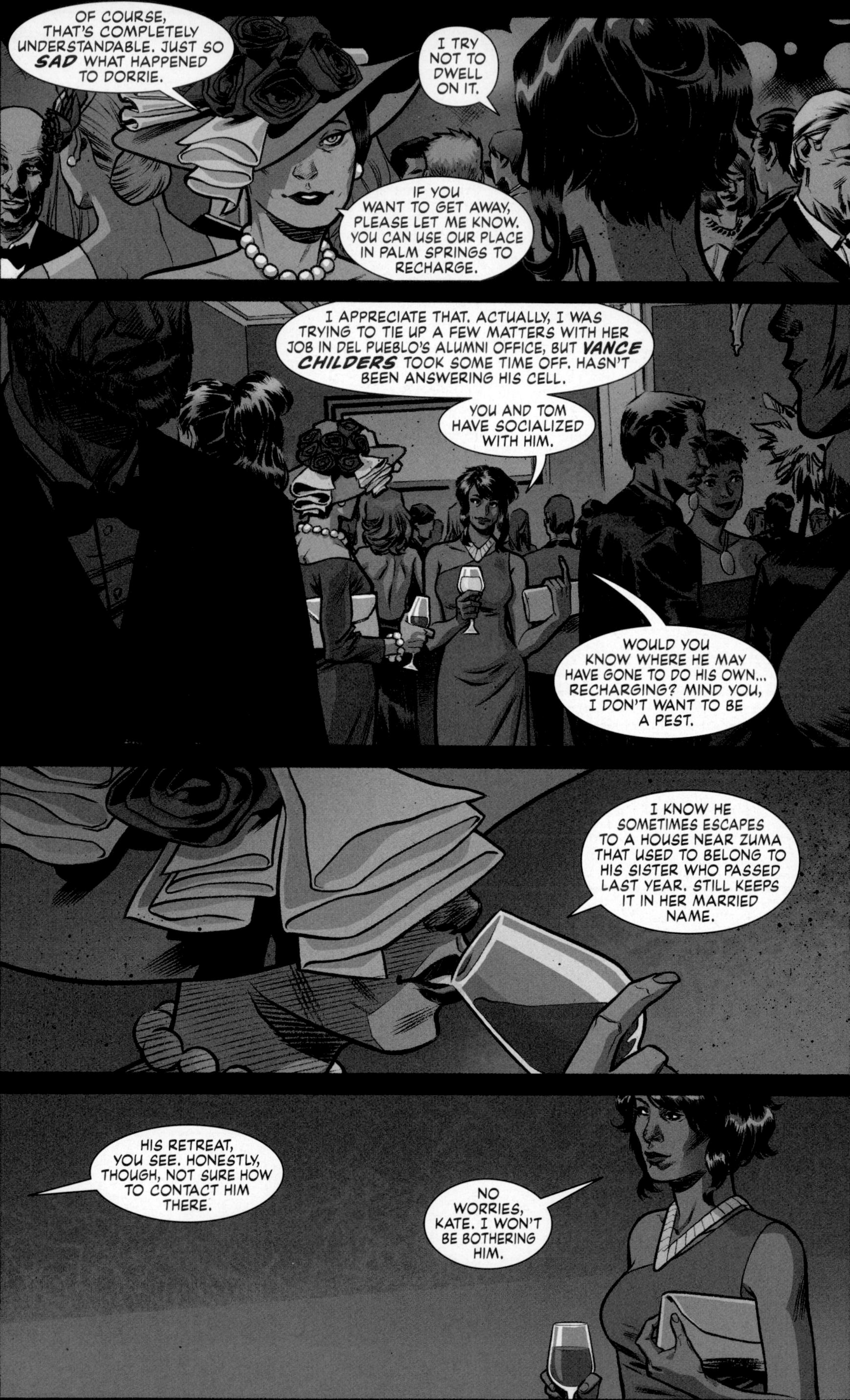
OF COURSE, THAT'S COMPLETELY UNDERSTANDABLE. JUST SO SAD WHAT HAPPENED TO DORRIE.
I TRY NOT TO DWELL ON IT.
IF YOU WANT TO GET AWAY, PLEASE LET ME KNOW. YOU CAN USE OUR PLACE IN PALM SPRINGS TO RECHARGE.
I APPRECIATE THAT. ACTUALLY, I WAS TRYING TO TIE UP A FEW MATTERS WITH HER JOB IN DEL PUEBLO'S ALUMNI OFFICE, BUT VANCE CHILDERS TOOK SOME TIME OFF. HASN'T BEEN ANSWERING HIS CELL.
YOU AND TOM HAVE SOCIALIZED WITH HIM.
WOULD YOU KNOW WHERE HE MAY HAVE GONE TO DO HIS OWN... RECHARGING? MIND YOU, I DON'T WANT TO BE A PEST.
I KNOW HE SOMETIMES ESCAPES TO A HOUSE NEAR ZUMA THAT USED TO BELONG TO HIS SISTER WHO PASSED LAST YEAR. STILL KEEPS IT IN HER MARRIED NAME.
HIS RETREAT, YOU SEE. HONESTLY, THOUGH, NOT SURE HOW TO CONTACT HIM THERE.
NO WORRIES, KATE. I WON'T BE BOTHERING HIM.

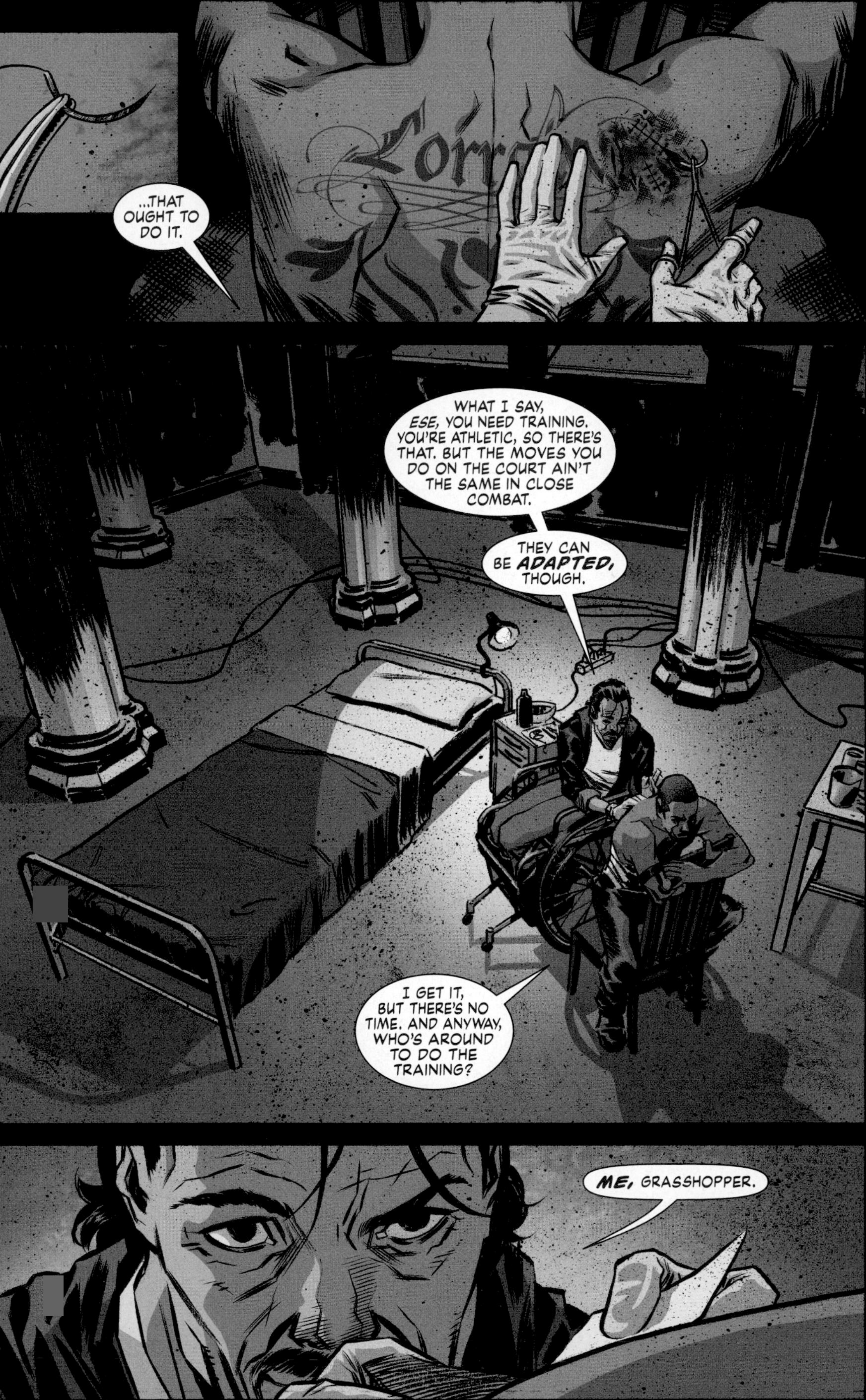

...THAT OUGHT TO DO IT.
WHAT I SAY, *ESE,* YOU NEED TRAINING. YOU'RE ATHLETIC, SO THERE'S THAT. BUT THE MOVES YOU DO ON THE COURT AIN'T THE SAME IN CLOSE COMBAT.
THEY CAN BE ***ADAPTED,*** THOUGH.
I GET IT, BUT THERE'S NO TIME. AND ANYWAY, WHO'S AROUND TO DO THE TRAINING?
ME, GRASSHOPPER.

NO DISRESPECT, MIKE, BUT HAVE YOU FORGOTTEN YOUR CURRENT CONDITION?

Miguel Ruben Regalado

Massachusetts Institute of Technology

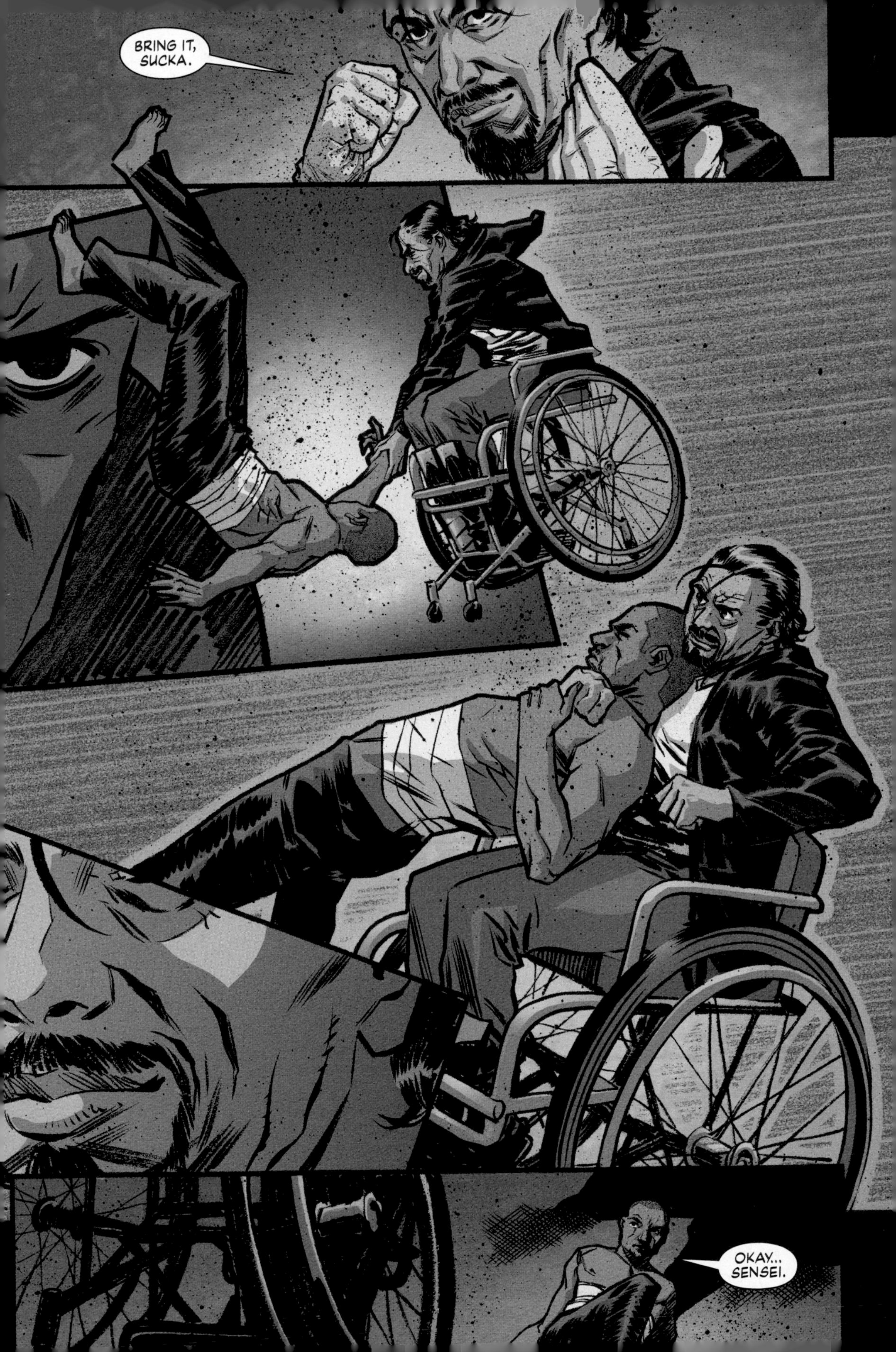
BRING IT, SUCKA.
OKAY... SENSEI.

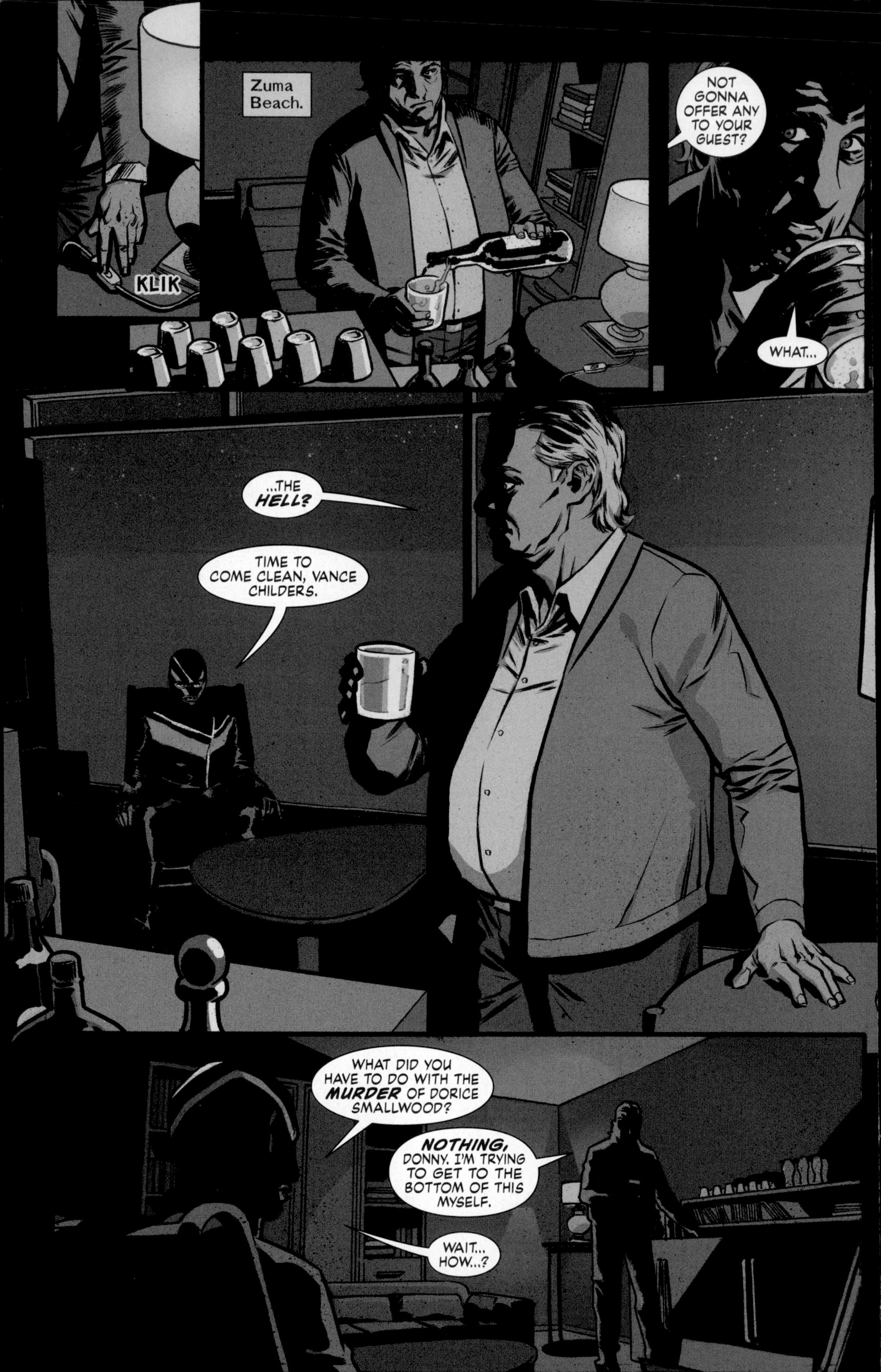

KLIK
Zuma Beach.
NOT GONNA OFFER ANY TO YOUR GUEST?
WHAT...
...THE HELL?
TIME TO COME CLEAN, VANCE CHILDERS.
WHAT DID YOU HAVE TO DO WITH THE MURDER OF DORICE SMALLWOOD?
NOTHING, DONNY. I'M TRYING TO GET TO THE BOTTOM OF THIS MYSELF.
WAIT... HOW...?

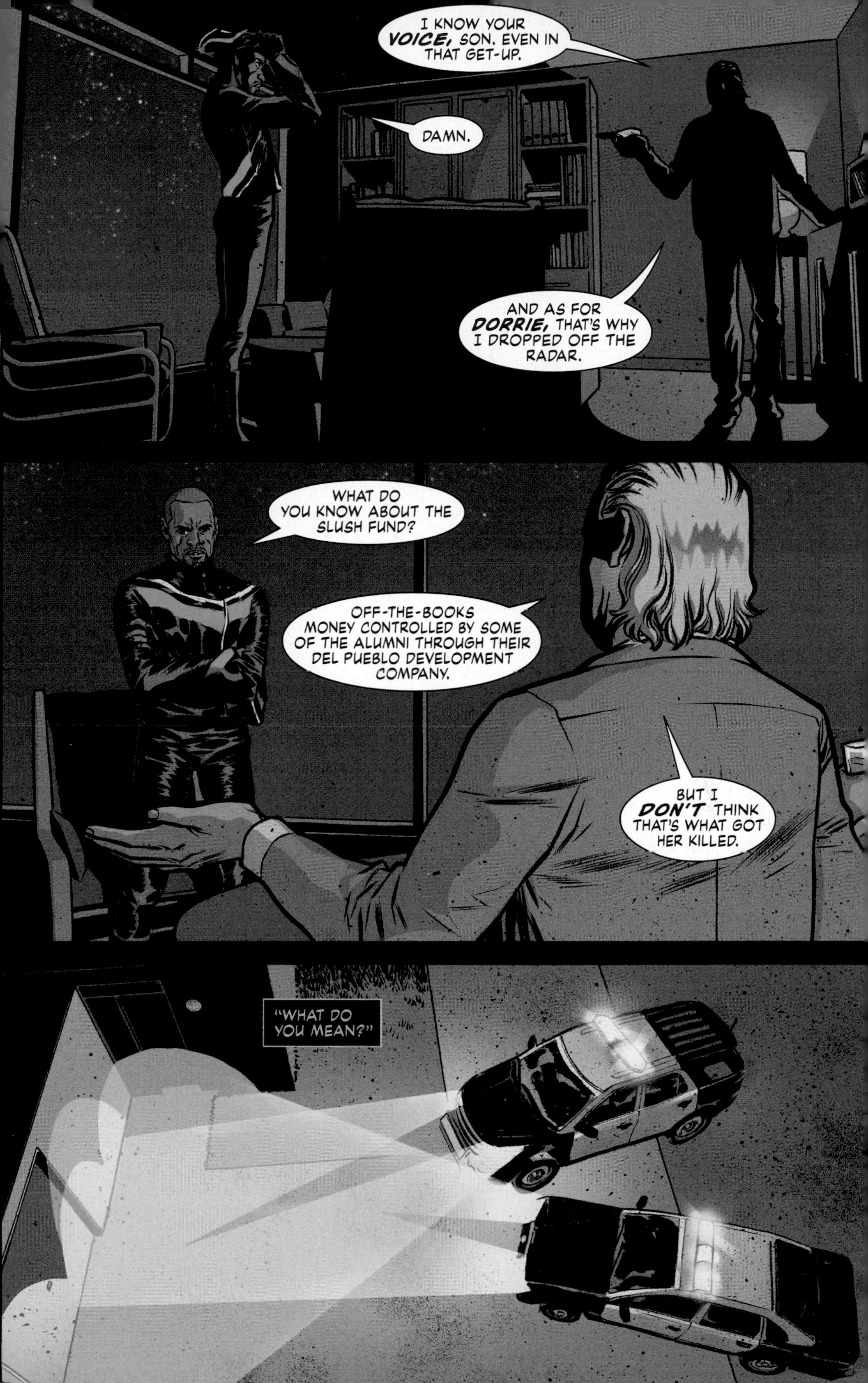
I KNOW YOUR VOICE, SON. EVEN IN THAT GET-UP.
DAMN.
AND AS FOR DORRIE, THAT'S WHY I DROPPED OFF THE RADAR.
WHAT DO YOU KNOW ABOUT THE SLUSH FUND?
OFF-THE-BOOKS MONEY CONTROLLED BY SOME OF THE ALUMNI THROUGH THEIR DEL PUEBLO DEVELOPMENT COMPANY.
BUT I DON'T THINK THAT'S WHAT GOT HER KILLED.
"WHAT DO YOU MEAN?"

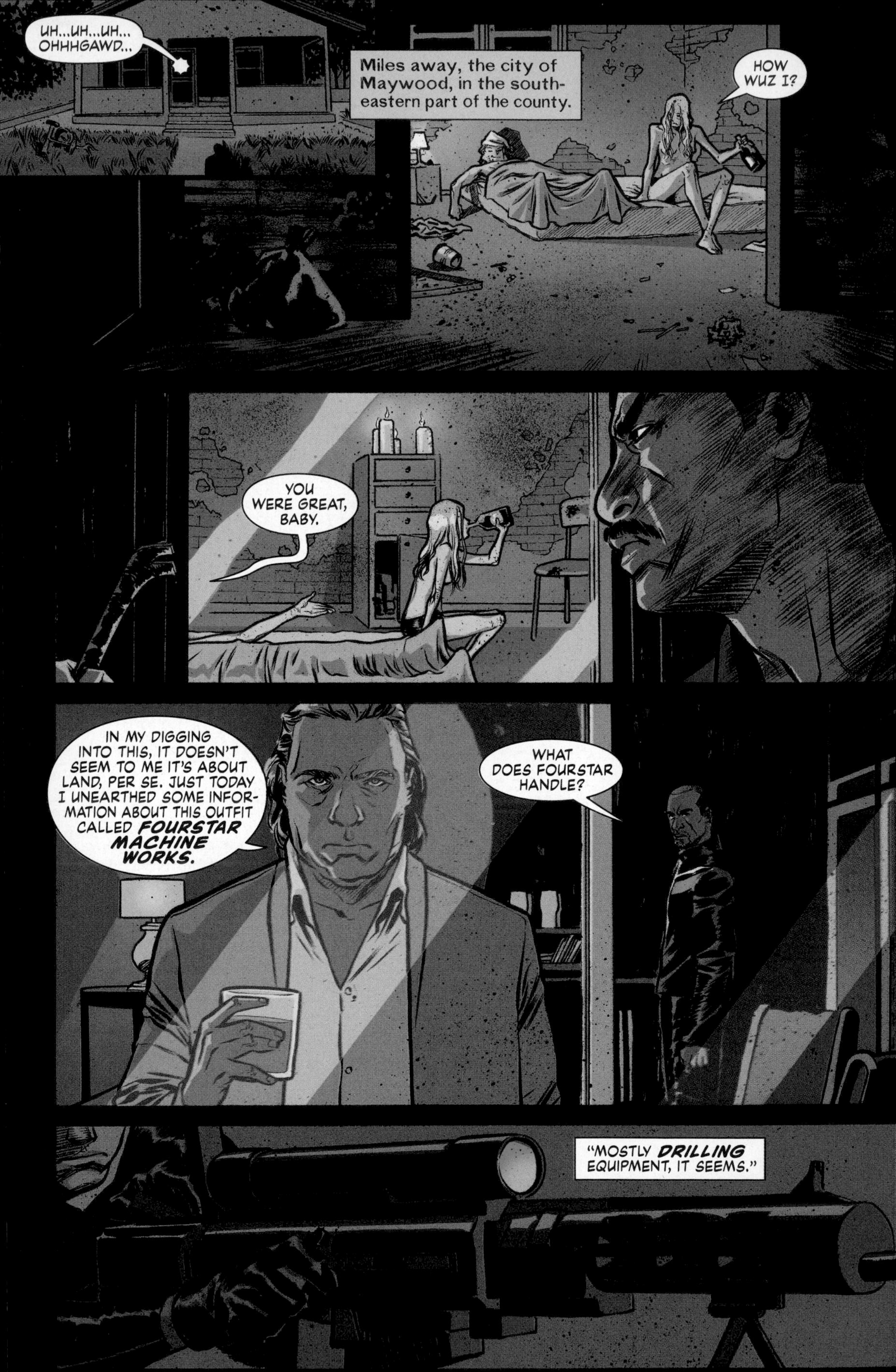
UH...UH...UH... OHHHGAWD...
Miles away, the city of Maywood, in the south-eastern part of the county.
HOW WUZ I?
YOU WERE GREAT, BABY.
IN MY DIGGING INTO THIS, IT DOESN'T SEEM TO ME IT'S ABOUT LAND, PER SE. JUST TODAY I UNEARTHED SOME INFORMATION ABOUT THIS OUTFIT CALLED FOURSTAR MACHINE WORKS.
WHAT DOES FOURSTAR HANDLE?
"MOSTLY DRILLING EQUIPMENT, IT SEEMS."

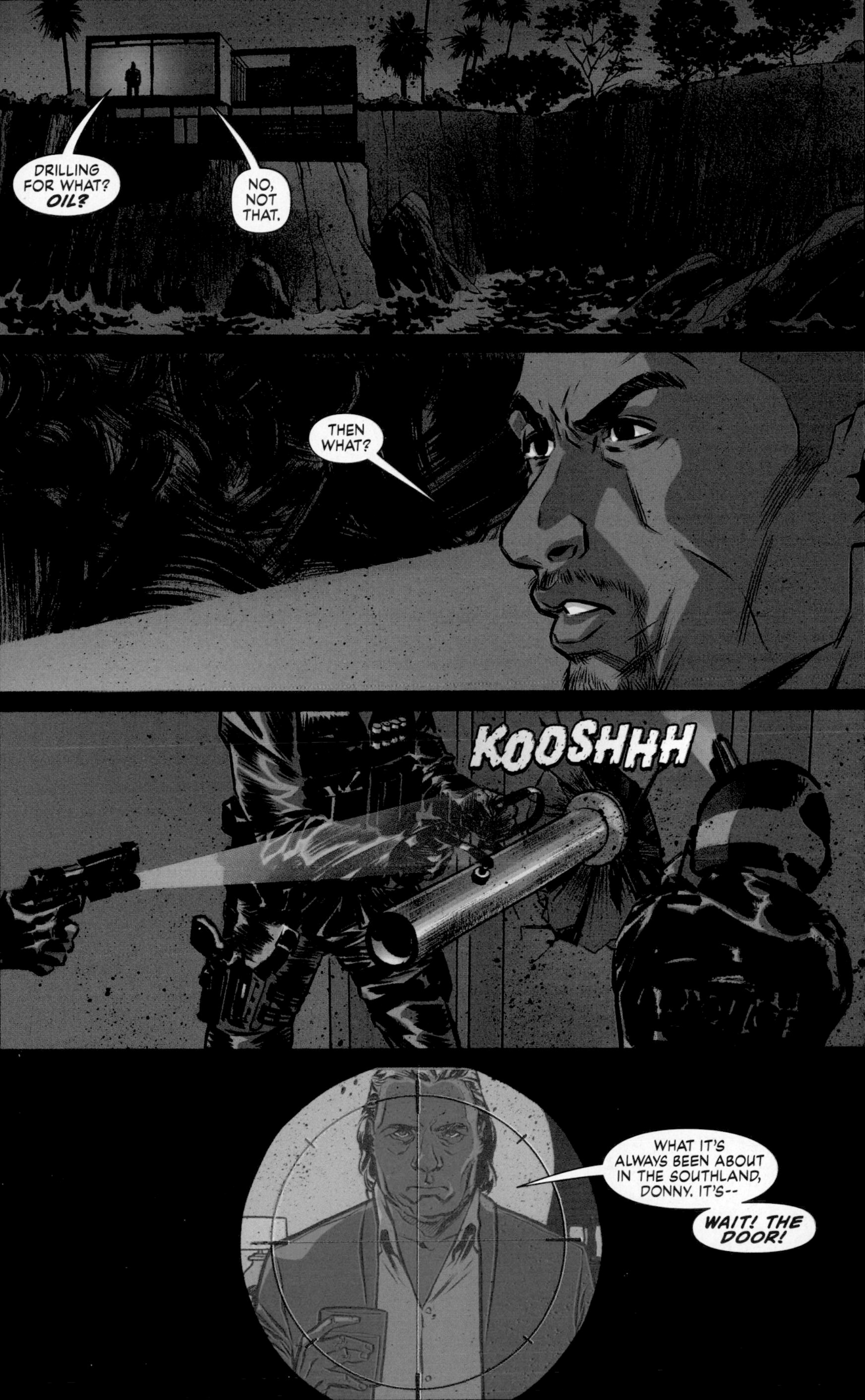
DRILLING FOR WHAT? OIL?
NO, NOT THAT.
THEN WHAT?
KOOSHHH
WHAT IT'S ALWAYS BEEN ABOUT IN THE SOUTHLAND, DONNY. IT'S--
WAIT! THE DOOR!

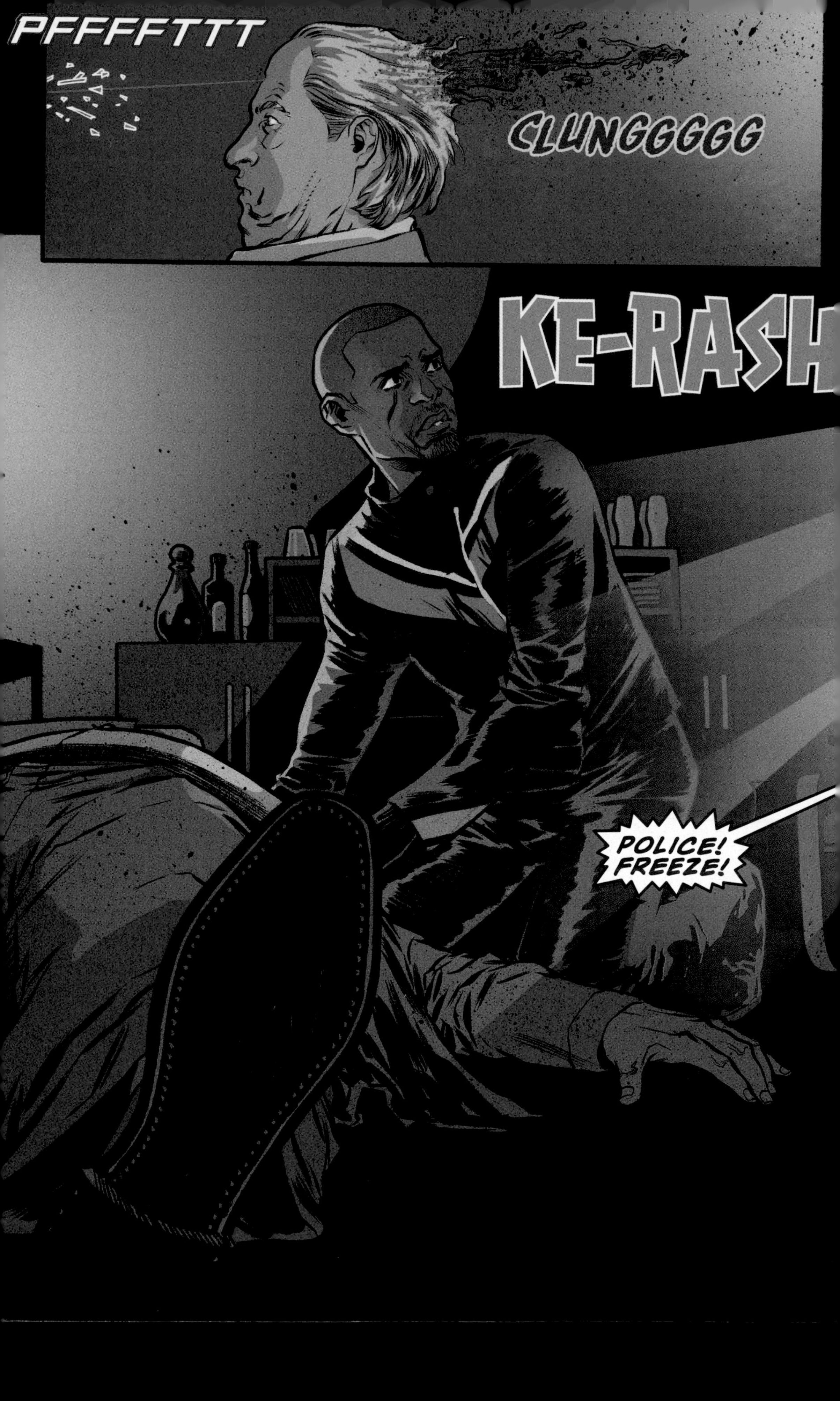
PFFFFTTT
CLUNGGGGG
KE-RASH
POLICE! FREEZE!

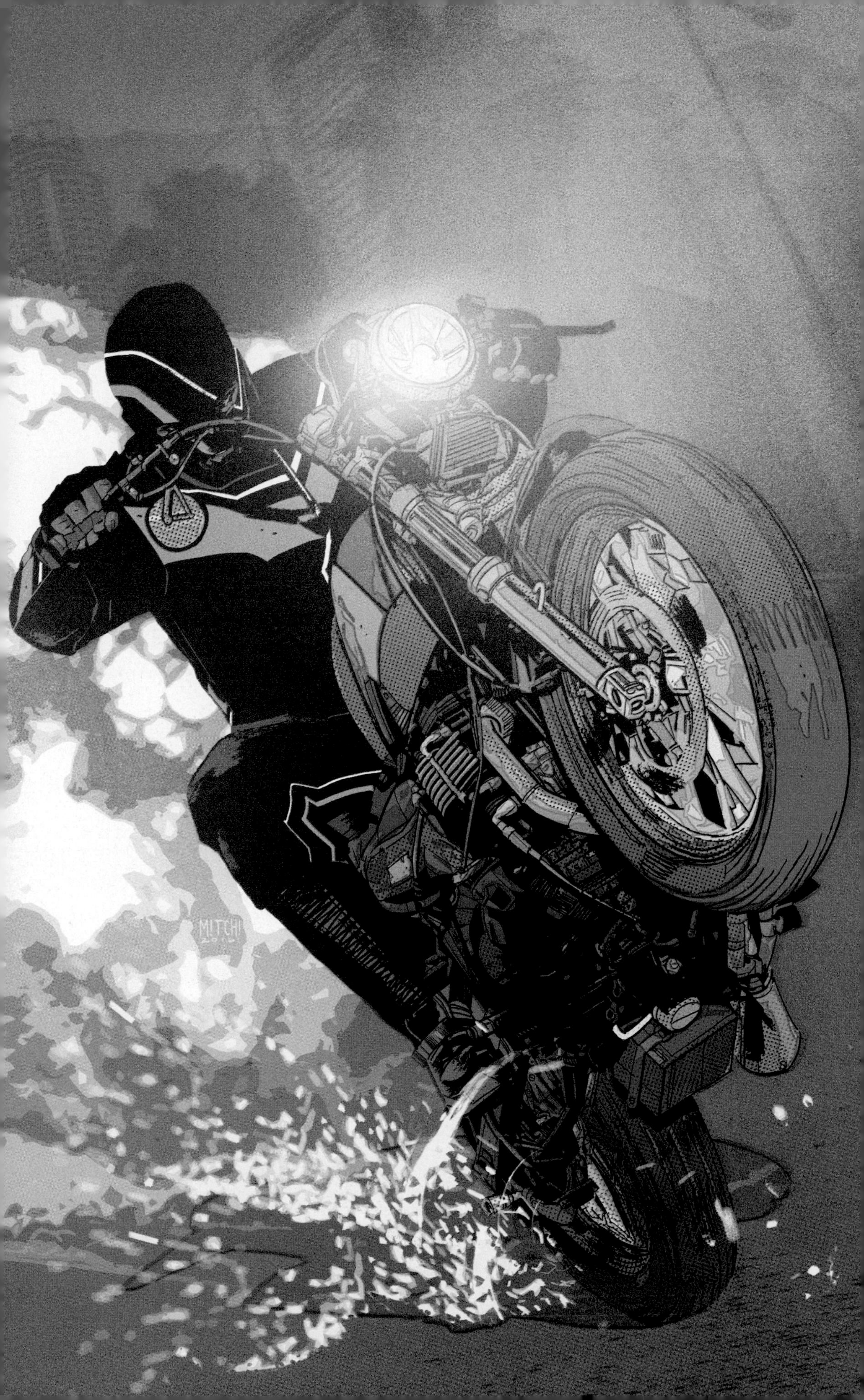
M!TCH!

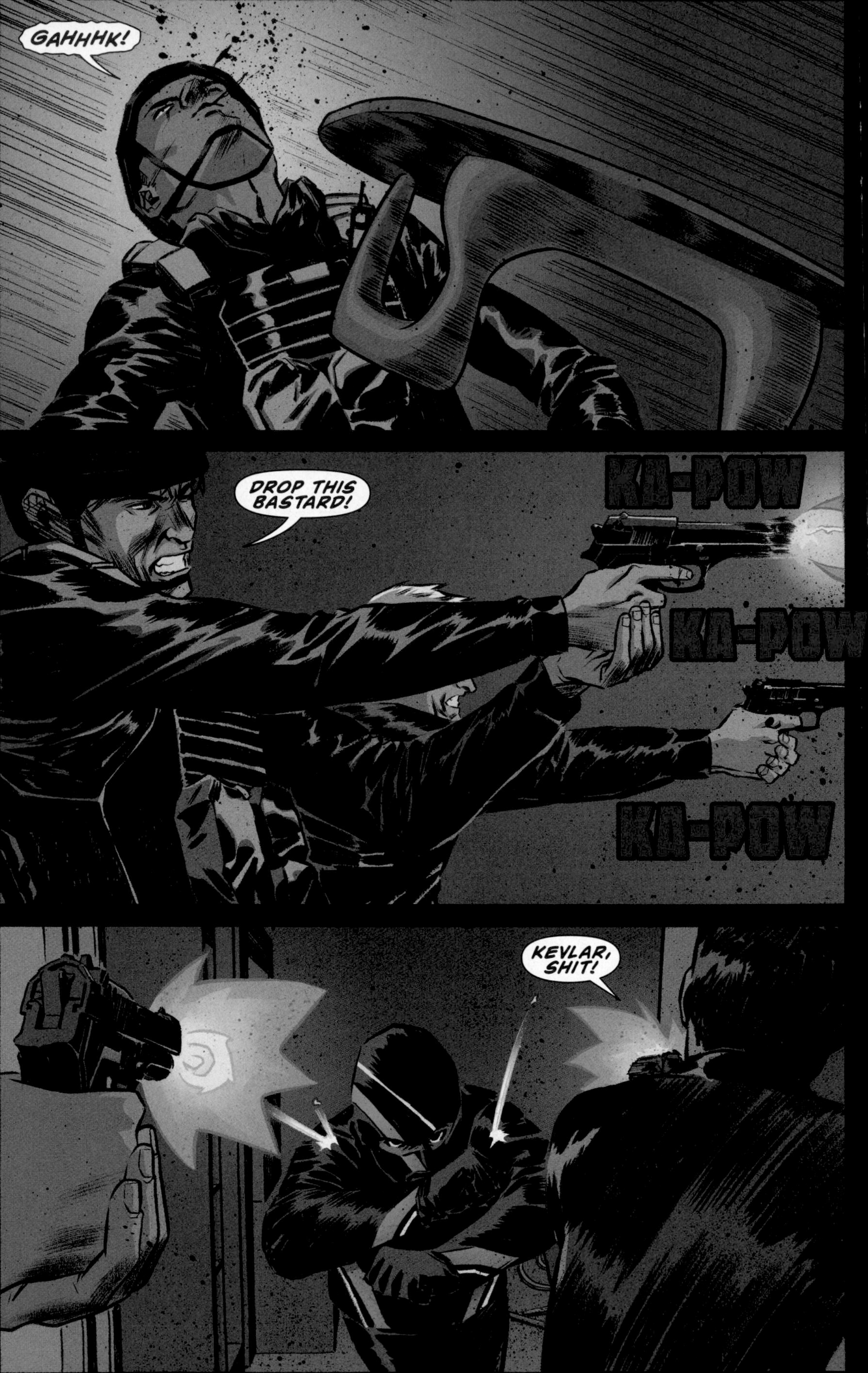
GAHHHK!
DROP THIS BASTARD!
KA-POW
KA-POW
KA-POW
KEVLAR, SHIT!

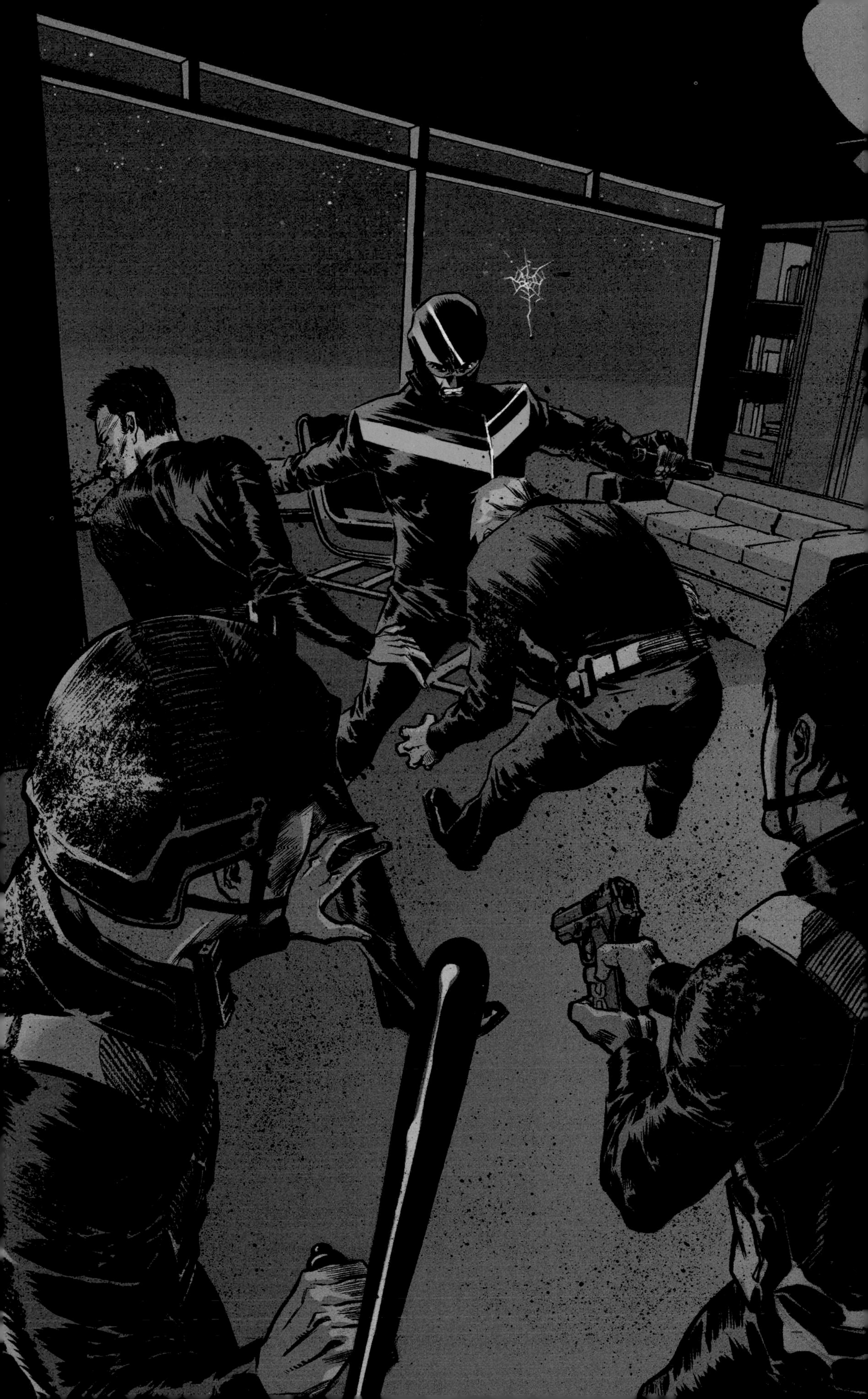

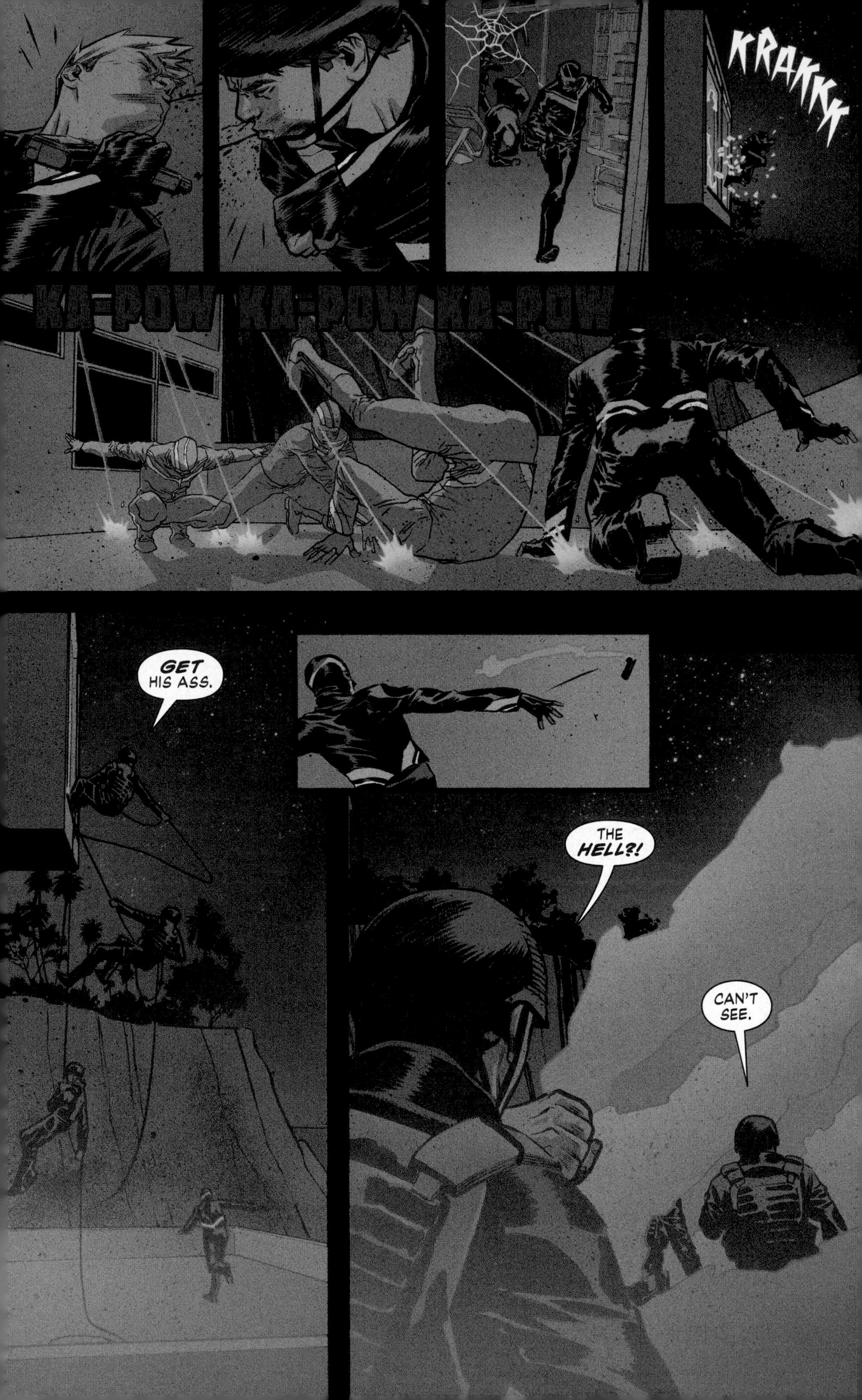
KRAKKK
KA-POW KA-POW KA-POW
GET HIS ASS.
THE HELL?!
CAN'T SEE.

SOMEBODY GET THE DAMN COAST GUARD ON THE LINE.

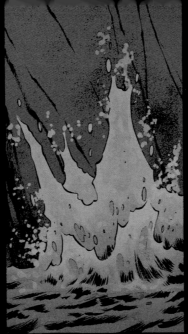

I'LL ATTEND TO YOU SOON...MR. FAIRCHILD.

WHAT THE HELL'S THE POINT OF WEARING A MASK IF EVERYONE KNOWS IT'S ME?

VHROOOOM

THIS IS THE *POLICE.* YOU THERE, IN THE WATER-- *HALT!*

WHUP WHUP WHUP

IT JUST KEEPS GETTING BETTER.

VIP VIP VIP VIP VIP VIP VIP

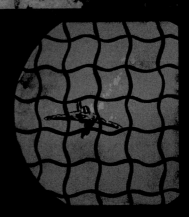

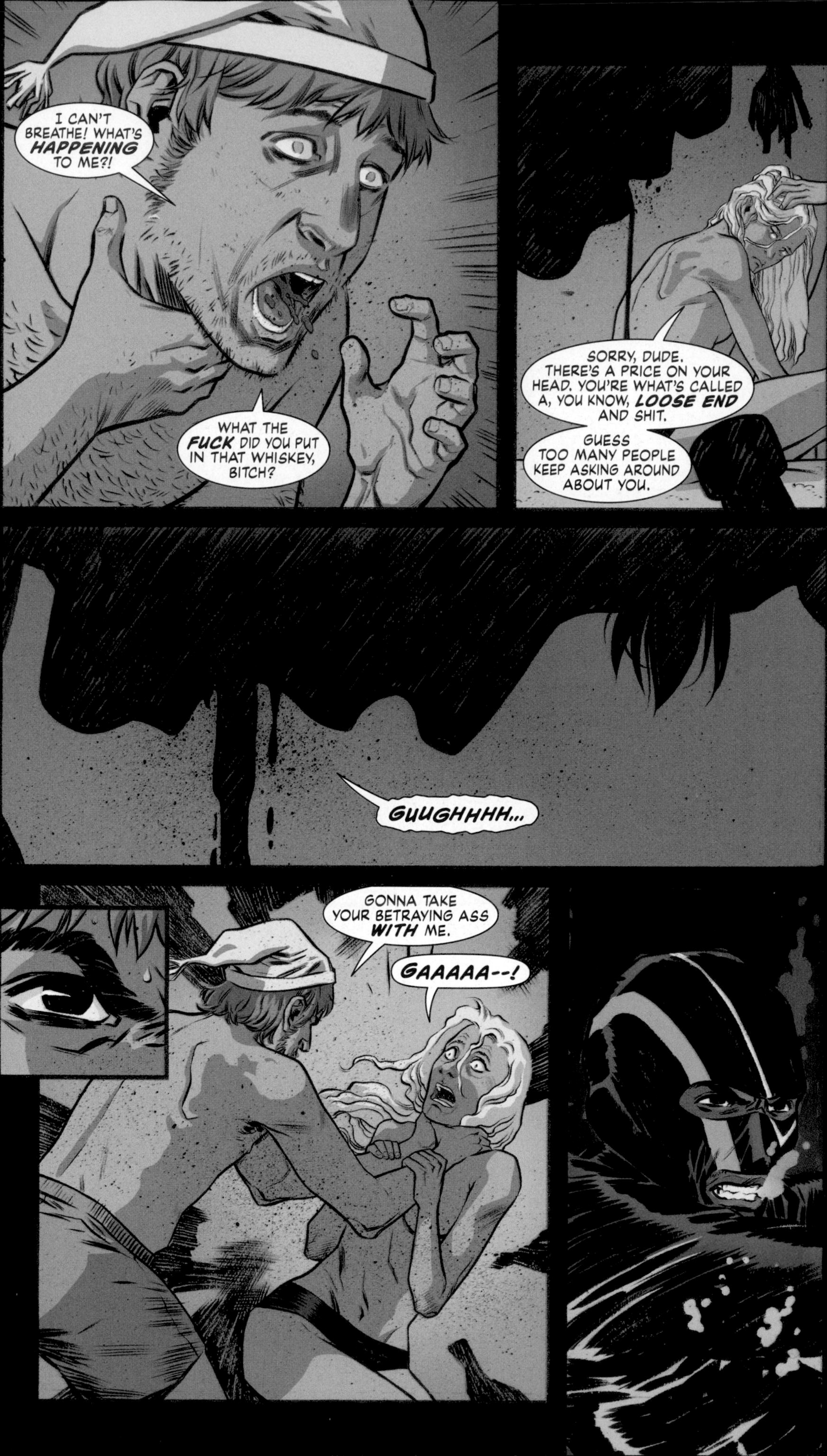
I CAN'T BREATHE! WHAT'S HAPPENING TO ME?!
WHAT THE FUCK DID YOU PUT IN THAT WHISKEY, BITCH?
SORRY, DUDE. THERE'S A PRICE ON YOUR HEAD. YOU'RE WHAT'S CALLED A, YOU KNOW, LOOSE END AND SHIT.
GUESS TOO MANY PEOPLE KEEP ASKING AROUND ABOUT YOU.
GUUGHHHH...
GONNA TAKE YOUR BETRAYING ASS WITH ME.
GAAAAA--!

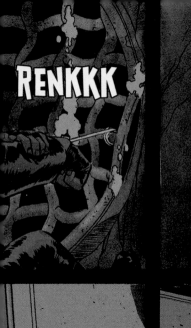

RENKKK

KRIIKKK

SLAM

THE FUCK?!

KAFF KAFF KAFF

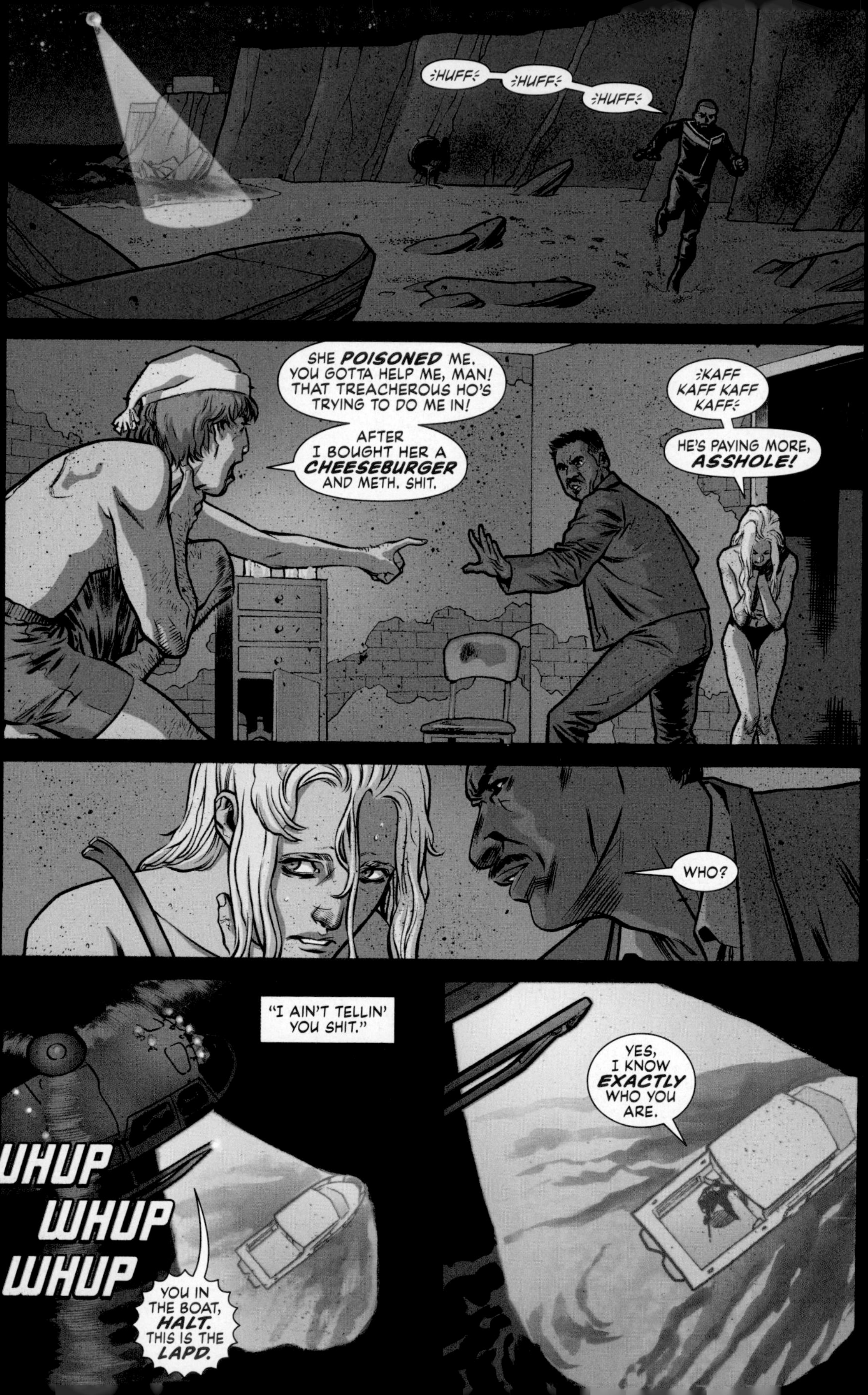

HUFF
HUFF
HUFF
SHE POISONED ME. YOU GOTTA HELP ME, MAN! THAT TREACHEROUS HO'S TRYING TO DO ME IN!
AFTER I BOUGHT HER A CHEESEBURGER AND METH. SHIT.
KAFF KAFF KAFF KAFF
HE'S PAYING MORE, ASSHOLE!
WHO?
"I AIN'T TELLIN' YOU SHIT."
WHUP WHUP WHUP
YOU IN THE BOAT, HALT. THIS IS THE LAPD.
YES, I KNOW EXACTLY WHO YOU ARE.

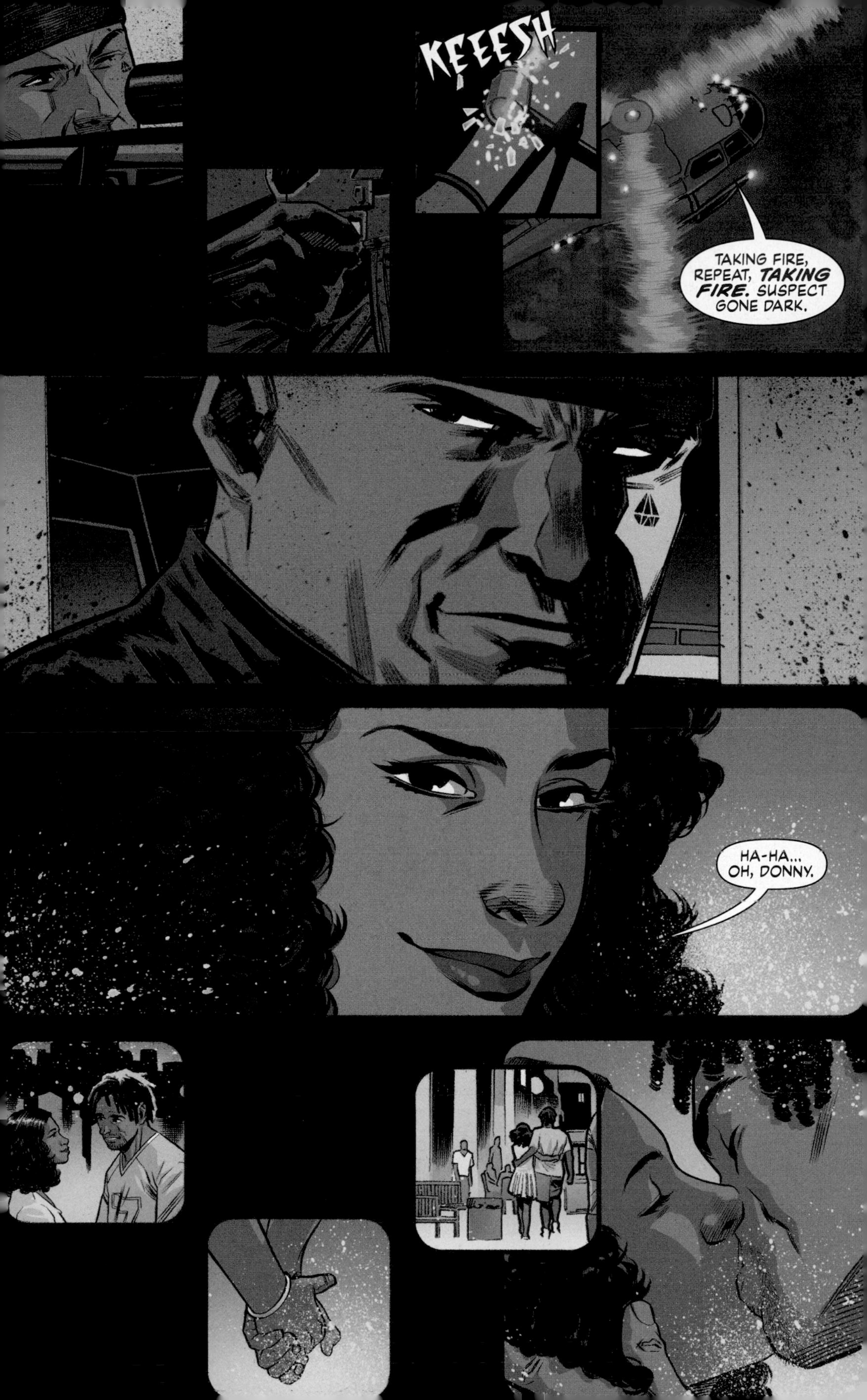
KEEESH
TAKING FIRE, REPEAT, TAKING FIRE. SUSPECT GONE DARK.
HA-HA... OH, DONNY.

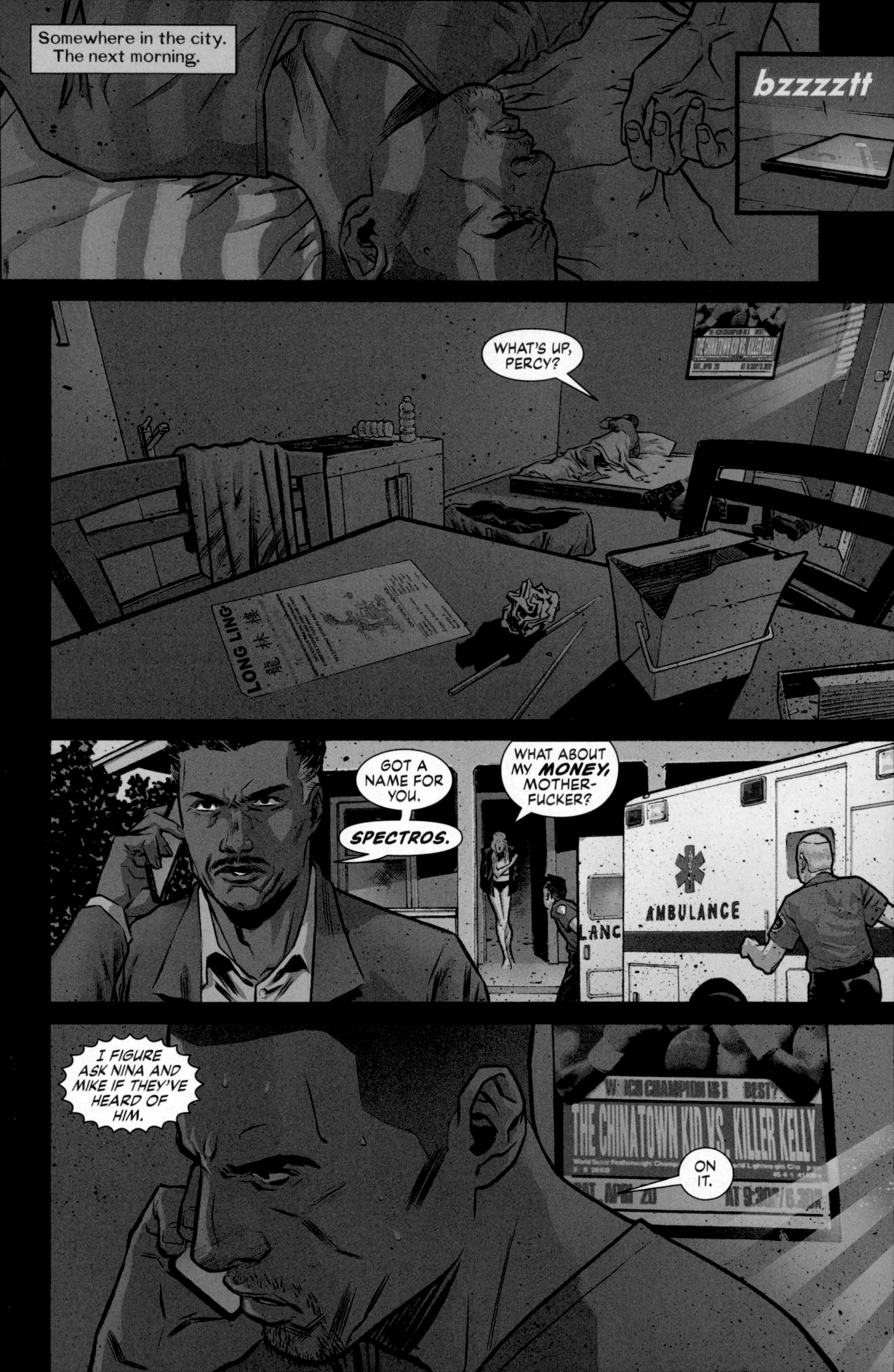

Somewhere in the city.
The next morning.
bzzzzztt
THE CHINATOWN KID VS. KILLER KELLY
WHAT'S UP, PERCY?
LONG LING
GOT A NAME FOR YOU.
SPECTROS.
WHAT ABOUT MY MONEY, MOTHER-FUCKER?
AMBULANCE
I FIGURE ASK NINA AND MIKE IF THEY'VE HEARD OF HIM.
THE CHINATOWN KID VS. KILLER KELLY
ON IT.

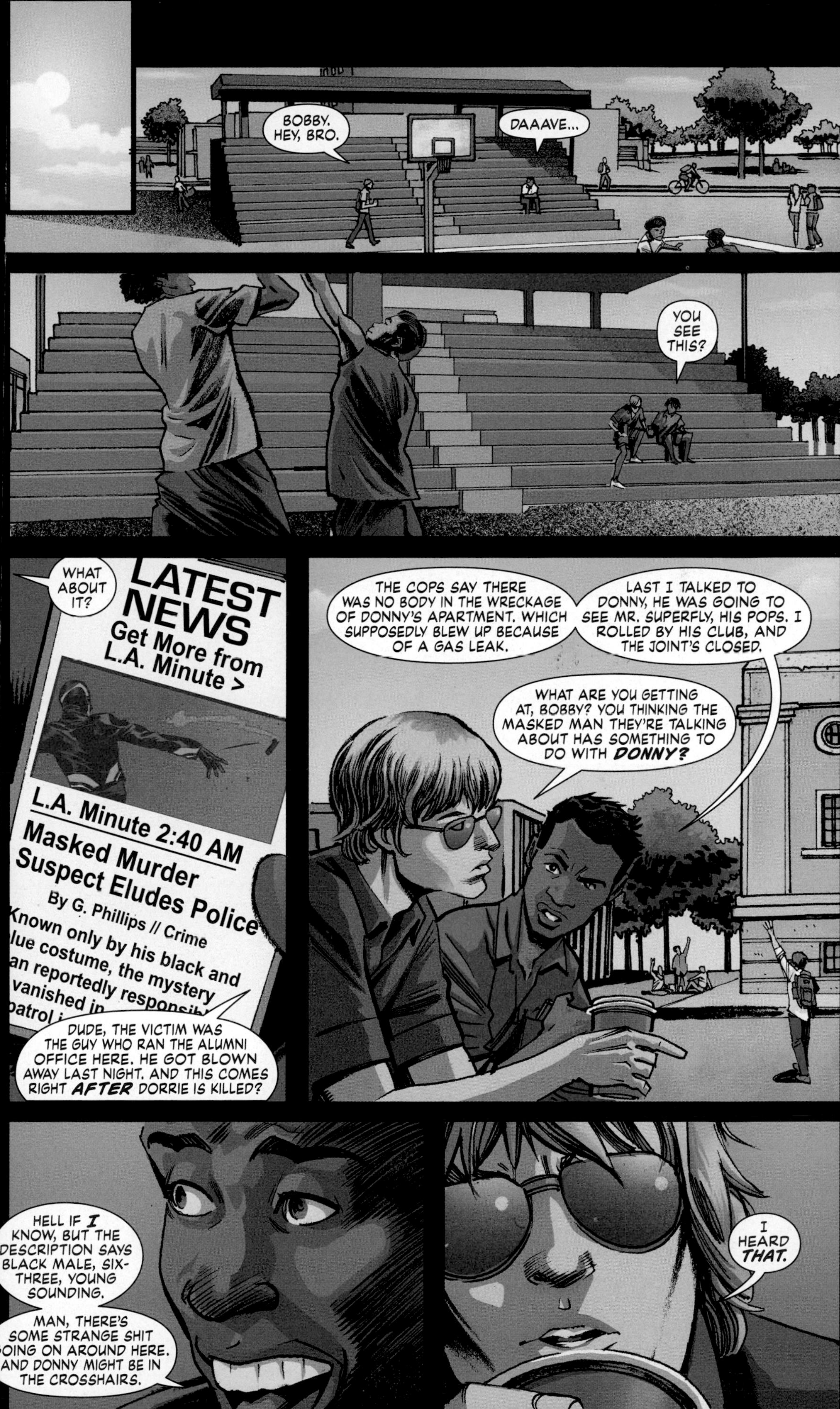
BOBBY. HEY, BRO.
DAAAVE...
YOU SEE THIS?
WHAT ABOUT IT?
LATEST NEWS
Get More from L.A. Minute >
L.A. Minute 2:40 AM
Masked Murder Suspect Eludes Police
By G. Phillips // Crime
Known only by his black and
lue costume, the mystery
an reportedly responsib
vanished in
patrol
DUDE, THE VICTIM WAS THE GUY WHO RAN THE ALUMNI OFFICE HERE. HE GOT BLOWN AWAY LAST NIGHT. AND THIS COMES RIGHT AFTER DORRIE IS KILLED?
THE COPS SAY THERE WAS NO BODY IN THE WRECKAGE OF DONNY'S APARTMENT. WHICH SUPPOSEDLY BLEW UP BECAUSE OF A GAS LEAK.
LAST I TALKED TO DONNY, HE WAS GOING TO SEE MR. SUPERFLY, HIS POPS. I ROLLED BY HIS CLUB, AND THE JOINT'S CLOSED.
WHAT ARE YOU GETTING AT, BOBBY? YOU THINKING THE MASKED MAN THEY'RE TALKING ABOUT HAS SOMETHING TO DO WITH DONNY?
HELL IF I KNOW, BUT THE DESCRIPTION SAYS BLACK MALE, SIX-THREE, YOUNG SOUNDING.
MAN, THERE'S SOME STRANGE SHIT GOING ON AROUND HERE. AND DONNY MIGHT BE IN THE CROSSHAIRS.
I HEARD THAT.

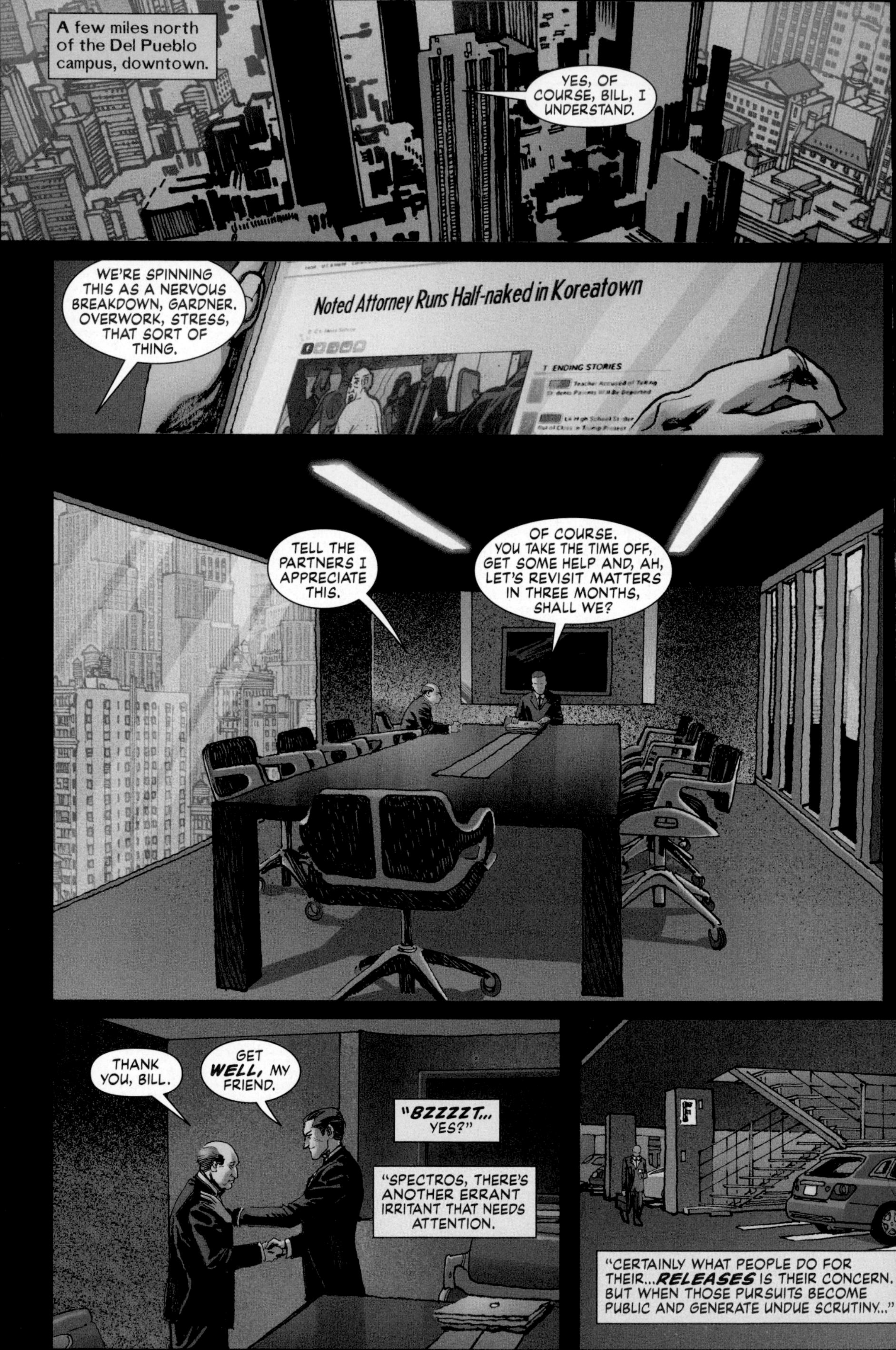
A few miles north of the Del Pueblo campus, downtown.
YES, OF COURSE, BILL, I UNDERSTAND.
WE'RE SPINNING THIS AS A NERVOUS BREAKDOWN, GARDNER. OVERWORK, STRESS, THAT SORT OF THING.
Noted Attorney Runs Half-naked in Koreatown
T ENDING STORIES
TELL THE PARTNERS I APPRECIATE THIS.
OF COURSE. YOU TAKE THE TIME OFF, GET SOME HELP AND, AH, LET'S REVISIT MATTERS IN THREE MONTHS, SHALL WE?
THANK YOU, BILL.
GET *WELL,* MY FRIEND.
"*BZZZZT...* YES?"
"SPECTROS, THERE'S ANOTHER ERRANT IRRITANT THAT NEEDS ATTENTION.
"CERTAINLY WHAT PEOPLE DO FOR THEIR...*RELEASES* IS THEIR CONCERN. BUT WHEN THOSE PURSUITS BECOME PUBLIC AND GENERATE UNDUE SCRUTINY..."

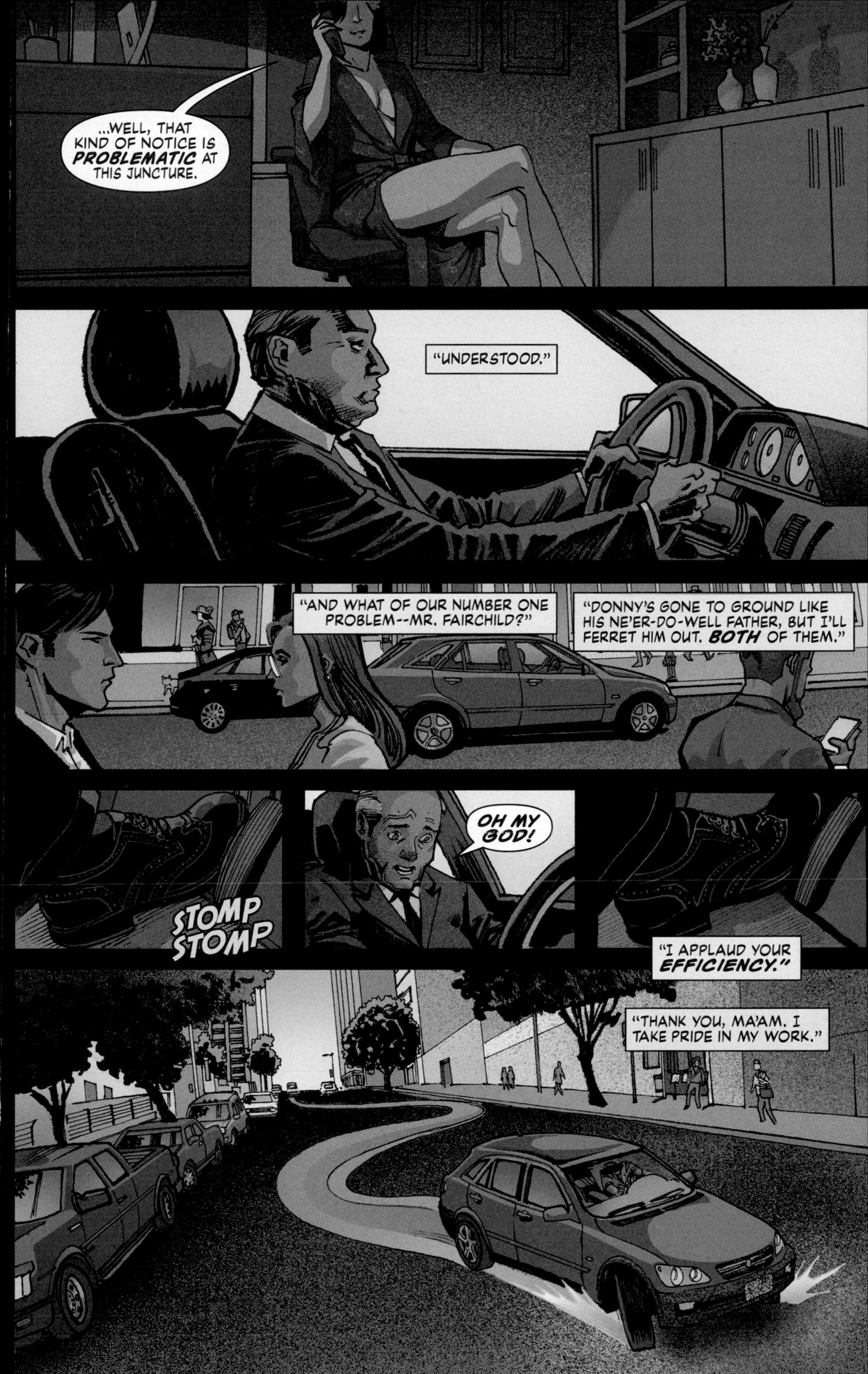
...WELL, THAT KIND OF NOTICE IS *PROBLEMATIC* AT THIS JUNCTURE.
"UNDERSTOOD."
"AND WHAT OF OUR NUMBER ONE PROBLEM--MR. FAIRCHILD?"
"DONNY'S GONE TO GROUND LIKE HIS NE'ER-DO-WELL FATHER, BUT I'LL FERRET HIM OUT. *BOTH* OF THEM."
STOMP STOMP
OH MY GOD!
"I APPLAUD YOUR *EFFICIENCY.*"
"THANK YOU, MA'AM. I TAKE PRIDE IN MY WORK."

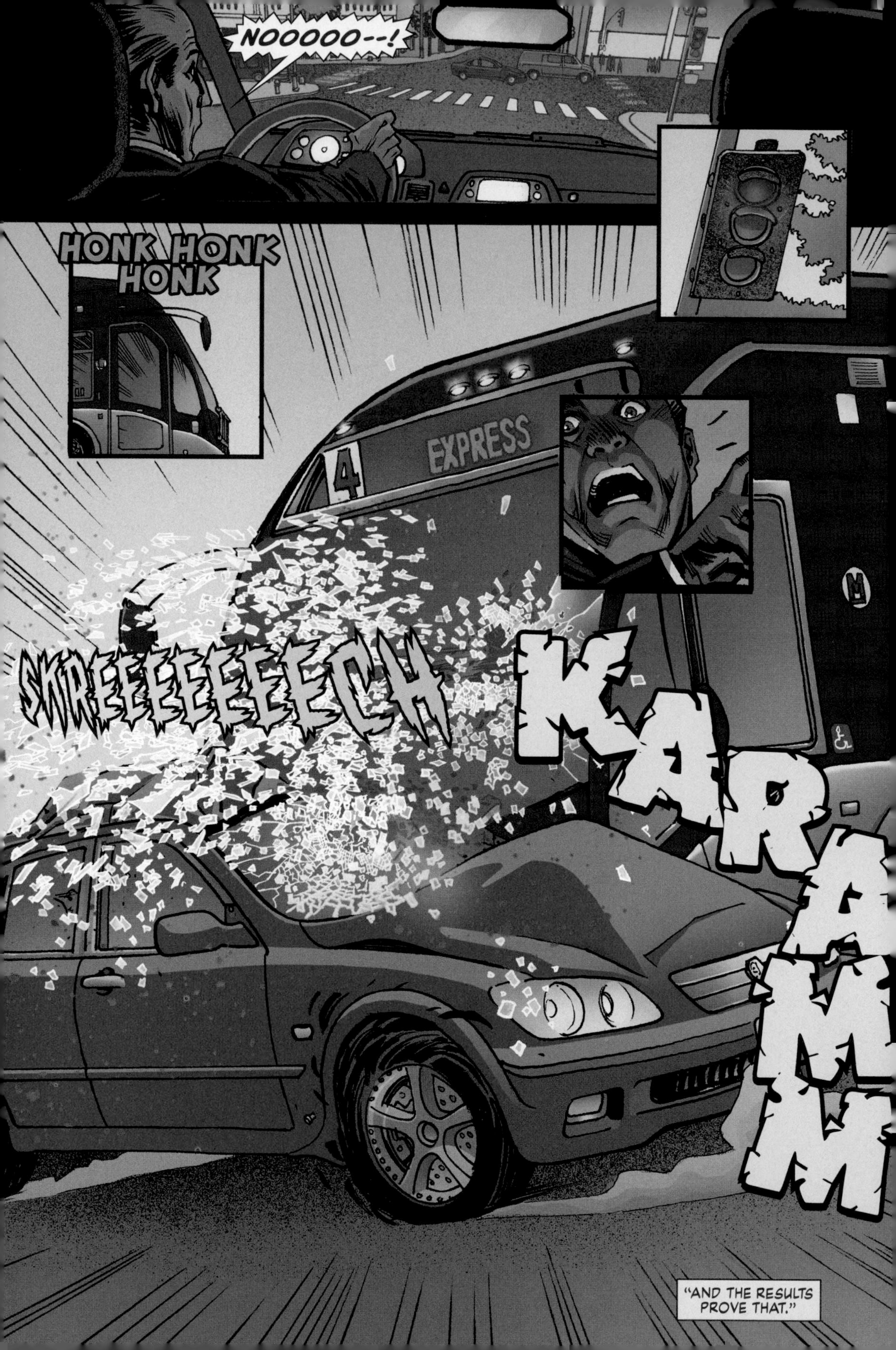
NOOOOO--!
HONK HONK HONK
EXPRESS
4
SKREEEEEEEECH
KARAMM
"AND THE RESULTS PROVE THAT."

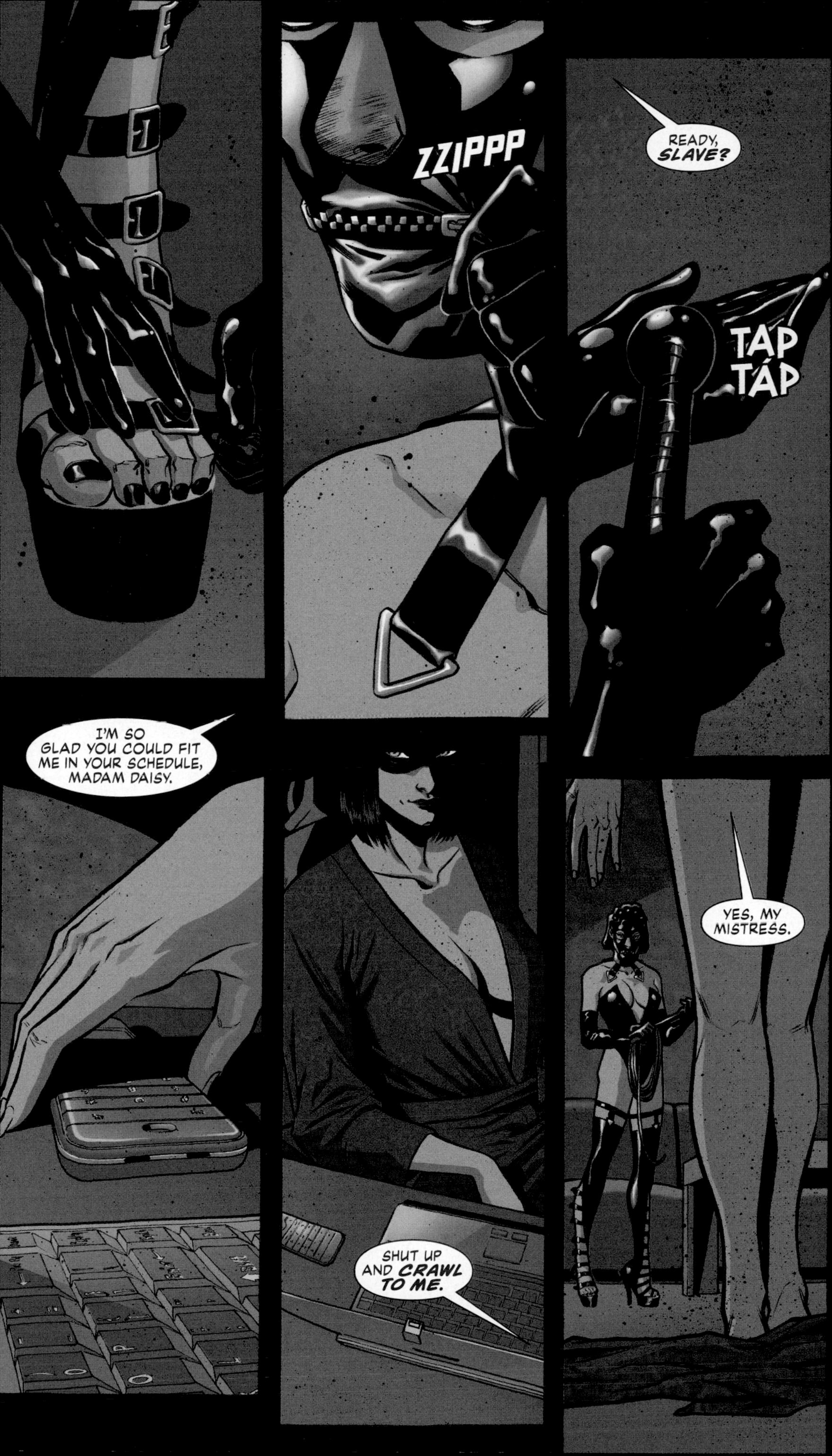
ZZIPPP
READY, SLAVE?
TAP TAP
I'M SO GLAD YOU COULD FIT ME IN YOUR SCHEDULE, MADAM DAISY.
SHUT UP AND CRAWL TO ME.
YES, MY MISTRESS.

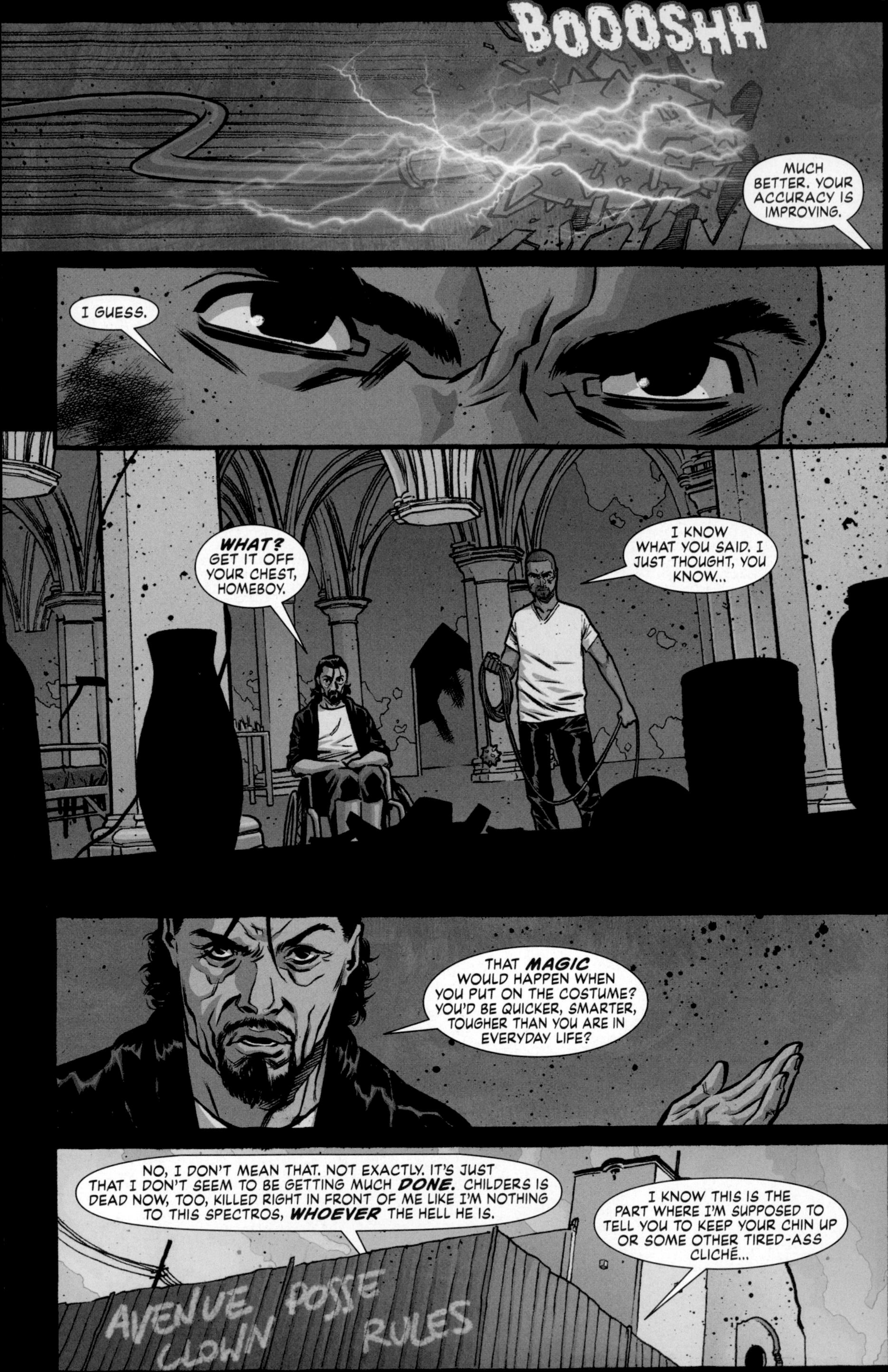
BOOOSHH
MUCH BETTER. YOUR ACCURACY IS IMPROVING.
I GUESS.
WHAT? GET IT OFF YOUR CHEST, HOMEBOY.
I KNOW WHAT YOU SAID. I JUST THOUGHT, YOU KNOW...
THAT MAGIC WOULD HAPPEN WHEN YOU PUT ON THE COSTUME? YOU'D BE QUICKER, SMARTER, TOUGHER THAN YOU ARE IN EVERYDAY LIFE?
NO, I DON'T MEAN THAT. NOT EXACTLY. IT'S JUST THAT I DON'T SEEM TO BE GETTING MUCH DONE. CHILDERS IS DEAD NOW, TOO, KILLED RIGHT IN FRONT OF ME LIKE I'M NOTHING TO THIS SPECTROS, WHOEVER THE HELL HE IS.
I KNOW THIS IS THE PART WHERE I'M SUPPOSED TO TELL YOU TO KEEP YOUR CHIN UP OR SOME OTHER TIRED-ASS CLICHÉ...
AVENUE CLOWN POSSE RULES

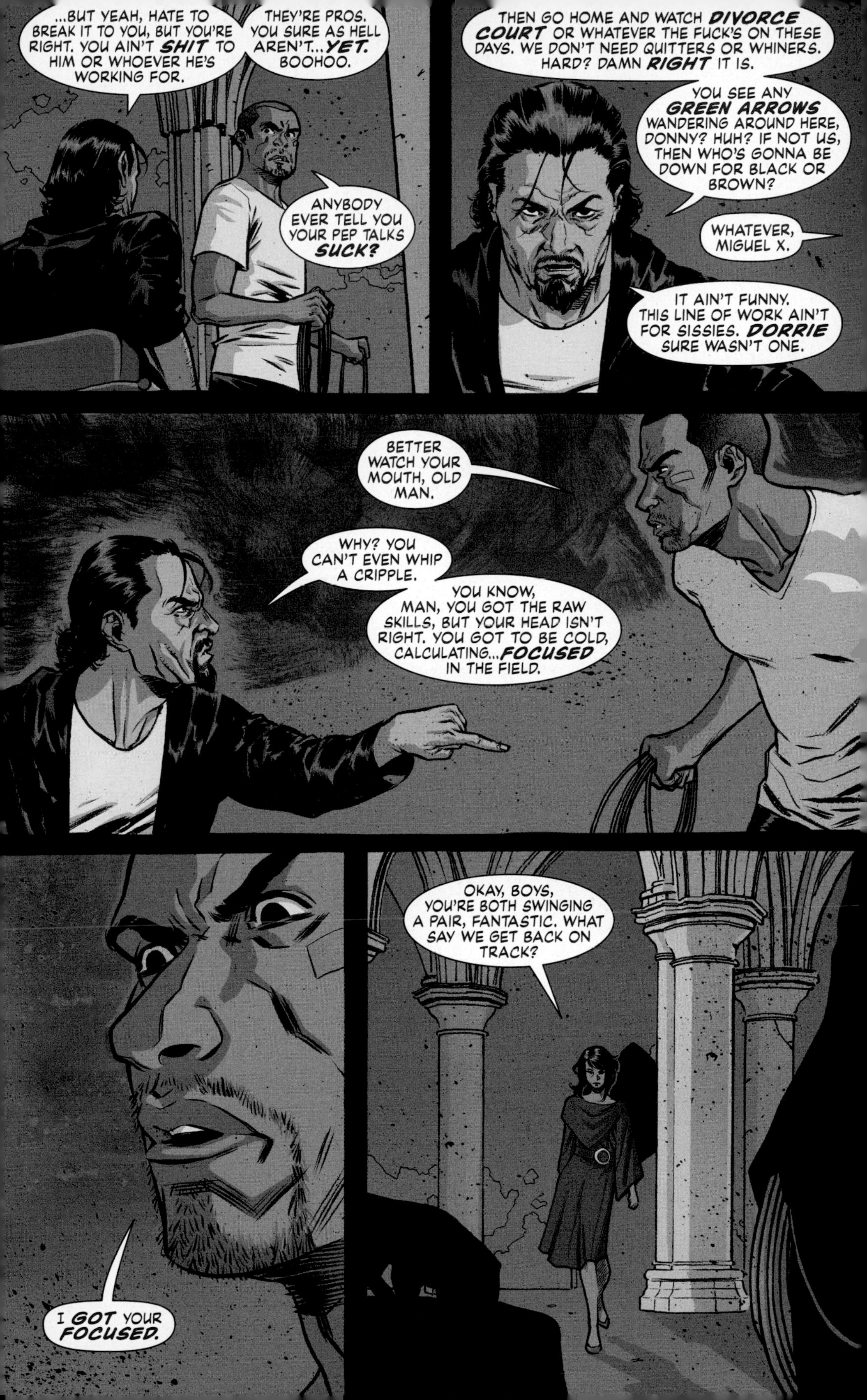
...BUT YEAH, HATE TO BREAK IT TO YOU, BUT YOU'RE RIGHT. YOU AIN'T SHIT TO HIM OR WHOEVER HE'S WORKING FOR.
THEY'RE PROS. YOU SURE AS HELL AREN'T...YET. BOOHOO.
ANYBODY EVER TELL YOU YOUR PEP TALKS SUCK?
THEN GO HOME AND WATCH DIVORCE COURT OR WHATEVER THE FUCK'S ON THESE DAYS. WE DON'T NEED QUITTERS OR WHINERS. HARD? DAMN RIGHT IT IS.
YOU SEE ANY GREEN ARROWS WANDERING AROUND HERE, DONNY? HUH? IF NOT US, THEN WHO'S GONNA BE DOWN FOR BLACK OR BROWN?
WHATEVER, MIGUEL X.
IT AIN'T FUNNY. THIS LINE OF WORK AIN'T FOR SISSIES. DORRIE SURE WASN'T ONE.
BETTER WATCH YOUR MOUTH, OLD MAN.
WHY? YOU CAN'T EVEN WHIP A CRIPPLE.
YOU KNOW, MAN, YOU GOT THE RAW SKILLS, BUT YOUR HEAD ISN'T RIGHT. YOU GOT TO BE COLD, CALCULATING...FOCUSED IN THE FIELD.
I GOT YOUR FOCUSED.
OKAY, BOYS, YOU'RE BOTH SWINGING A PAIR, FANTASTIC. WHAT SAY WE GET BACK ON TRACK?

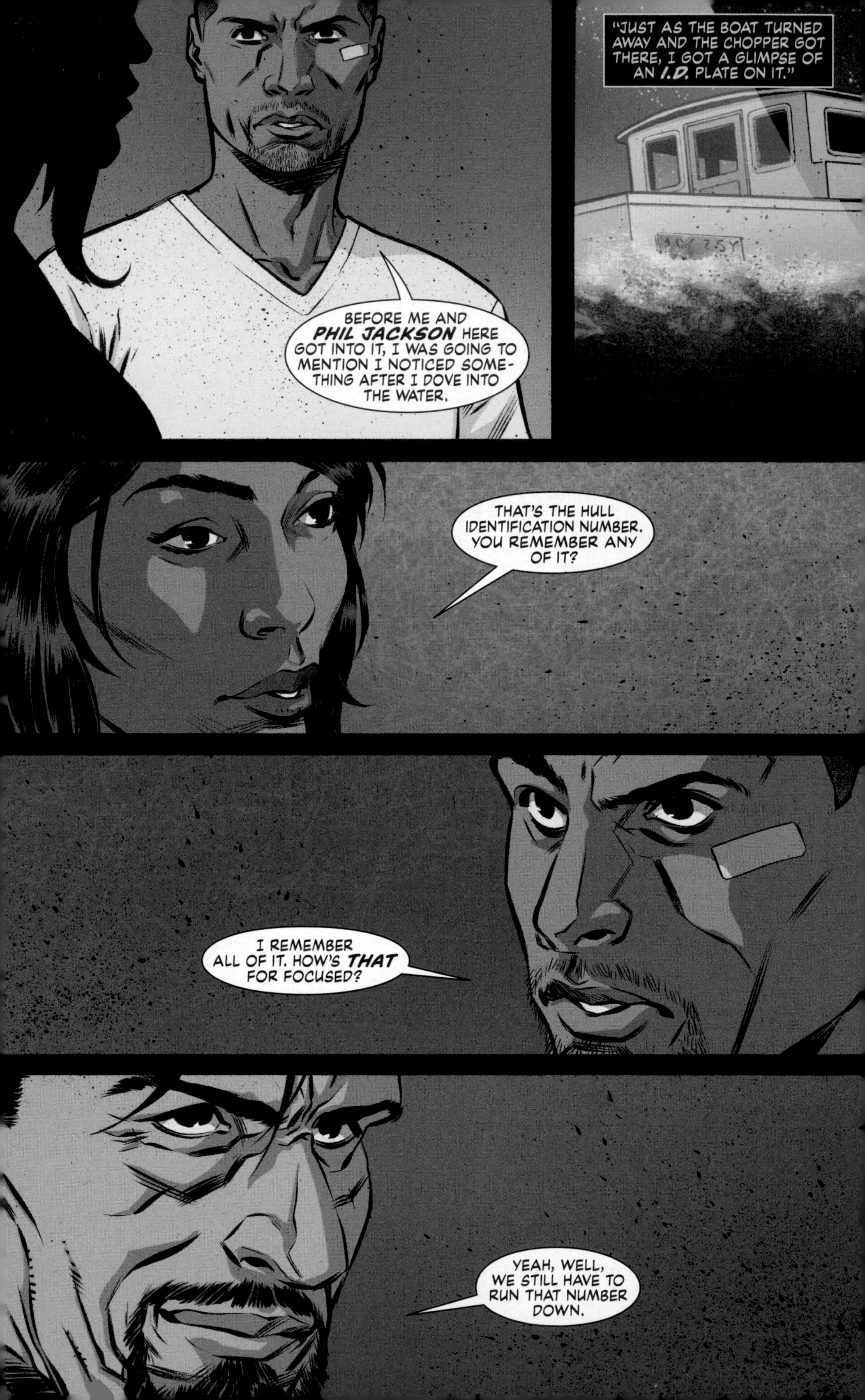
BEFORE ME AND PHIL JACKSON HERE GOT INTO IT, I WAS GOING TO MENTION I NOTICED SOME-THING AFTER I DOVE INTO THE WATER.
"JUST AS THE BOAT TURNED AWAY AND THE CHOPPER GOT THERE, I GOT A GLIMPSE OF AN I.D. PLATE ON IT."
THAT'S THE HULL IDENTIFICATION NUMBER. YOU REMEMBER ANY OF IT?
I REMEMBER ALL OF IT. HOW'S THAT FOR FOCUSED?
YEAH, WELL, WE STILL HAVE TO RUN THAT NUMBER DOWN.

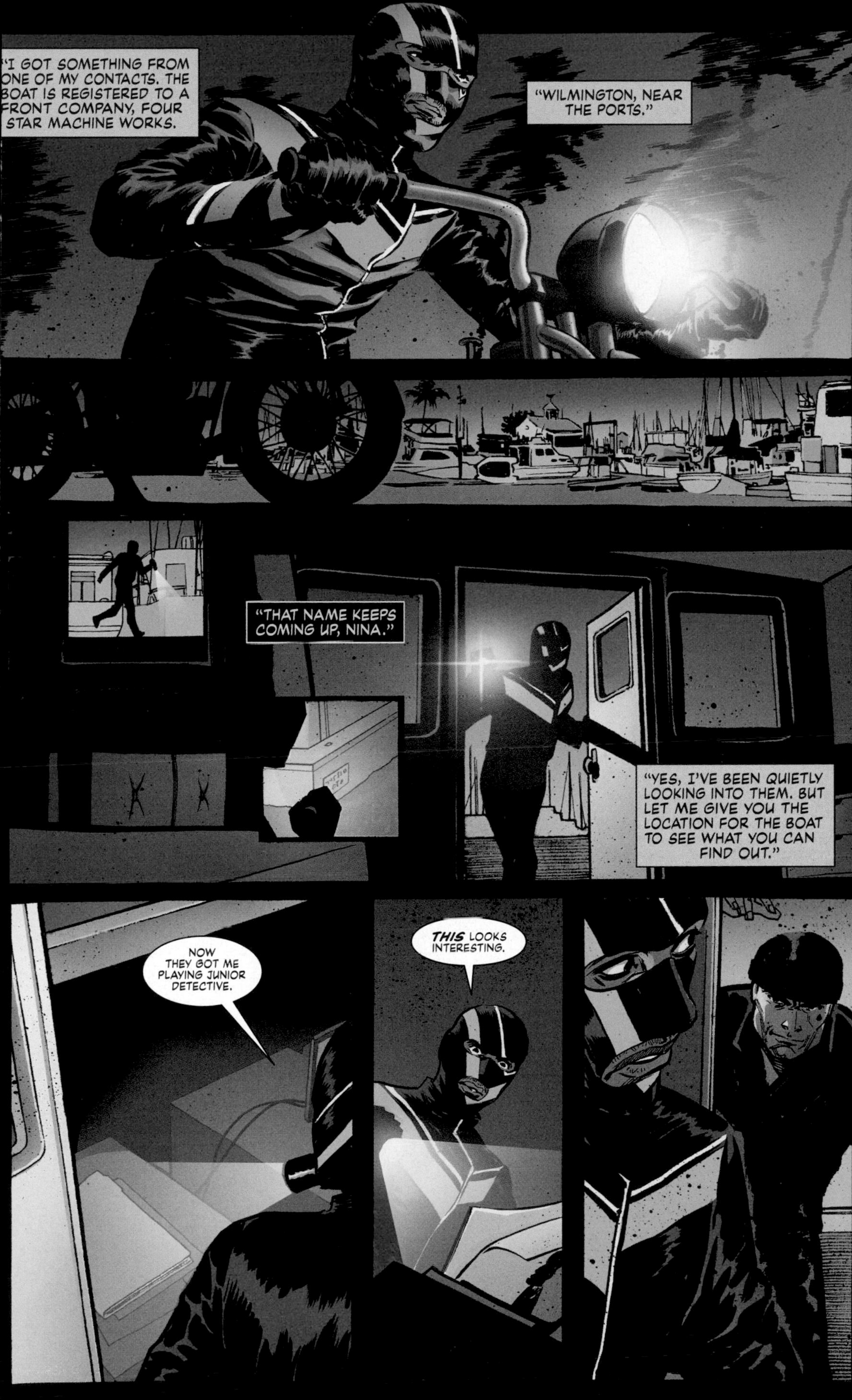
"I GOT SOMETHING FROM ONE OF MY CONTACTS. THE BOAT IS REGISTERED TO A FRONT COMPANY, FOUR STAR MACHINE WORKS.
"WILMINGTON, NEAR THE PORTS."
"THAT NAME KEEPS COMING UP, NINA."
"YES, I'VE BEEN QUIETLY LOOKING INTO THEM. BUT LET ME GIVE YOU THE LOCATION FOR THE BOAT TO SEE WHAT YOU CAN FIND OUT."
NOW THEY GOT ME PLAYING JUNIOR DETECTIVE.
THIS LOOKS INTERESTING.

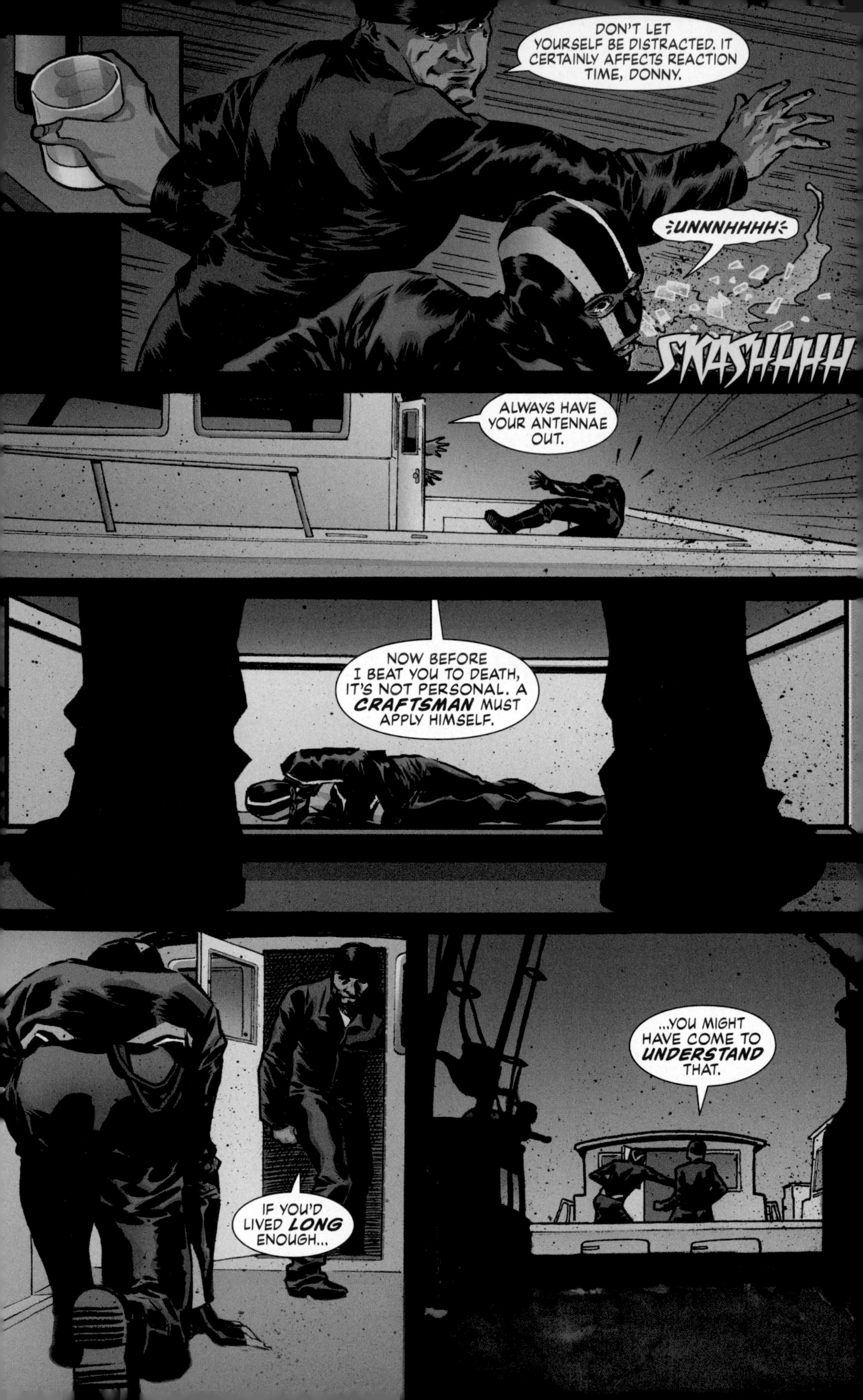
DON'T LET YOURSELF BE DISTRACTED. IT CERTAINLY AFFECTS REACTION TIME, DONNY.
UNNNHHHH
SKASHHHH
ALWAYS HAVE YOUR ANTENNAE OUT.
NOW BEFORE I BEAT YOU TO DEATH, IT'S NOT PERSONAL. A CRAFTSMAN MUST APPLY HIMSELF.
IF YOU'D LIVED LONG ENOUGH...
...YOU MIGHT HAVE COME TO UNDERSTAND THAT.

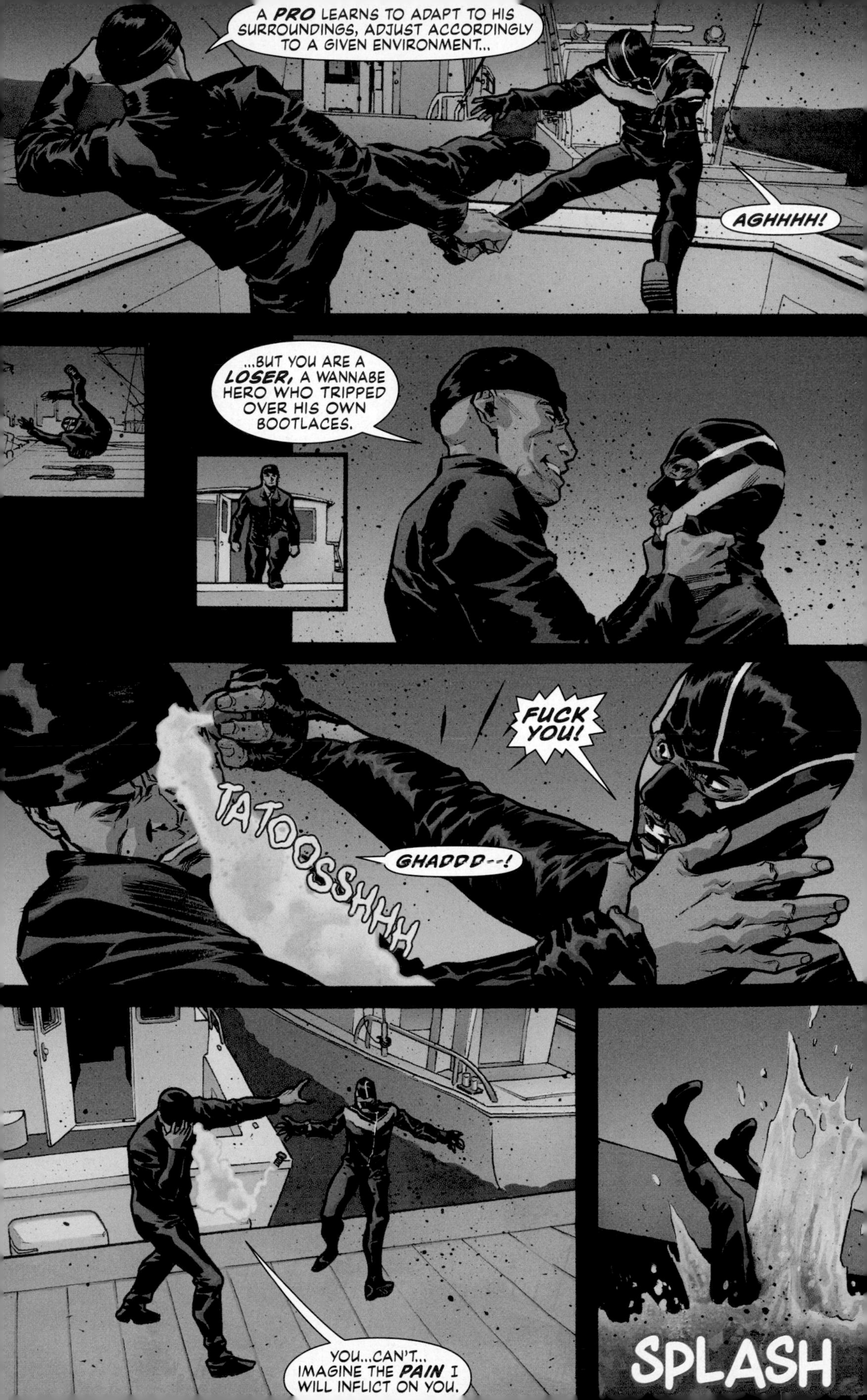
A PRO LEARNS TO ADAPT TO HIS SURROUNDINGS, ADJUST ACCORDINGLY TO A GIVEN ENVIRONMENT...
AGHHHH!
...BUT YOU ARE A LOSER, A WANNABE HERO WHO TRIPPED OVER HIS OWN BOOTLACES.
FUCK YOU!
TATOOSSHHH
GHADDD--!
YOU...CAN'T... IMAGINE THE PAIN I WILL INFLICT ON YOU.
SPLASH

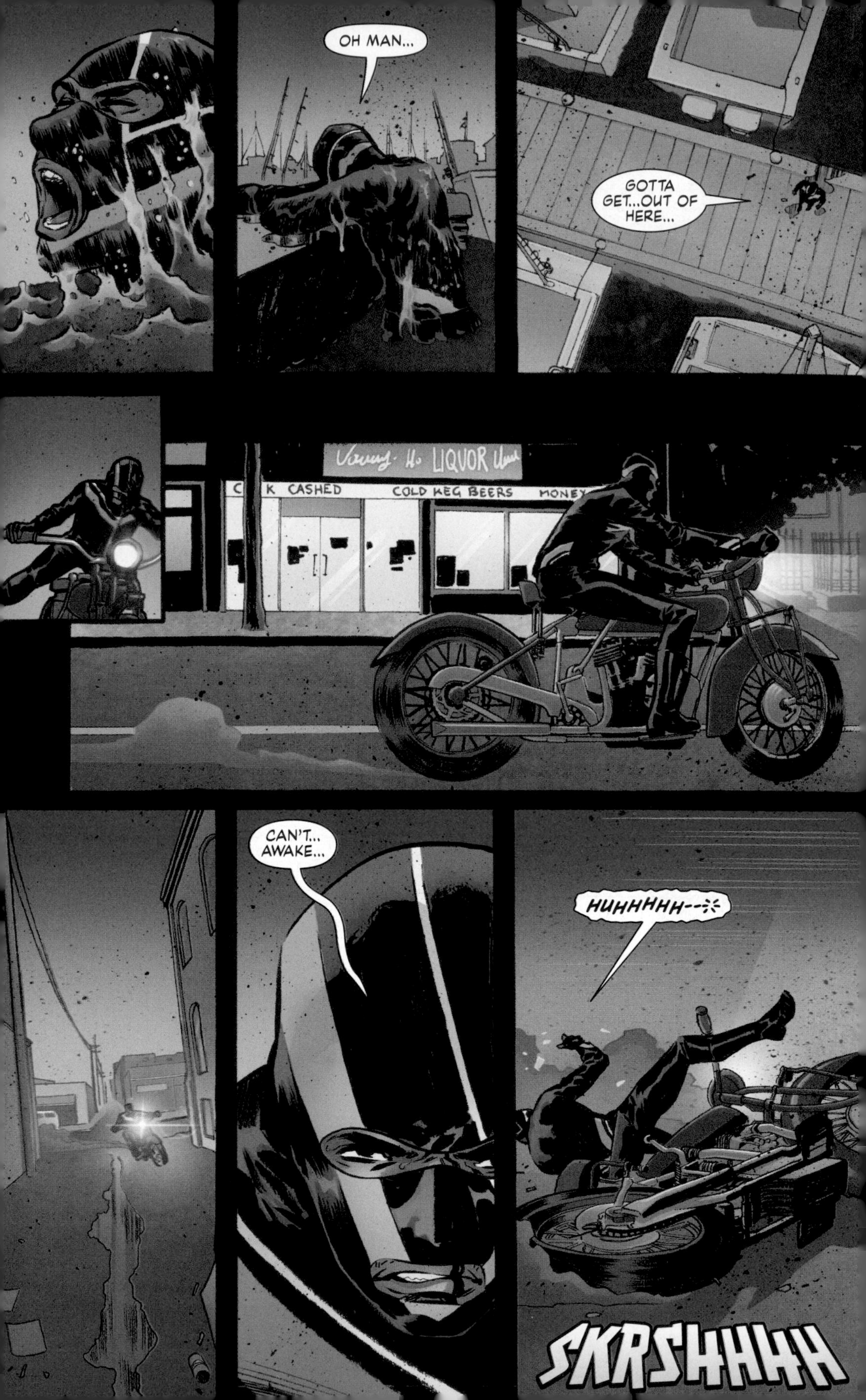
OH MAN...
GOTTA GET...OUT OF HERE...
LIQUOR
K CASHED
COLD KEG BEERS
MONEY
CAN'T... AWAKE...
HUHHHHH--
SKRSHHHH

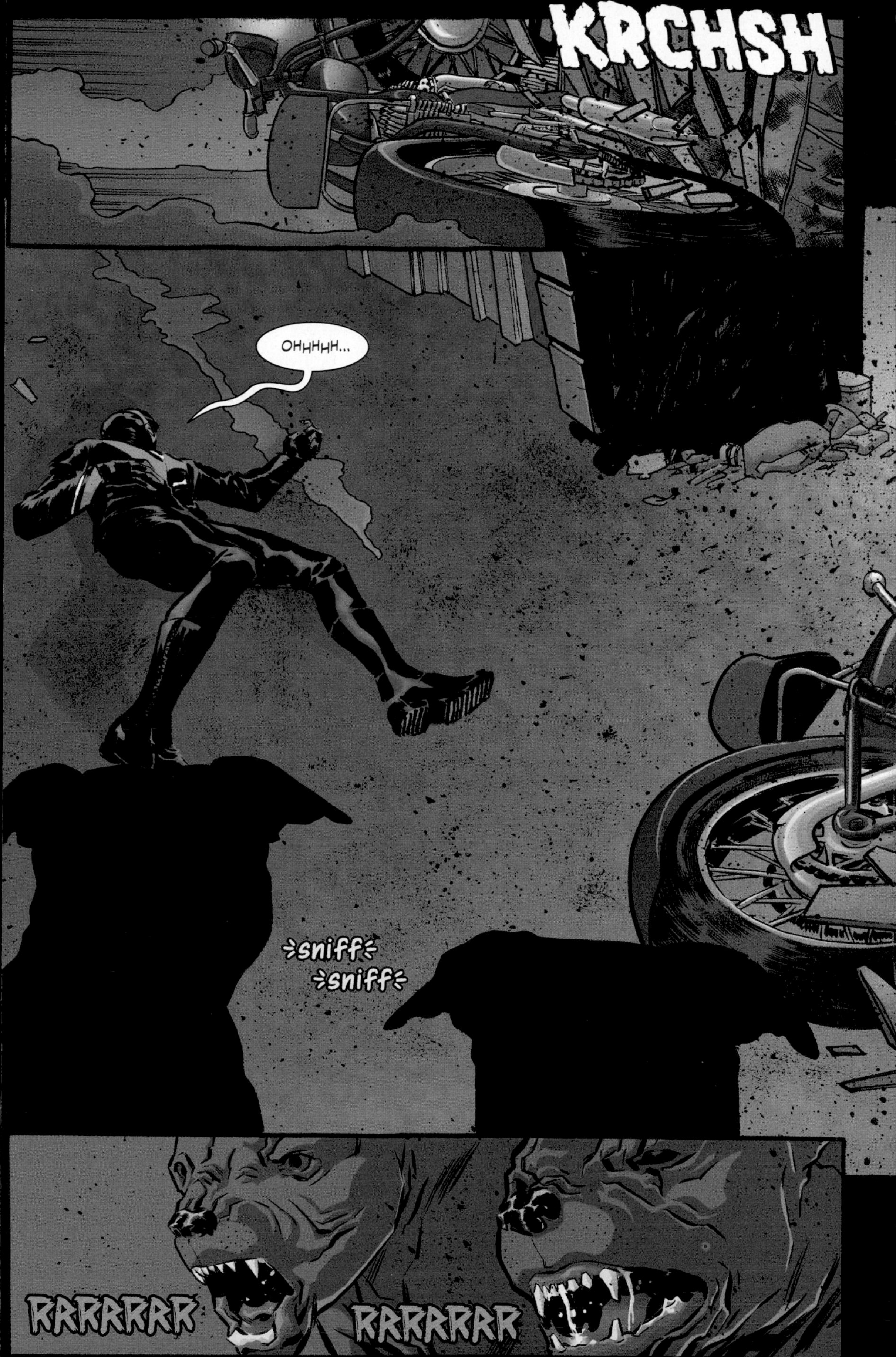
KRCHSH
OHHHHH...
sniff
sniff
RRRRRRR
RRRRRRR

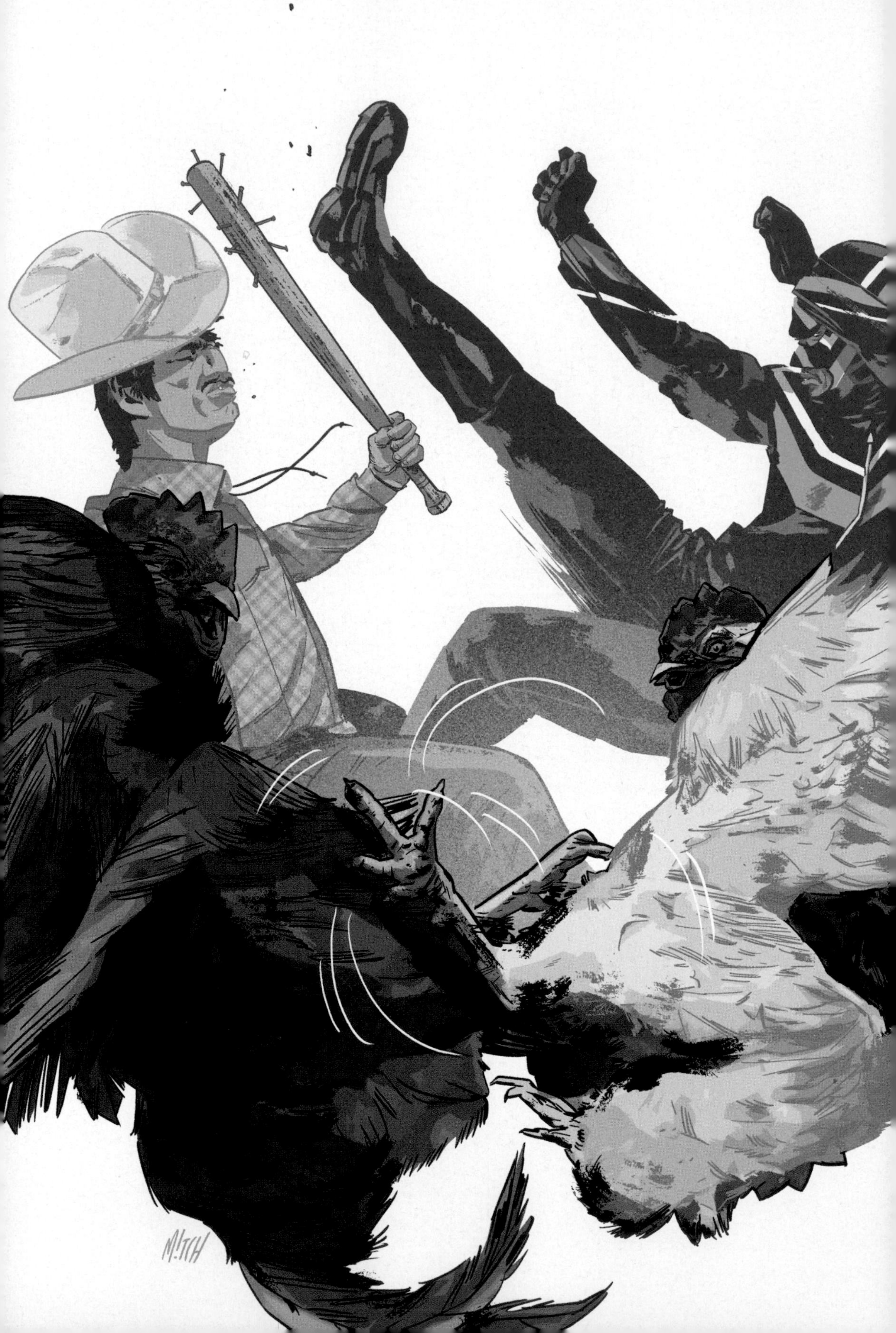

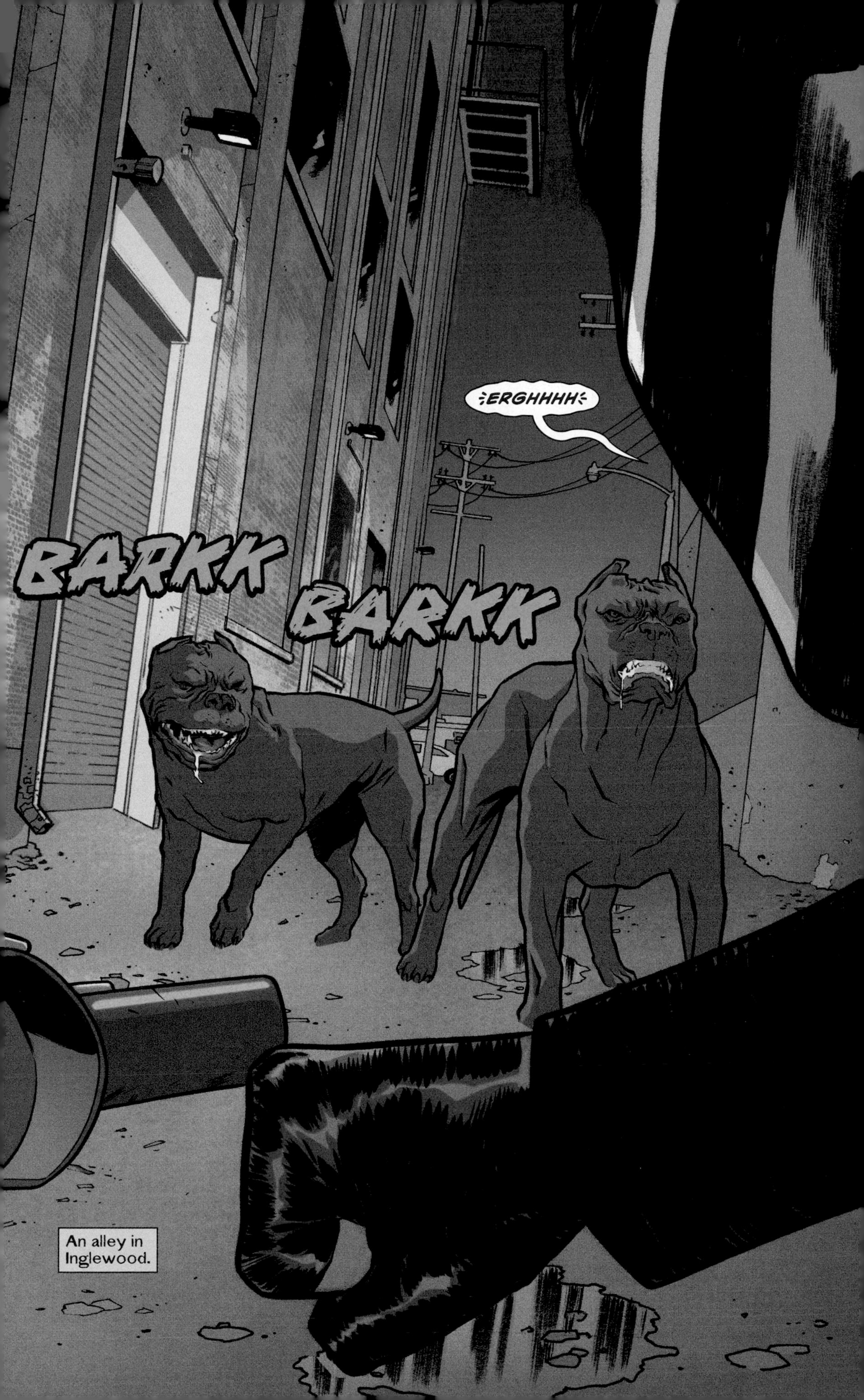
BARKK
BARKK
ERGHHHH
An alley in Inglewood.

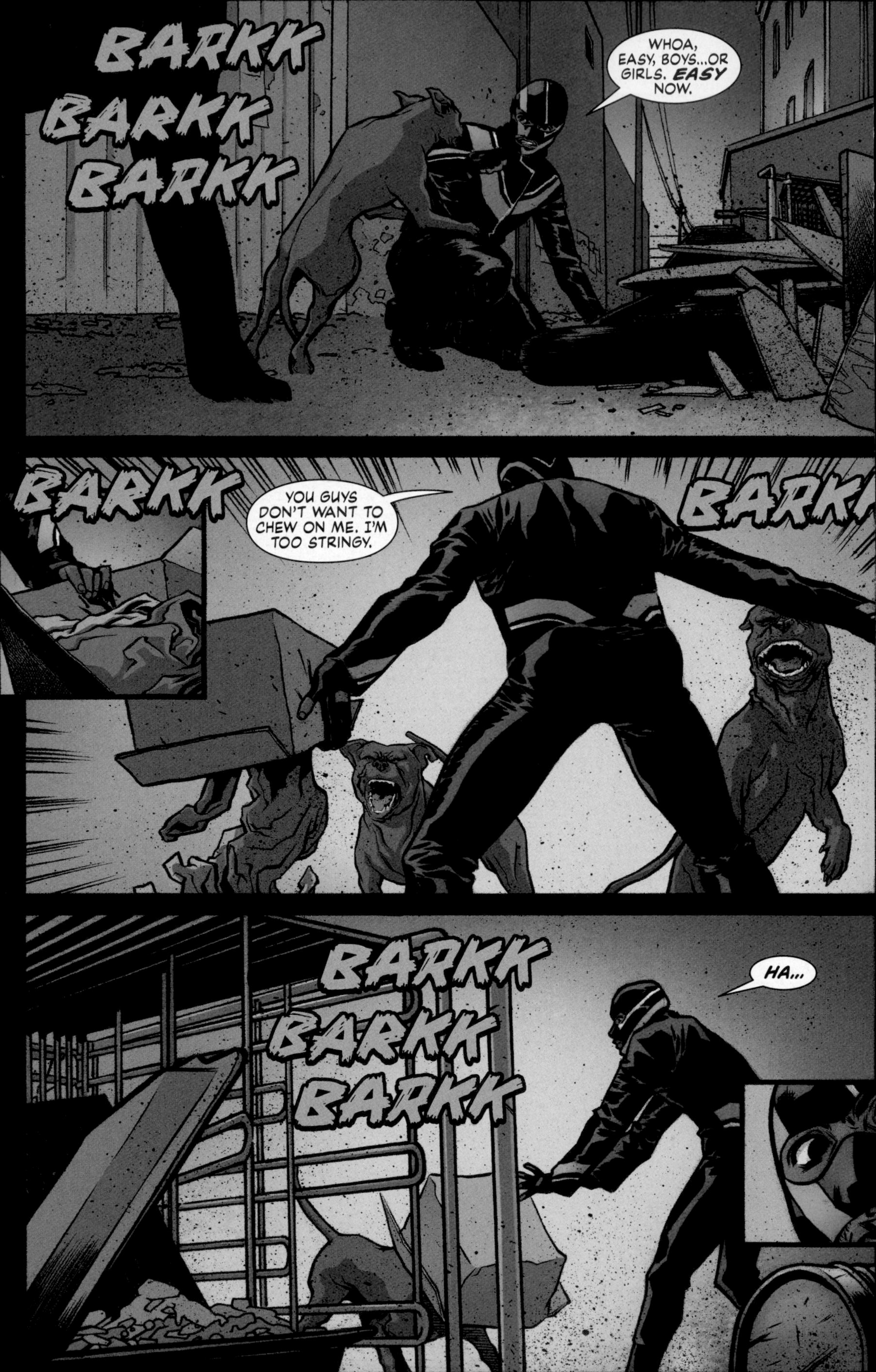
BARKK
BARKK
BARKK
WHOA, EASY, BOYS...OR GIRLS. EASY NOW.
BARKK
YOU GUYS DON'T WANT TO CHEW ON ME. I'M TOO STRINGY.
BARKK
BARKK
BARKK
BARKK
HA...

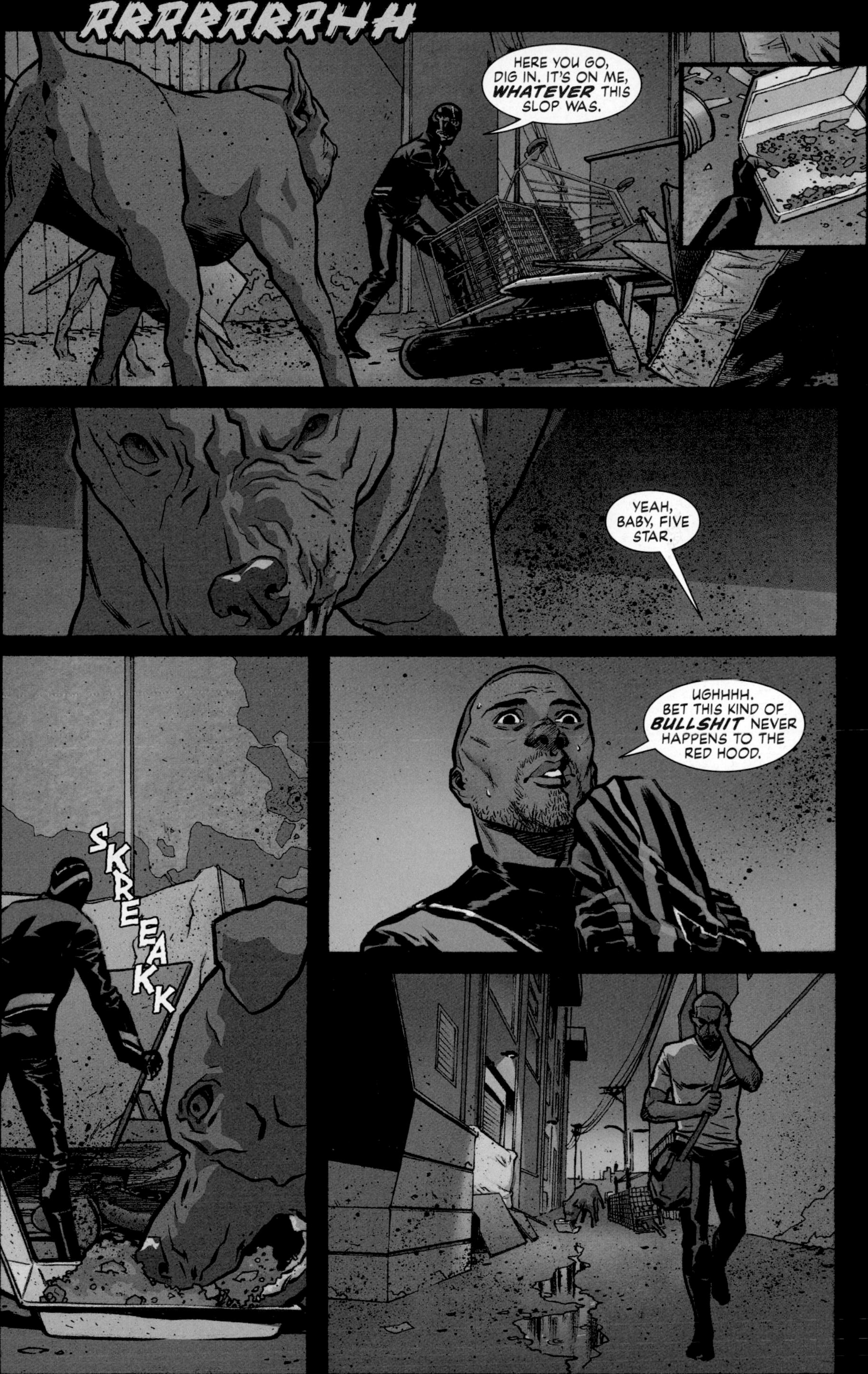
RRRRRRRHH
HERE YOU GO, DIG IN. IT'S ON ME, WHATEVER THIS SLOP WAS.
YEAH, BABY, FIVE STAR.
SKREEAKK
UGHHHH. BET THIS KIND OF BULLSHIT NEVER HAPPENS TO THE RED HOOD.

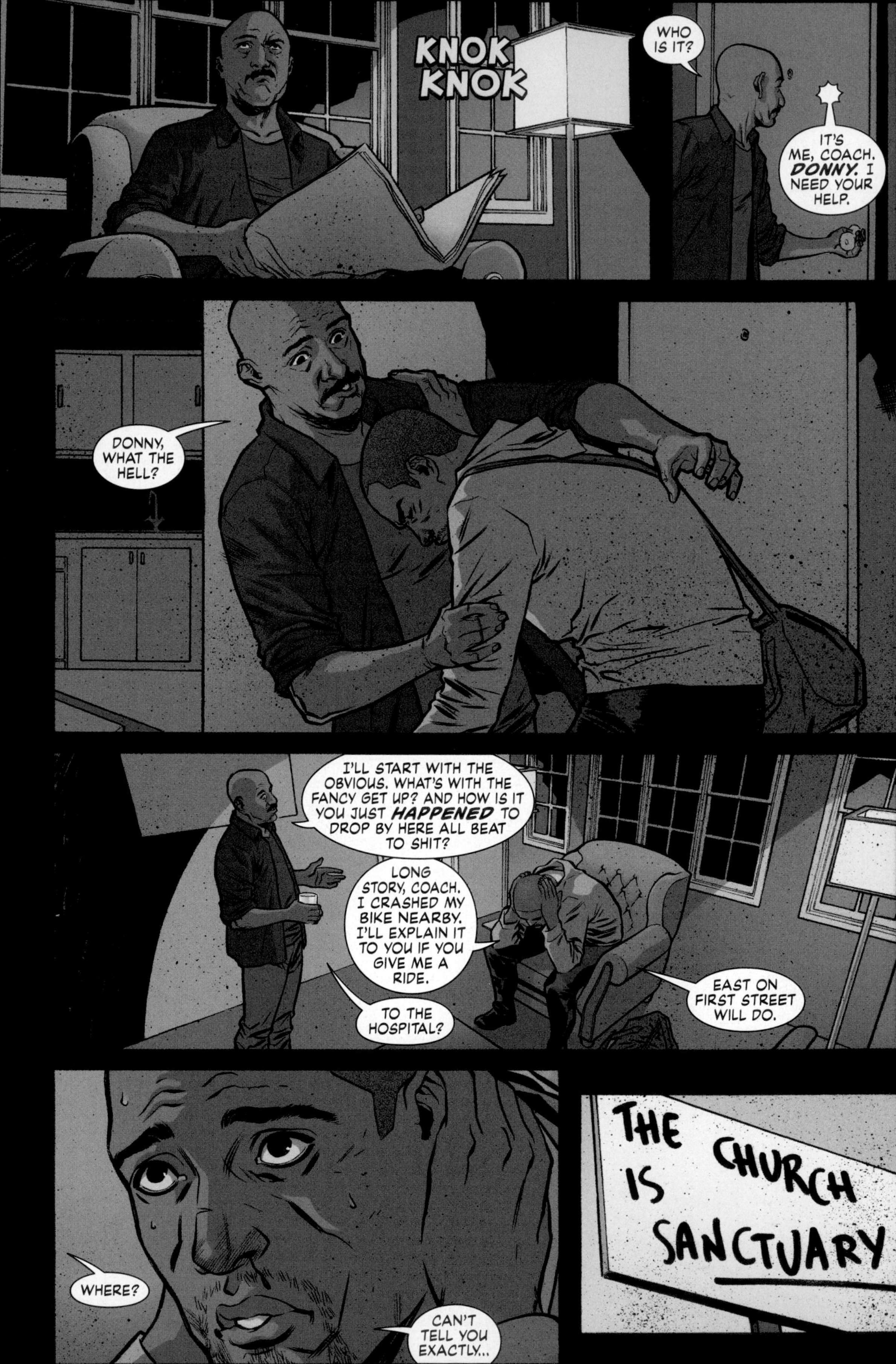
KNOK KNOK
WHO IS IT?
IT'S ME, COACH. DONNY. I NEED YOUR HELP.
DONNY, WHAT THE HELL?
I'LL START WITH THE OBVIOUS. WHAT'S WITH THE FANCY GET UP? AND HOW IS IT YOU JUST HAPPENED TO DROP BY HERE ALL BEAT TO SHIT?
LONG STORY, COACH. I CRASHED MY BIKE NEARBY. I'LL EXPLAIN IT TO YOU IF YOU GIVE ME A RIDE.
TO THE HOSPITAL?
EAST ON FIRST STREET WILL DO.
WHERE?
CAN'T TELL YOU EXACTLY...
THE CHURCH IS SANCTUARY

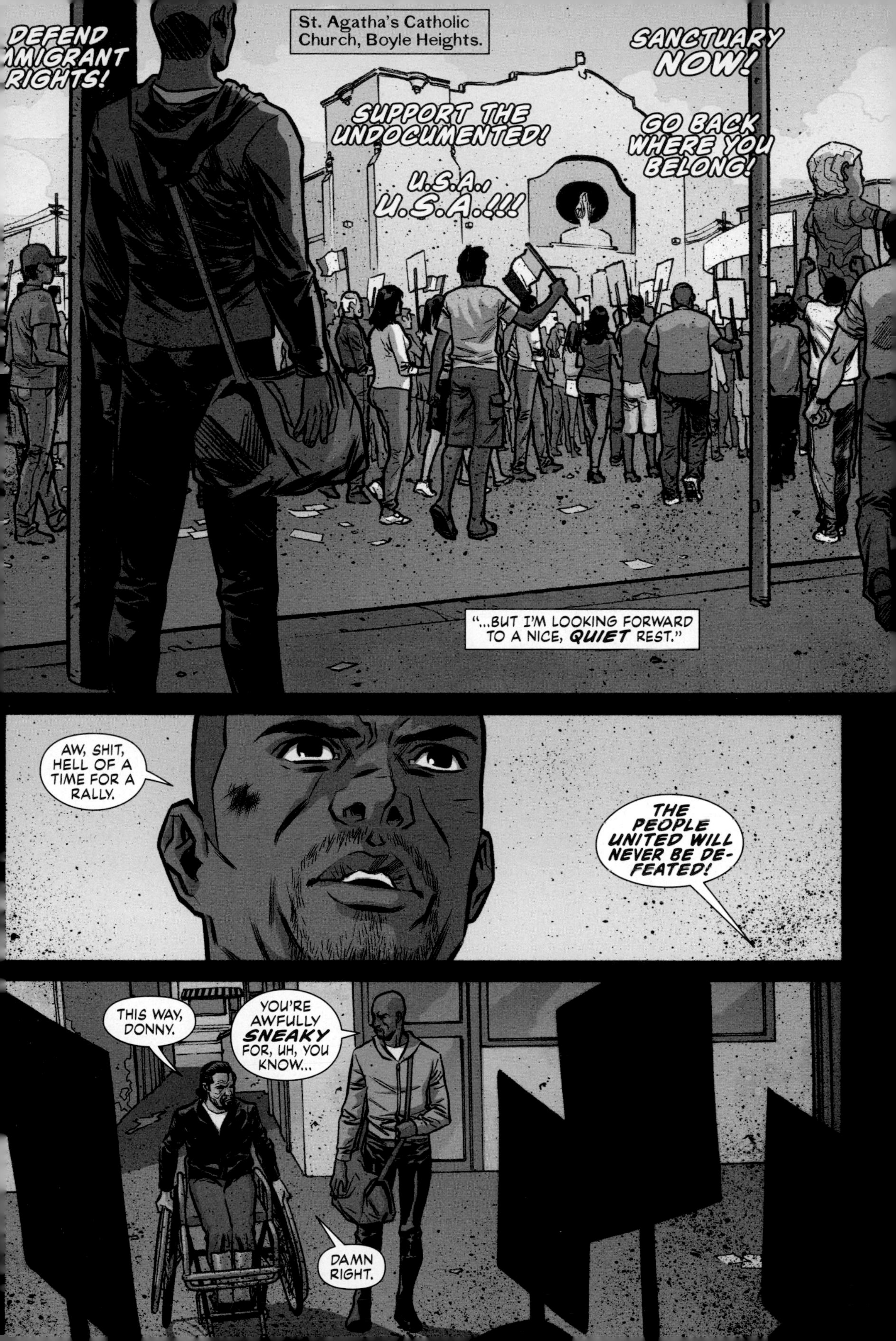
St. Agatha's Catholic Church, Boyle Heights.
DEFEND IMMIGRANT RIGHTS!
SANCTUARY NOW!
SUPPORT THE UNDOCUMENTED!
GO BACK WHERE YOU BELONG!
U.S.A., U.S.A.!!!
"...BUT I'M LOOKING FORWARD TO A NICE, QUIET REST."
AW, SHIT, HELL OF A TIME FOR A RALLY.
THE PEOPLE UNITED WILL NEVER BE DE-FEATED!
THIS WAY, DONNY.
YOU'RE AWFULLY SNEAKY FOR, UH, YOU KNOW...
DAMN RIGHT.

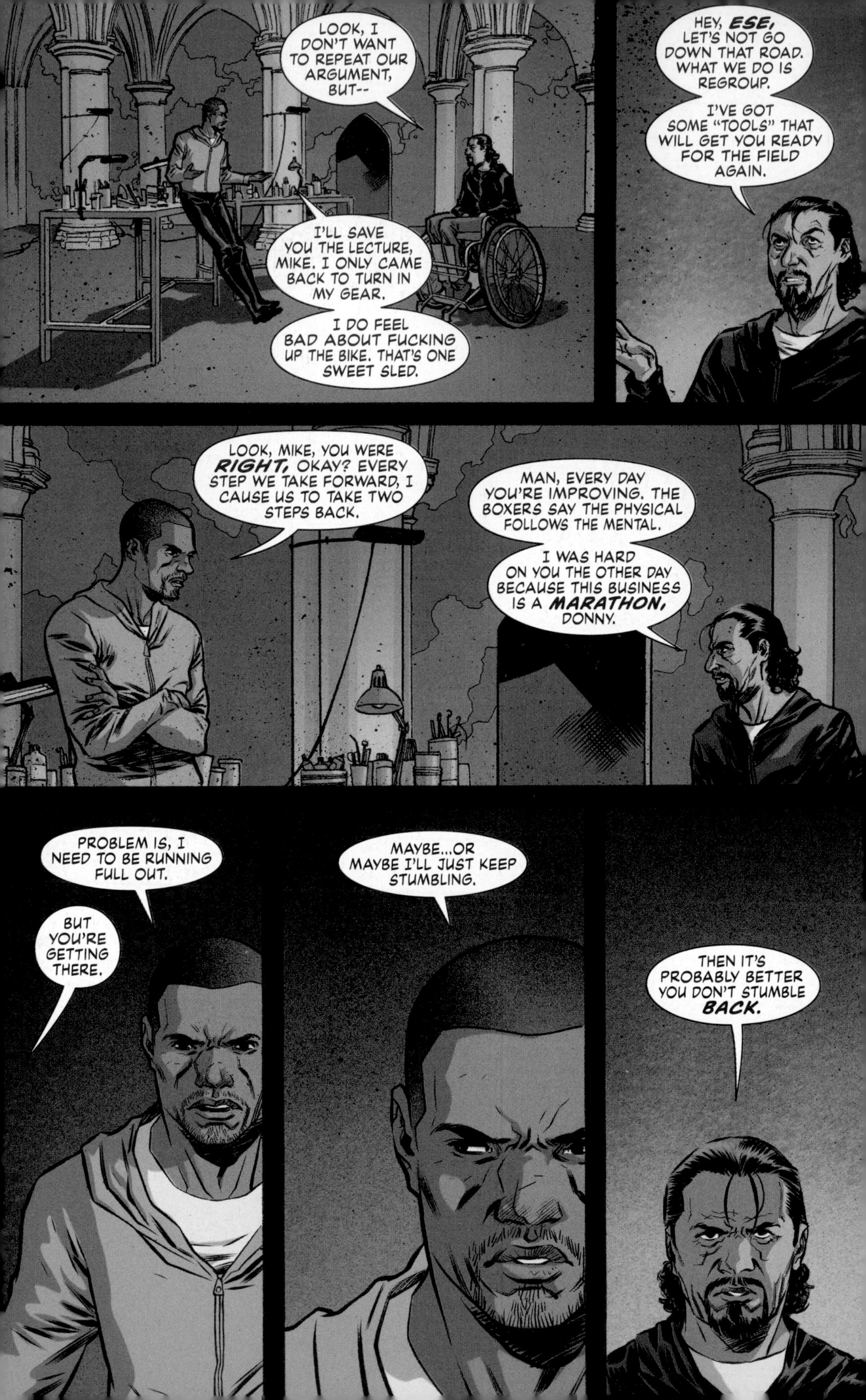

LOOK, I DON'T WANT TO REPEAT OUR ARGUMENT, BUT--
I'LL SAVE YOU THE LECTURE, MIKE. I ONLY CAME BACK TO TURN IN MY GEAR.
I DO FEEL BAD ABOUT FUCKING UP THE BIKE. THAT'S ONE SWEET SLED.
HEY, ESE, LET'S NOT GO DOWN THAT ROAD. WHAT WE DO IS REGROUP.
I'VE GOT SOME "TOOLS" THAT WILL GET YOU READY FOR THE FIELD AGAIN.
LOOK, MIKE, YOU WERE RIGHT, OKAY? EVERY STEP WE TAKE FORWARD, I CAUSE US TO TAKE TWO STEPS BACK.
MAN, EVERY DAY YOU'RE IMPROVING. THE BOXERS SAY THE PHYSICAL FOLLOWS THE MENTAL.
I WAS HARD ON YOU THE OTHER DAY BECAUSE THIS BUSINESS IS A MARATHON, DONNY.
PROBLEM IS, I NEED TO BE RUNNING FULL OUT.
BUT YOU'RE GETTING THERE.
MAYBE...OR MAYBE I'LL JUST KEEP STUMBLING.
THEN IT'S PROBABLY BETTER YOU DON'T STUMBLE BACK.

South L.A.

WHO IS IT?

OPEN UP, MY NIGGA. HEH.

KNOCK KNOCK

DONNY!

BACK FROM THE DEAD. YOU JUST GONNA LEAVE A BROTHER HANGIN'?

FOR SURE, COME ON IN.

WHERE YOU BEEN, DONNY? WHAT THE HELL'S GOING ON? ARE *YOU* THE ONE RUNNING AROUND IN THE MASK FIGHTING WITH THE COPS?

I DIDN'T COME HERE TO PLAY *TWENTY QUESTIONS*, DAVE.

I CAME TO GET US *FADED.* THIS SHIT IS CALLED "PURPLE JADE FAZE."

NOW YOU'RE *TALKING!*

MEDIC
MARIJ

FOR DO
MEDIC
KEEP

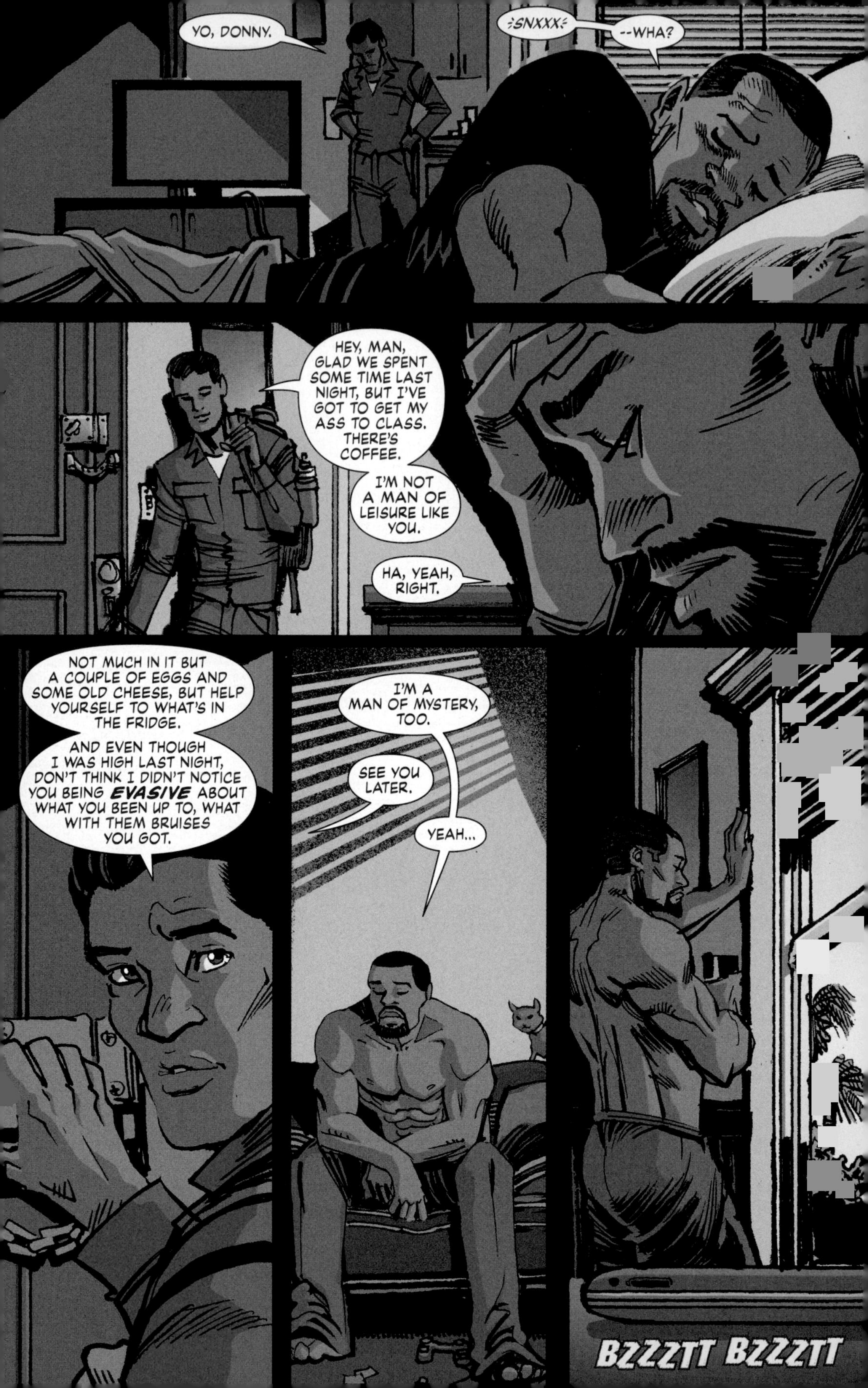
YO, DONNY.
:SNXXX:
--WHA?
HEY, MAN, GLAD WE SPENT SOME TIME LAST NIGHT, BUT I'VE GOT TO GET MY ASS TO CLASS. THERE'S COFFEE.
I'M NOT A MAN OF LEISURE LIKE YOU.
HA, YEAH, RIGHT.
NOT MUCH IN IT BUT A COUPLE OF EGGS AND SOME OLD CHEESE, BUT HELP YOURSELF TO WHAT'S IN THE FRIDGE.
AND EVEN THOUGH I WAS HIGH LAST NIGHT, DON'T THINK I DIDN'T NOTICE YOU BEING EVASIVE ABOUT WHAT YOU BEEN UP TO, WHAT WITH THEM BRUISES YOU GOT.
I'M A MAN OF MYSTERY, TOO.
SEE YOU LATER.
YEAH...
BZZZTT BZZZTT

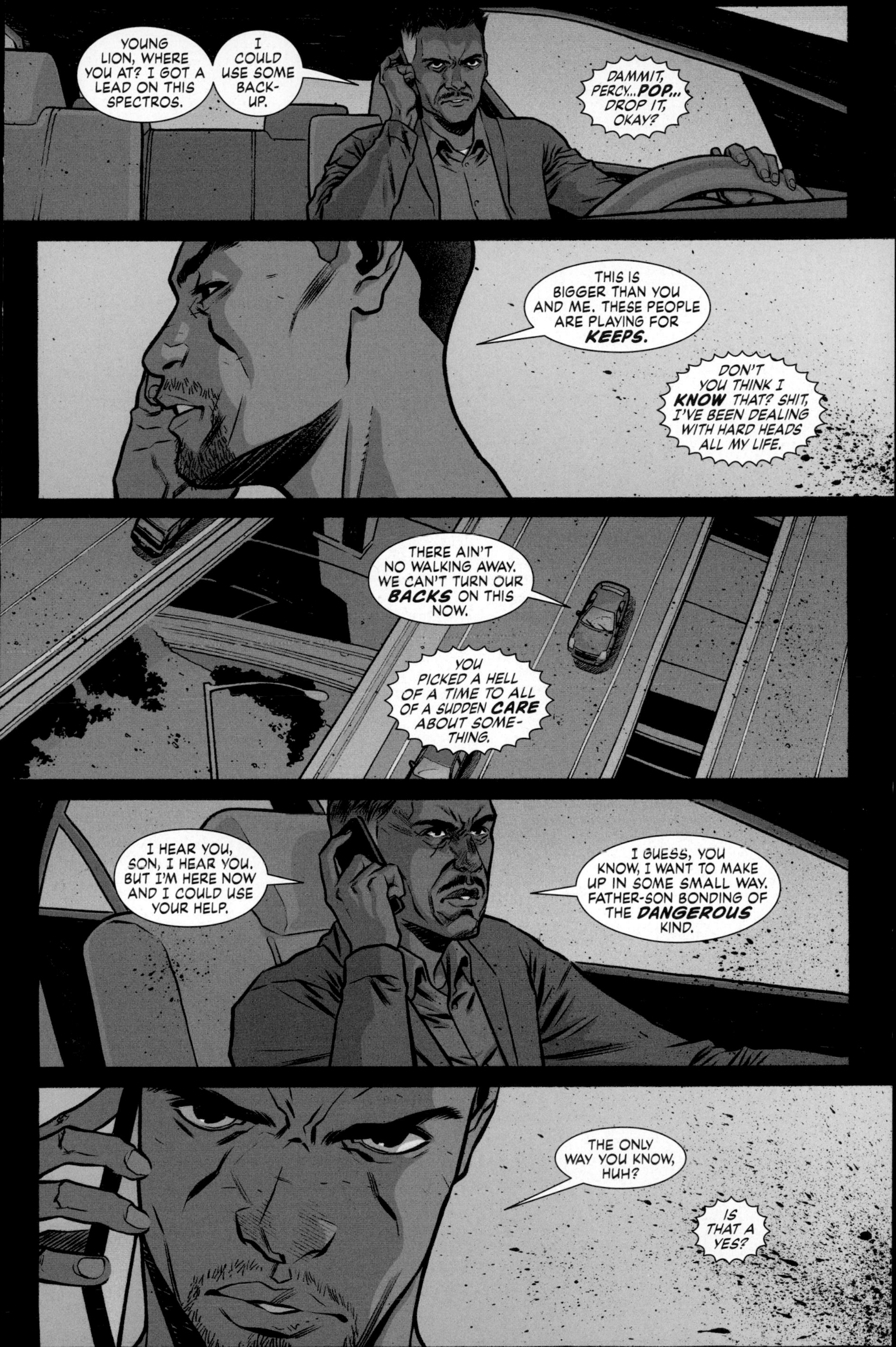
YOUNG LION, WHERE YOU AT? I GOT A LEAD ON THIS SPECTROS.
I COULD USE SOME BACK-UP.
DAMMIT, PERCY...POP... DROP IT, OKAY?
THIS IS BIGGER THAN YOU AND ME. THESE PEOPLE ARE PLAYING FOR KEEPS.
DON'T YOU THINK I KNOW THAT? SHIT, I'VE BEEN DEALING WITH HARD HEADS ALL MY LIFE.
THERE AIN'T NO WALKING AWAY. WE CAN'T TURN OUR BACKS ON THIS NOW.
YOU PICKED A HELL OF A TIME TO ALL OF A SUDDEN CARE ABOUT SOME-THING.
I HEAR YOU, SON, I HEAR YOU. BUT I'M HERE NOW AND I COULD USE YOUR HELP.
I GUESS, YOU KNOW, I WANT TO MAKE UP IN SOME SMALL WAY. FATHER-SON BONDING OF THE DANGEROUS KIND.
THE ONLY WAY YOU KNOW, HUH?
IS THAT A YES?

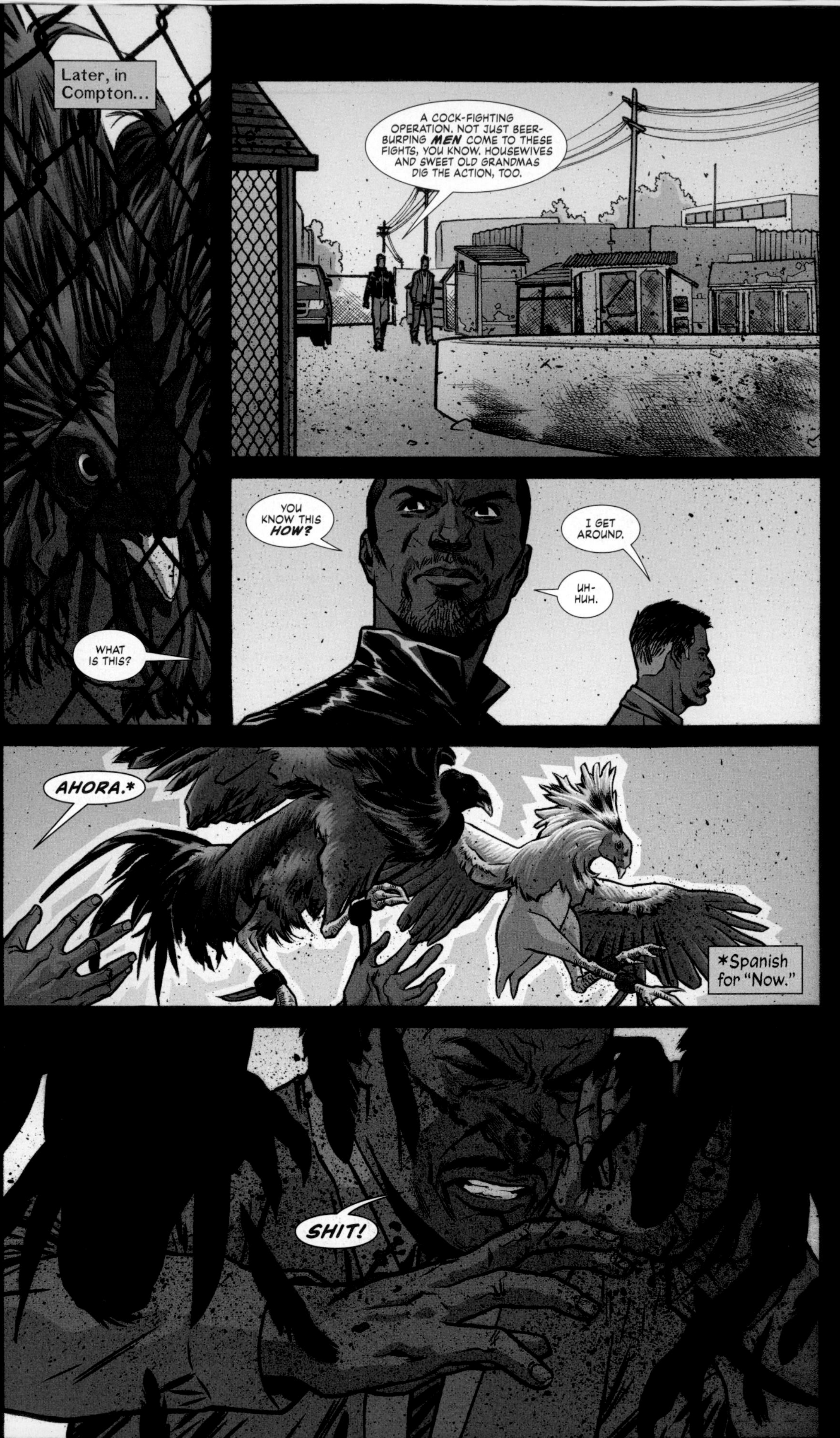
Later, in Compton...
A COCK-FIGHTING OPERATION. NOT JUST BEER-BURPING MEN COME TO THESE FIGHTS, YOU KNOW. HOUSEWIVES AND SWEET OLD GRANDMAS DIG THE ACTION, TOO.
WHAT IS THIS?
YOU KNOW THIS HOW?
I GET AROUND.
UH-HUH.
AHORA.*
*Spanish for "Now."
SHIT!

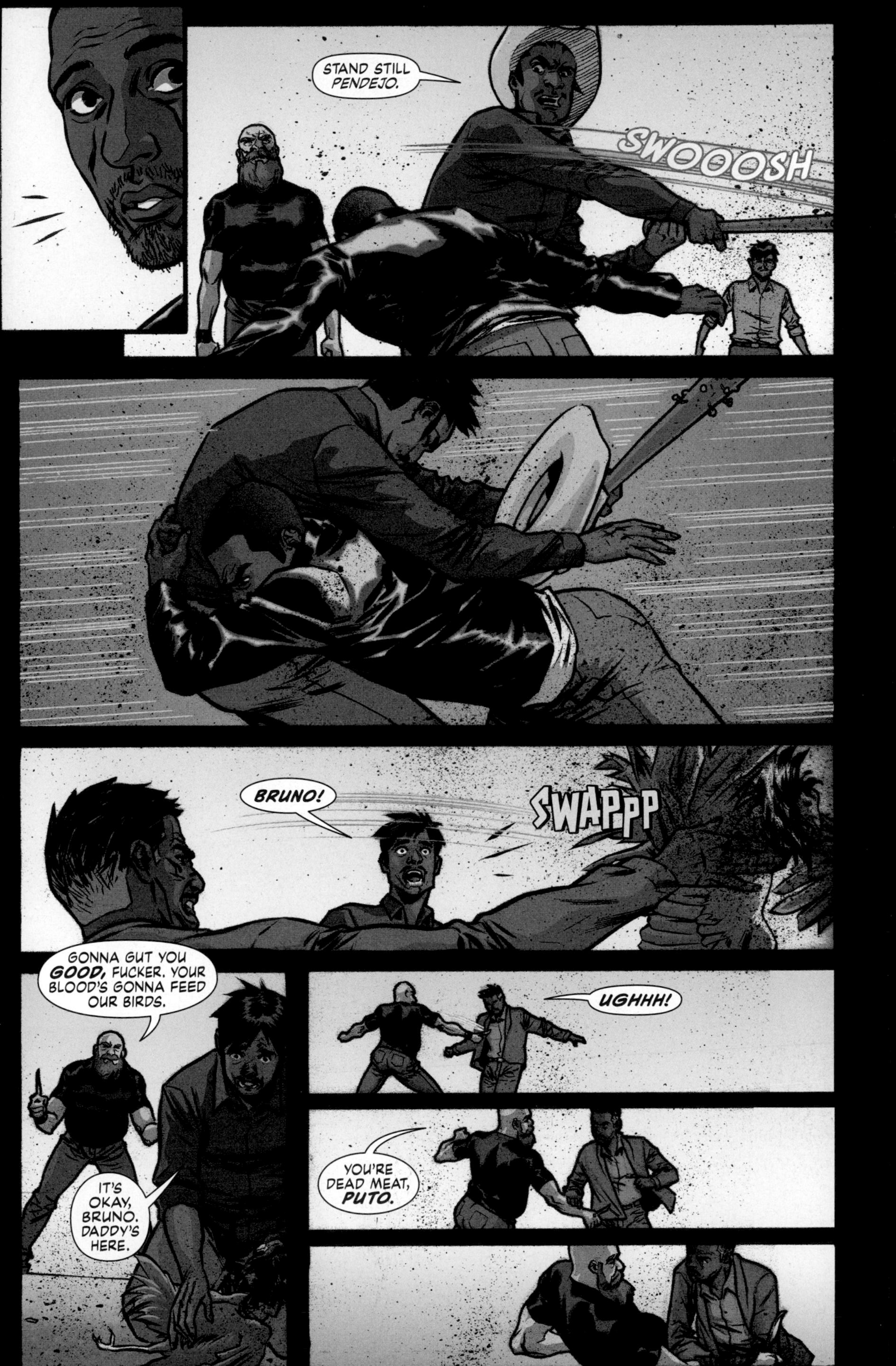
STAND STILL PENDEJO.
SWOOOSH
BRUNO!
SWAPPP
GONNA GUT YOU GOOD, FUCKER. YOUR BLOOD'S GONNA FEED OUR BIRDS.
IT'S OKAY, BRUNO. DADDY'S HERE.
UGHHH!
YOU'RE DEAD MEAT, PUTO.

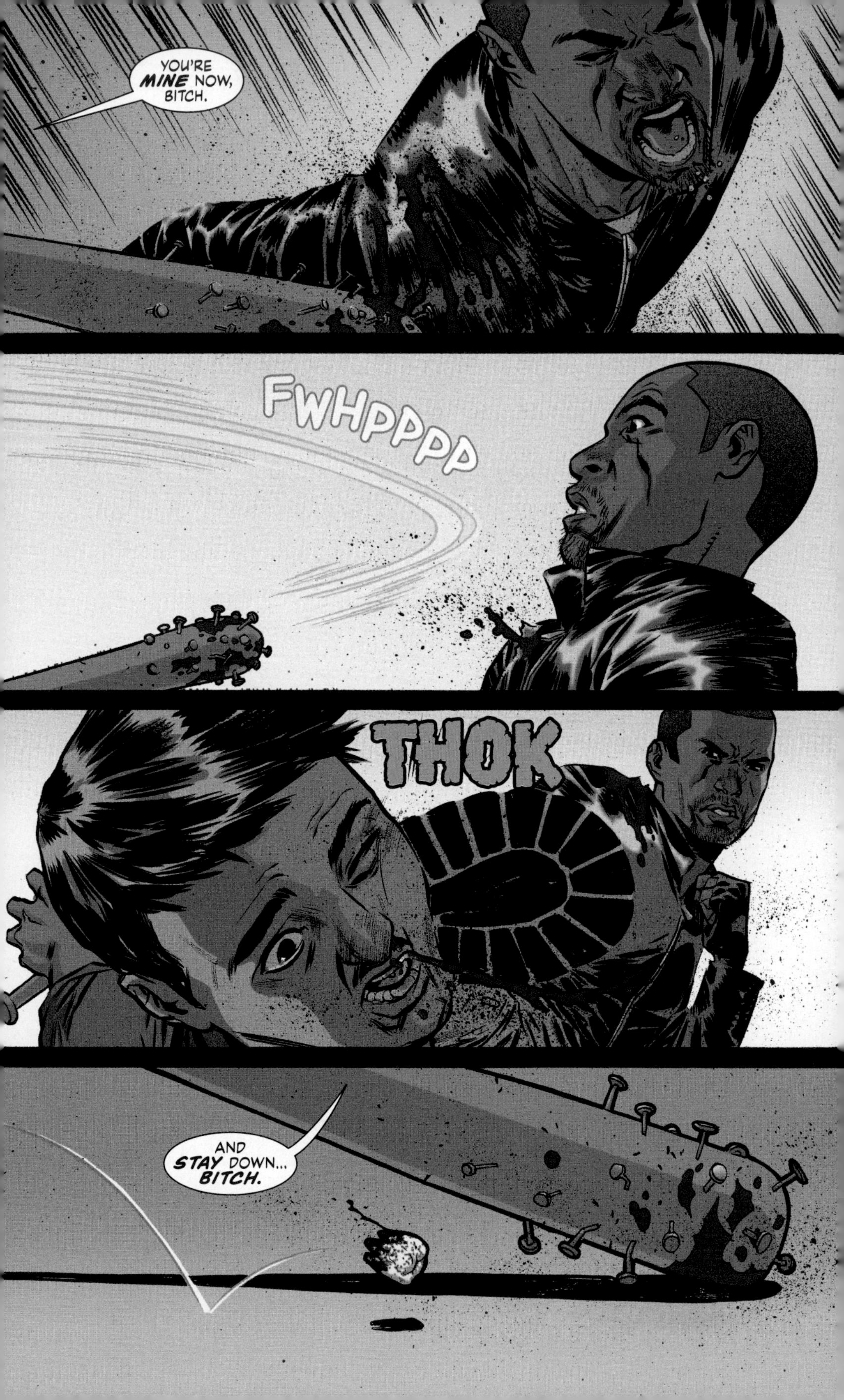
YOU'RE *MINE* NOW, BITCH.
FWHPPPP
THOK
AND *STAY* DOWN... *BITCH.*

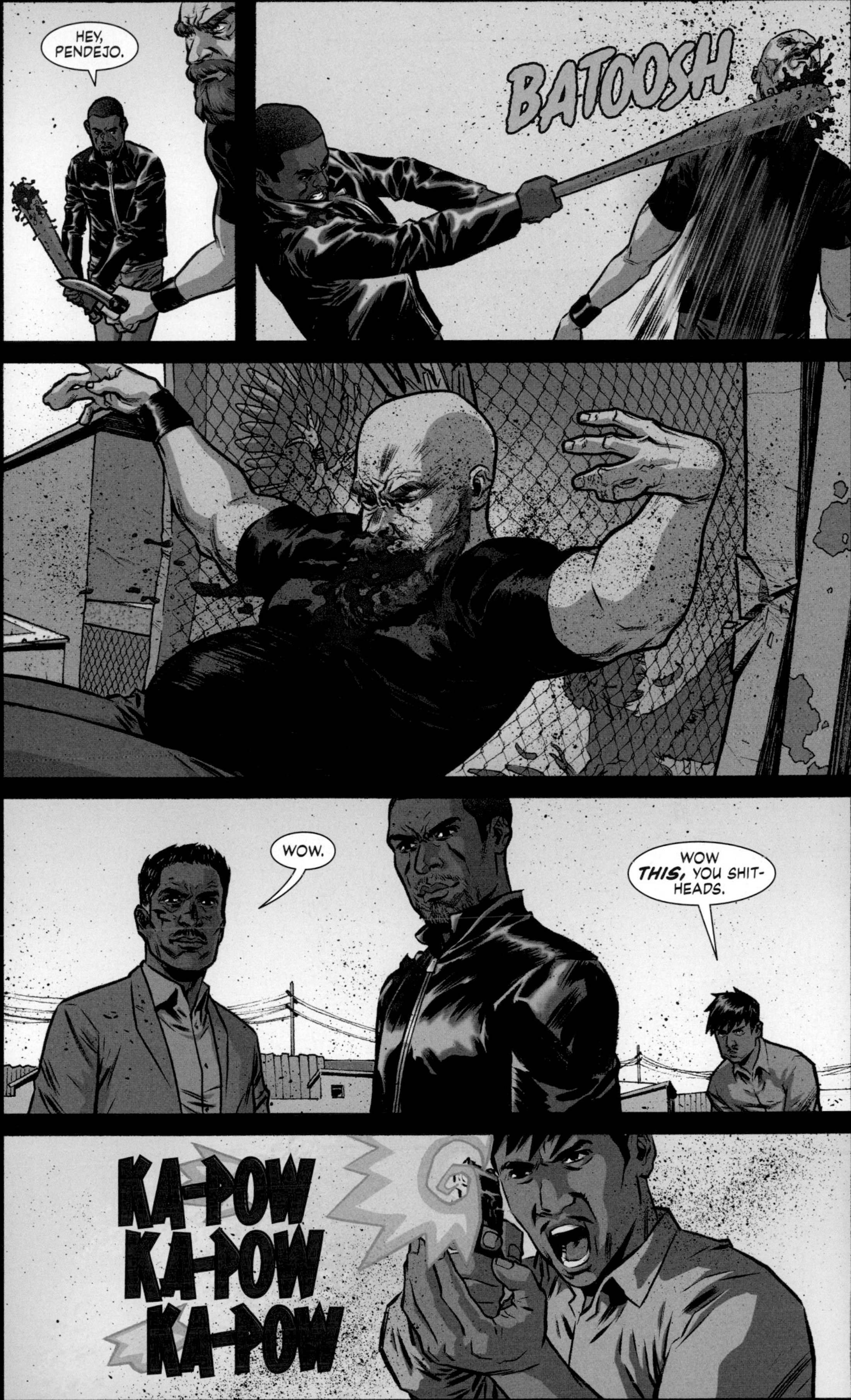
HEY, PENDEJO.
BATOOSH
WOW.
WOW THIS, YOU SHIT-HEADS.
KA-POW
KA-POW
KA-POW

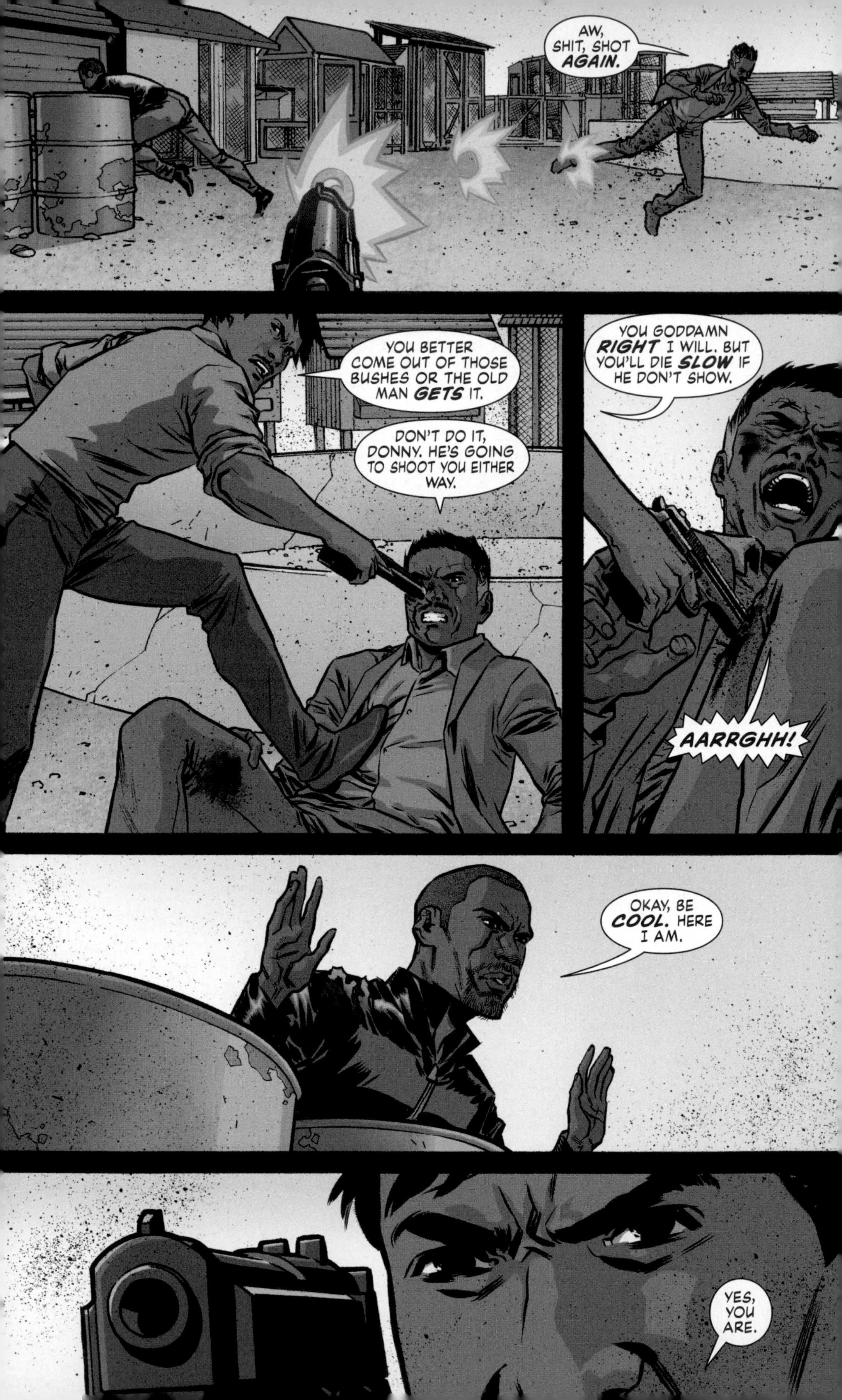
AW, SHIT, SHOT AGAIN.
YOU BETTER COME OUT OF THOSE BUSHES OR THE OLD MAN GETS IT.
DON'T DO IT, DONNY. HE'S GOING TO SHOOT YOU EITHER WAY.
YOU GODDAMN RIGHT I WILL. BUT YOU'LL DIE SLOW IF HE DON'T SHOW.
AARRGHH!
OKAY, BE COOL. HERE I AM.
YES, YOU ARE.

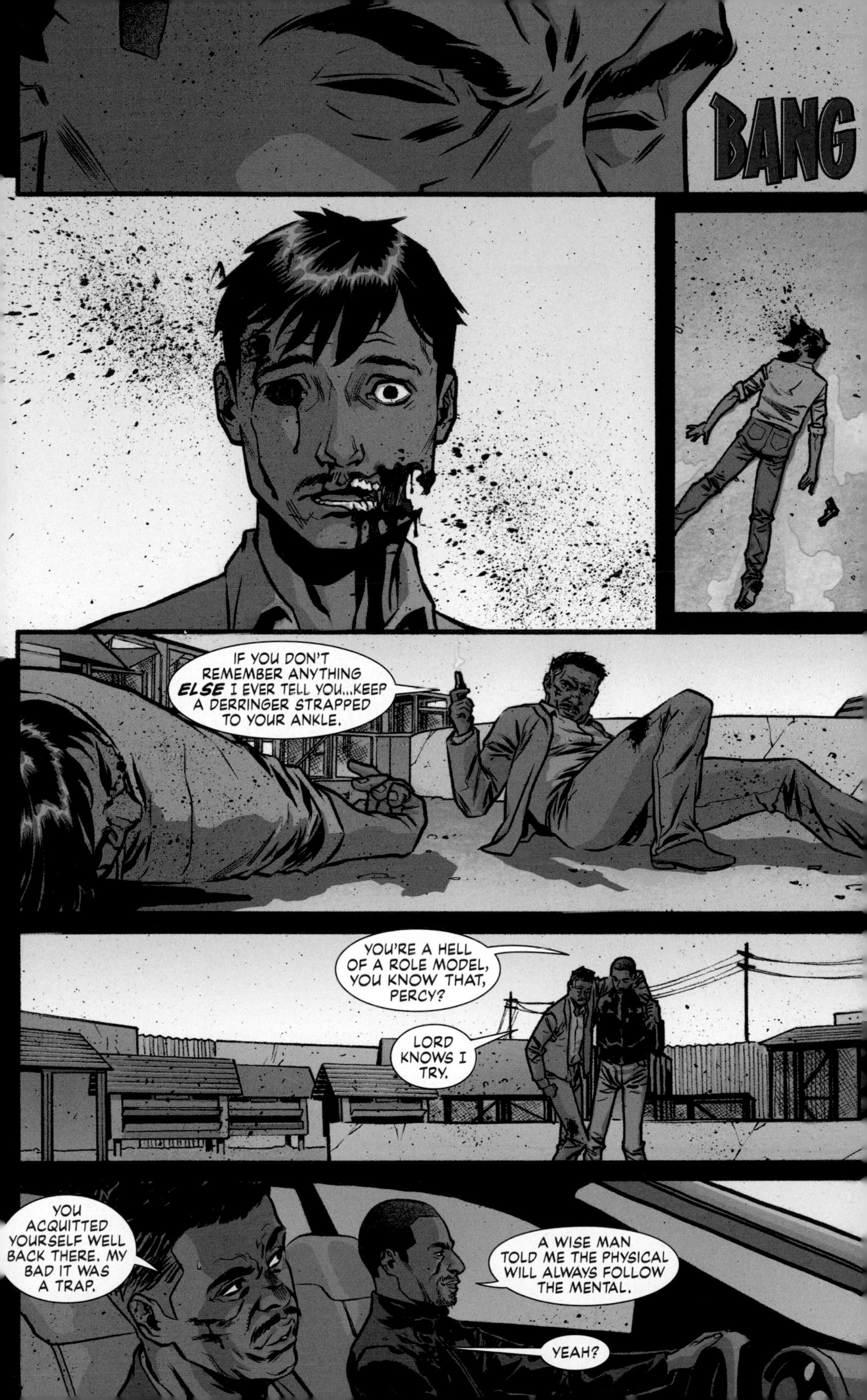
BANG
IF YOU DON'T REMEMBER ANYTHING *ELSE* I EVER TELL YOU...KEEP A DERRINGER STRAPPED TO YOUR ANKLE.
YOU'RE A HELL OF A ROLE MODEL, YOU KNOW THAT, PERCY?
LORD KNOWS I TRY.
YOU ACQUITTED YOURSELF WELL BACK THERE. MY BAD IT WAS A TRAP.
A WISE MAN TOLD ME THE PHYSICAL WILL ALWAYS FOLLOW THE MENTAL.
YEAH?

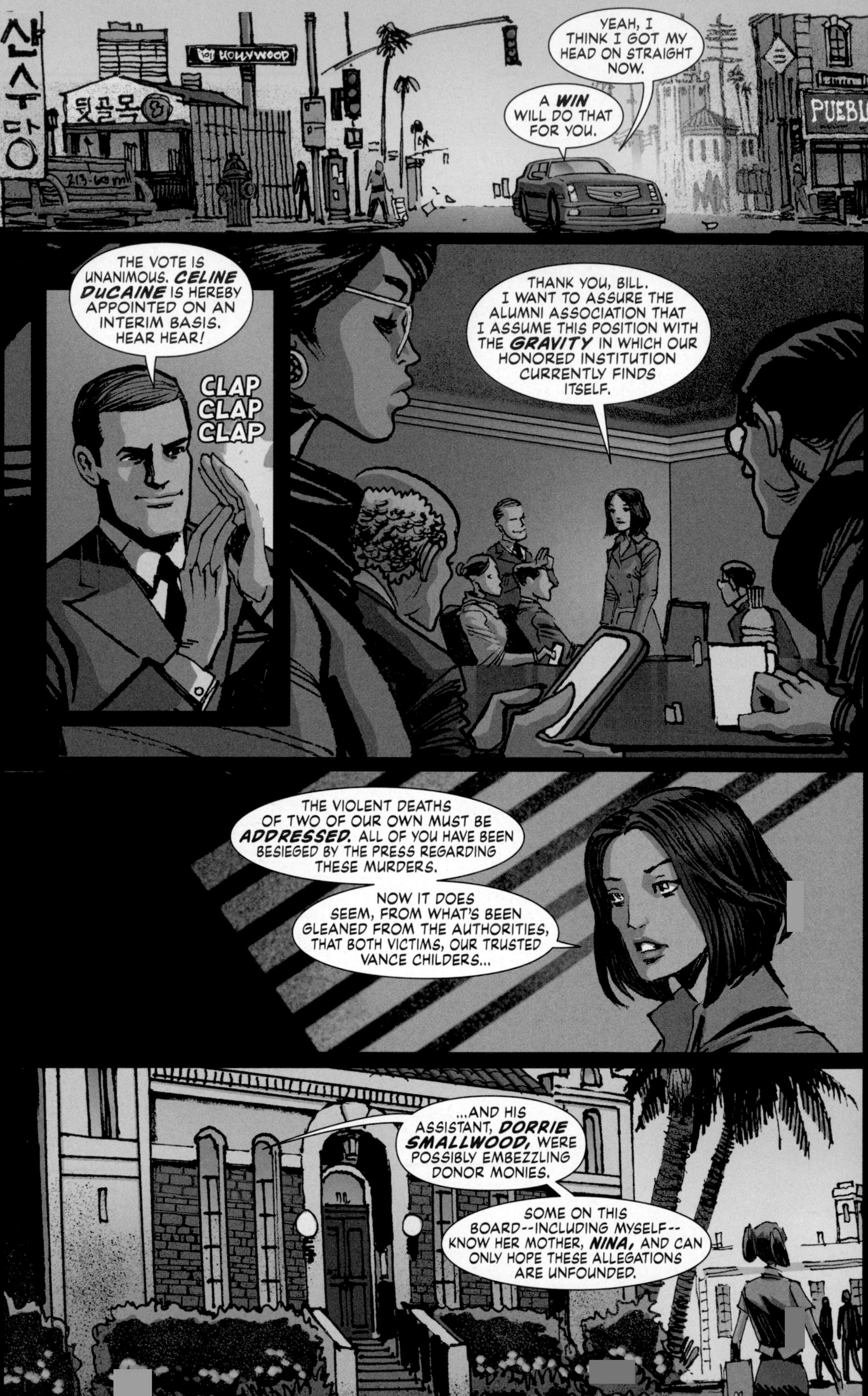
HOLLYWOOD
YEAH, I THINK I GOT MY HEAD ON STRAIGHT NOW.
A WIN WILL DO THAT FOR YOU.
THE VOTE IS UNANIMOUS. CELINE DUCAINE IS HEREBY APPOINTED ON AN INTERIM BASIS. HEAR HEAR!
CLAP CLAP CLAP
THANK YOU, BILL. I WANT TO ASSURE THE ALUMNI ASSOCIATION THAT I ASSUME THIS POSITION WITH THE GRAVITY IN WHICH OUR HONORED INSTITUTION CURRENTLY FINDS ITSELF.
THE VIOLENT DEATHS OF TWO OF OUR OWN MUST BE ADDRESSED. ALL OF YOU HAVE BEEN BESIEGED BY THE PRESS REGARDING THESE MURDERS.
NOW IT DOES SEEM, FROM WHAT'S BEEN GLEANED FROM THE AUTHORITIES, THAT BOTH VICTIMS, OUR TRUSTED VANCE CHILDERS...
...AND HIS ASSISTANT, DORRIE SMALLWOOD, WERE POSSIBLY EMBEZZLING DONOR MONIES.
SOME ON THIS BOARD--INCLUDING MYSELF--KNOW HER MOTHER, NINA, AND CAN ONLY HOPE THESE ALLEGATIONS ARE UNFOUNDED.

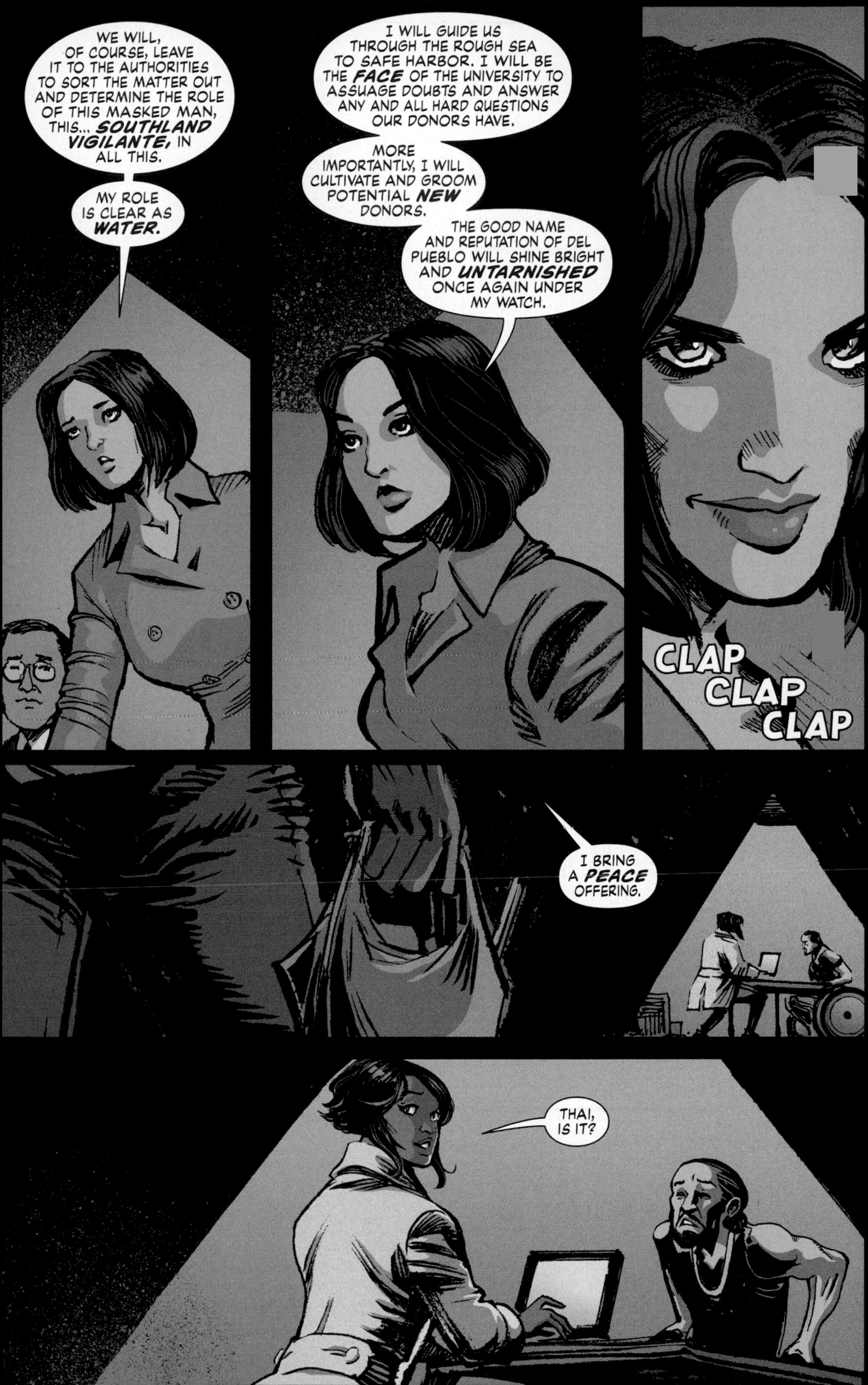
WE WILL, OF COURSE, LEAVE IT TO THE AUTHORITIES TO SORT THE MATTER OUT AND DETERMINE THE ROLE OF THIS MASKED MAN, THIS... SOUTHLAND VIGILANTE, IN ALL THIS.
MY ROLE IS CLEAR AS WATER.
I WILL GUIDE US THROUGH THE ROUGH SEA TO SAFE HARBOR. I WILL BE THE FACE OF THE UNIVERSITY TO ASSUAGE DOUBTS AND ANSWER ANY AND ALL HARD QUESTIONS OUR DONORS HAVE.
MORE IMPORTANTLY, I WILL CULTIVATE AND GROOM POTENTIAL NEW DONORS.
THE GOOD NAME AND REPUTATION OF DEL PUEBLO WILL SHINE BRIGHT AND UNTARNISHED ONCE AGAIN UNDER MY WATCH.
CLAP CLAP CLAP
I BRING A PEACE OFFERING.
THAI, IS IT?

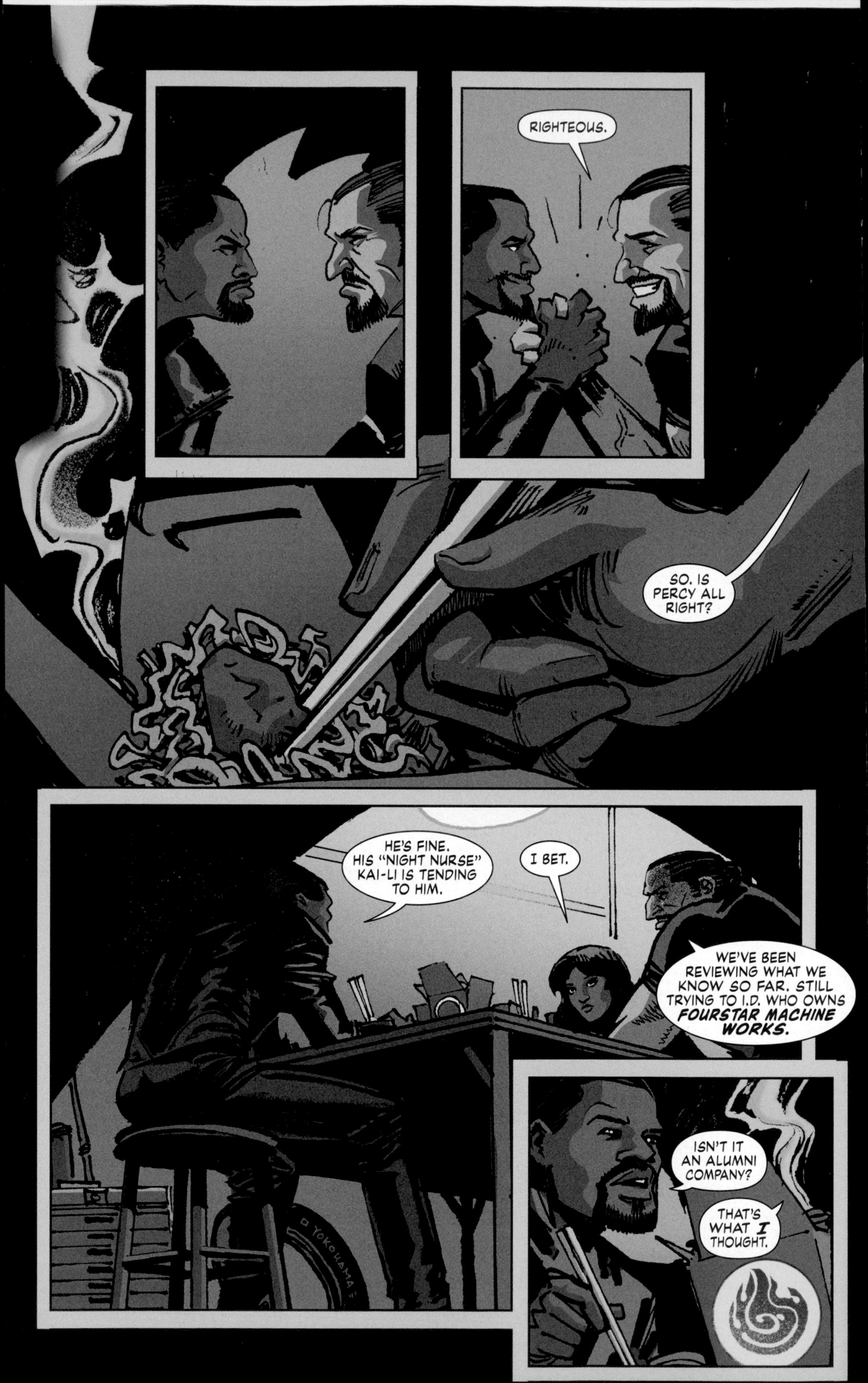
RIGHTEOUS.
SO. IS PERCY ALL RIGHT?
HE'S FINE. HIS "NIGHT NURSE" KAI-LI IS TENDING TO HIM.
I BET.
WE'VE BEEN REVIEWING WHAT WE KNOW SO FAR. STILL TRYING TO I.D. WHO OWNS **FOURSTAR MACHINE WORKS.**
ISN'T IT AN ALUMNI COMPANY?
THAT'S WHAT ***I*** THOUGHT.
YOKOHAMA

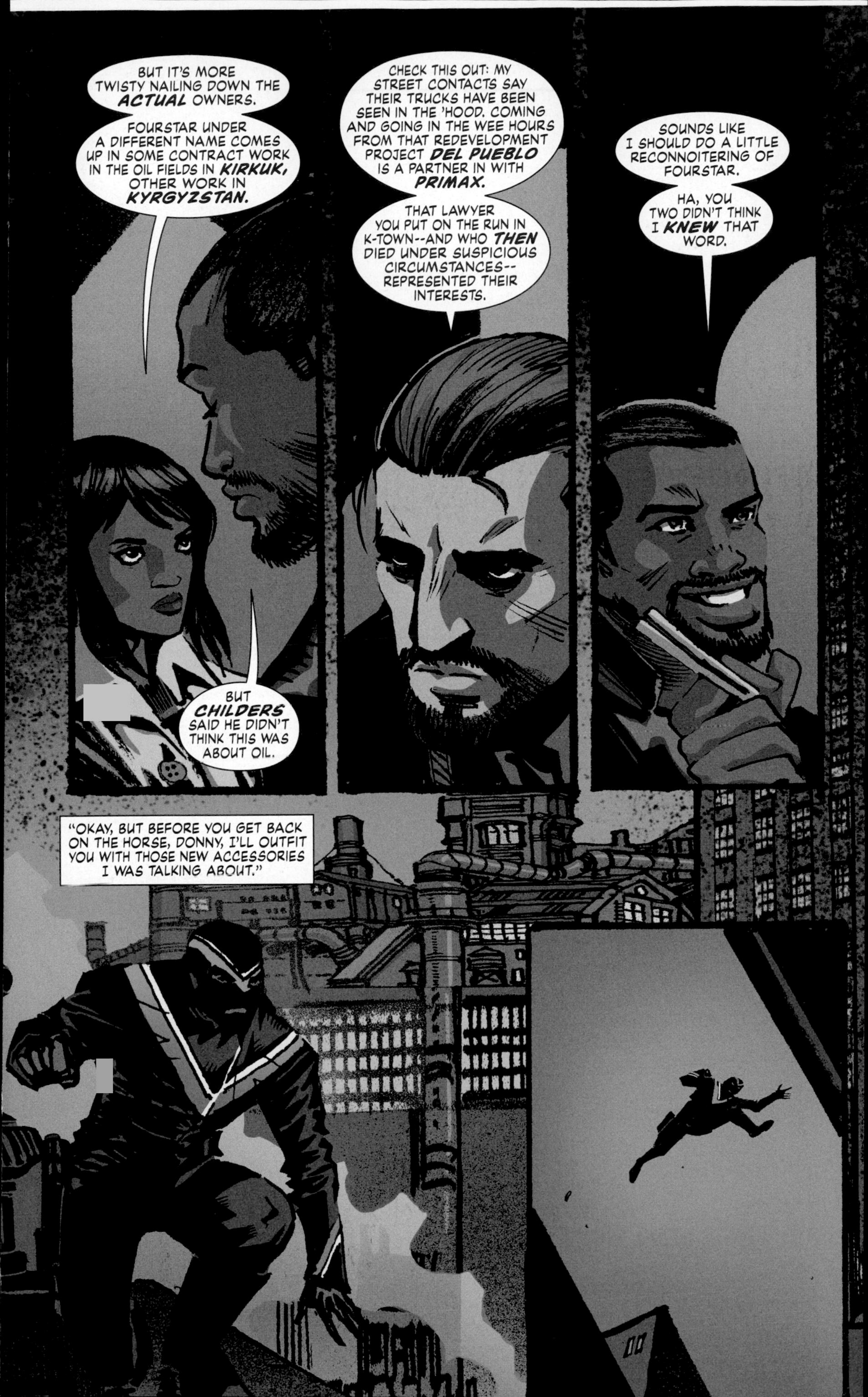
BUT IT'S MORE TWISTY NAILING DOWN THE ACTUAL OWNERS.
FOURSTAR UNDER A DIFFERENT NAME COMES UP IN SOME CONTRACT WORK IN THE OIL FIELDS IN KIRKUK, OTHER WORK IN KYRGYZSTAN.
BUT CHILDERS SAID HE DIDN'T THINK THIS WAS ABOUT OIL.
CHECK THIS OUT: MY STREET CONTACTS SAY THEIR TRUCKS HAVE BEEN SEEN IN THE 'HOOD. COMING AND GOING IN THE WEE HOURS FROM THAT REDEVELOPMENT PROJECT DEL PUEBLO IS A PARTNER IN WITH PRIMAX.
THAT LAWYER YOU PUT ON THE RUN IN K-TOWN--AND WHO THEN DIED UNDER SUSPICIOUS CIRCUMSTANCES--REPRESENTED THEIR INTERESTS.
SOUNDS LIKE I SHOULD DO A LITTLE RECONNOITERING OF FOURSTAR.
HA, YOU TWO DIDN'T THINK I KNEW THAT WORD.
"OKAY, BUT BEFORE YOU GET BACK ON THE HORSE, DONNY, I'LL OUTFIT YOU WITH THOSE NEW ACCESSORIES I WAS TALKING ABOUT."

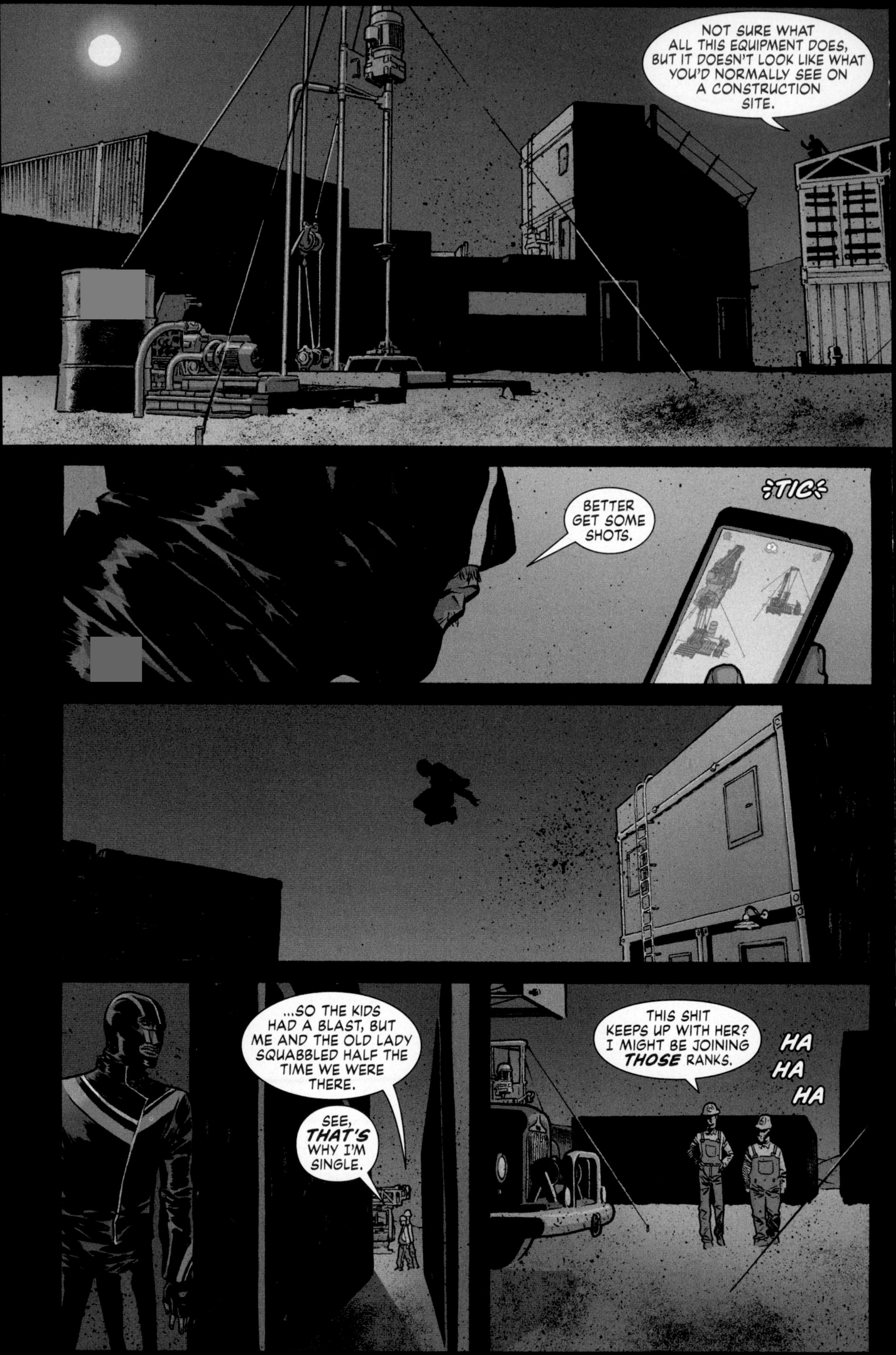
NOT SURE WHAT ALL THIS EQUIPMENT DOES, BUT IT DOESN'T LOOK LIKE WHAT YOU'D NORMALLY SEE ON A CONSTRUCTION SITE.
TIC
BETTER GET SOME SHOTS.
...SO THE KIDS HAD A BLAST, BUT ME AND THE OLD LADY SQUABBLED HALF THE TIME WE WERE THERE.
SEE, THAT'S WHY I'M SINGLE.
THIS SHIT KEEPS UP WITH HER? I MIGHT BE JOINING THOSE RANKS.
HA HA HA

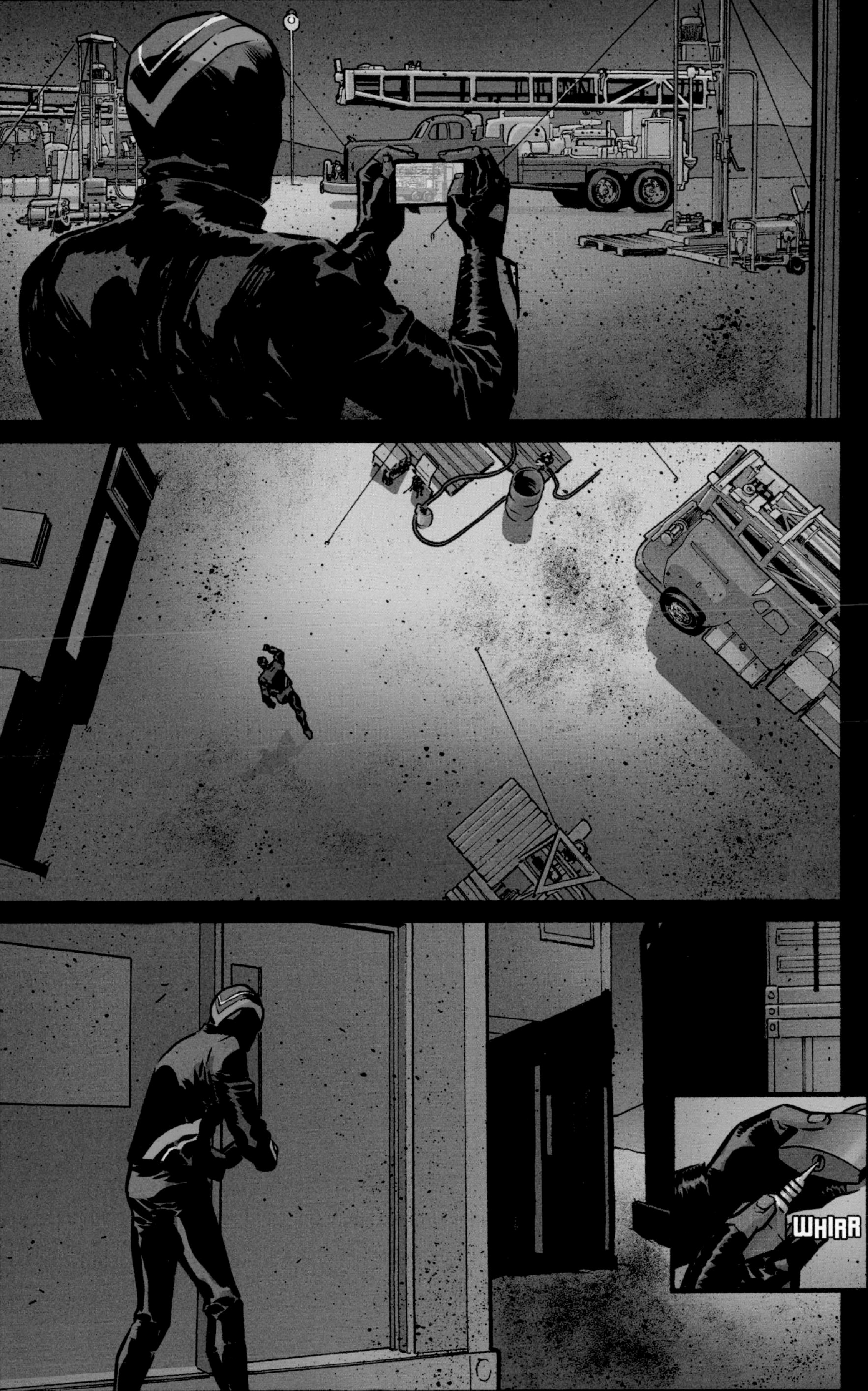
WHIRR

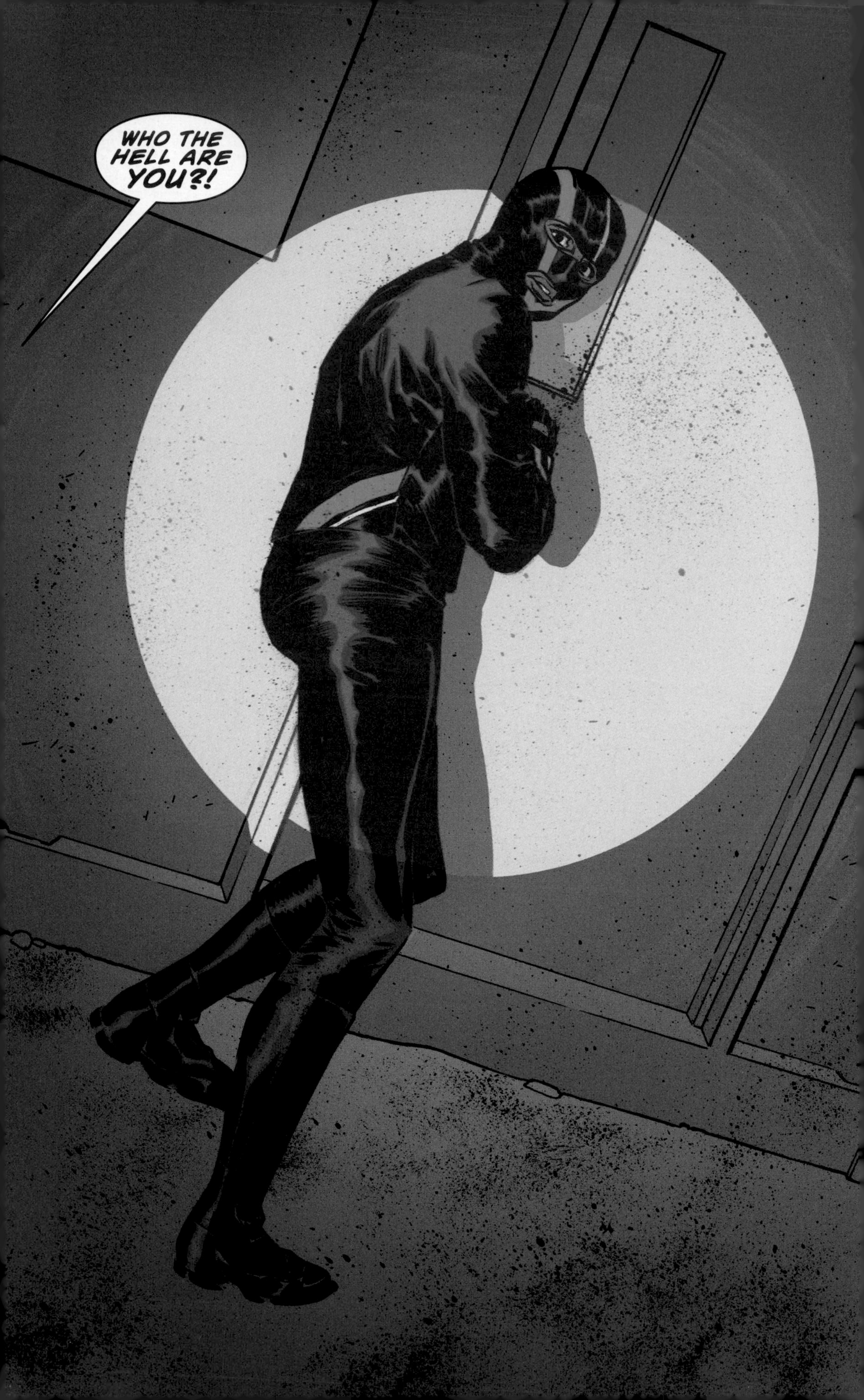
WHO THE HELL ARE YOU?!

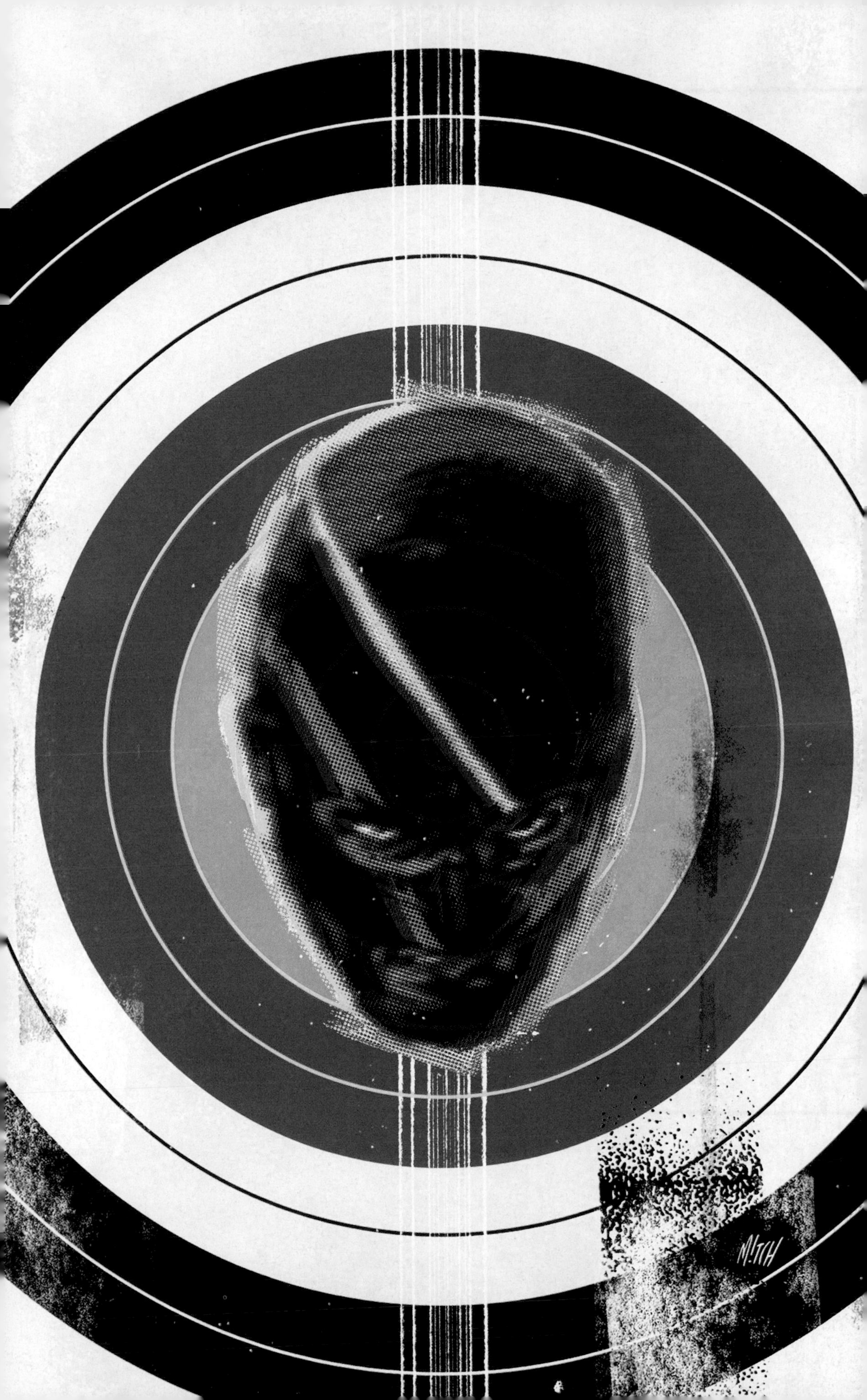
MITCH

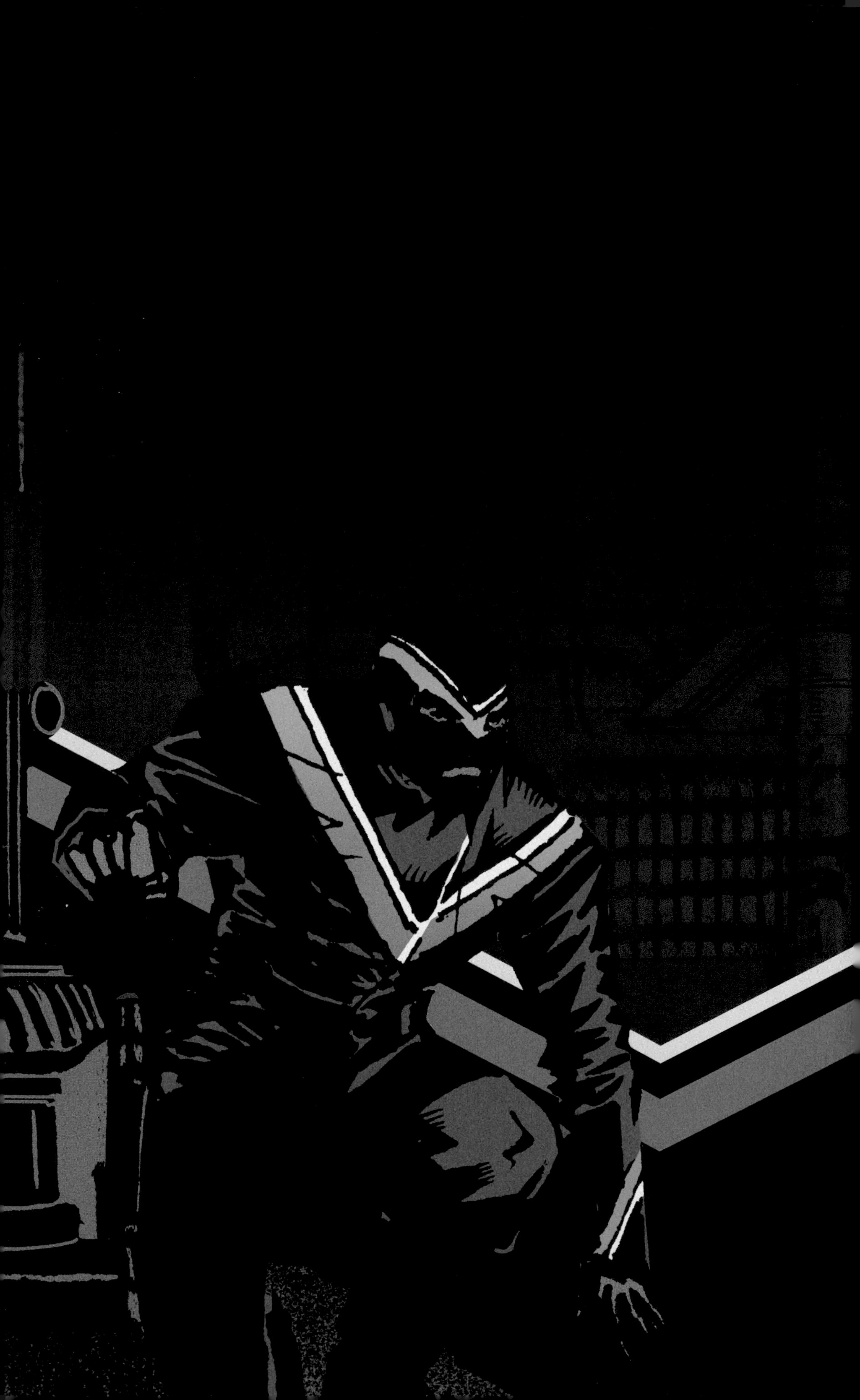

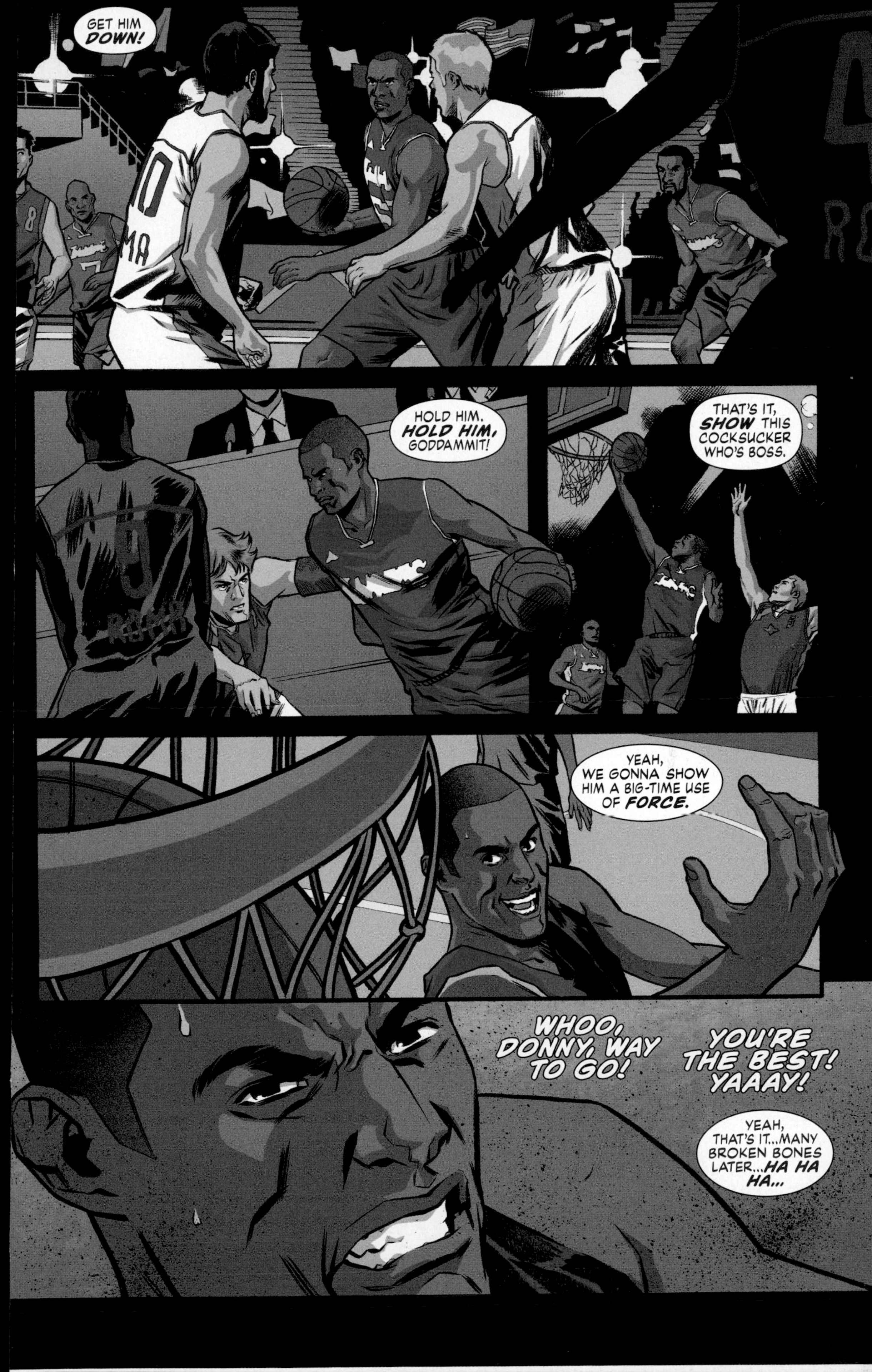
GET HIM DOWN!
HOLD HIM. HOLD HIM, GODDAMMIT!
THAT'S IT, SHOW THIS COCKSUCKER WHO'S BOSS.
YEAH, WE GONNA SHOW HIM A BIG-TIME USE OF FORCE.
WHOO, DONNY, WAY TO GO!
YOU'RE THE BEST! YAAAY!
YEAH, THAT'S IT...MANY BROKEN BONES LATER...HA HA HA...

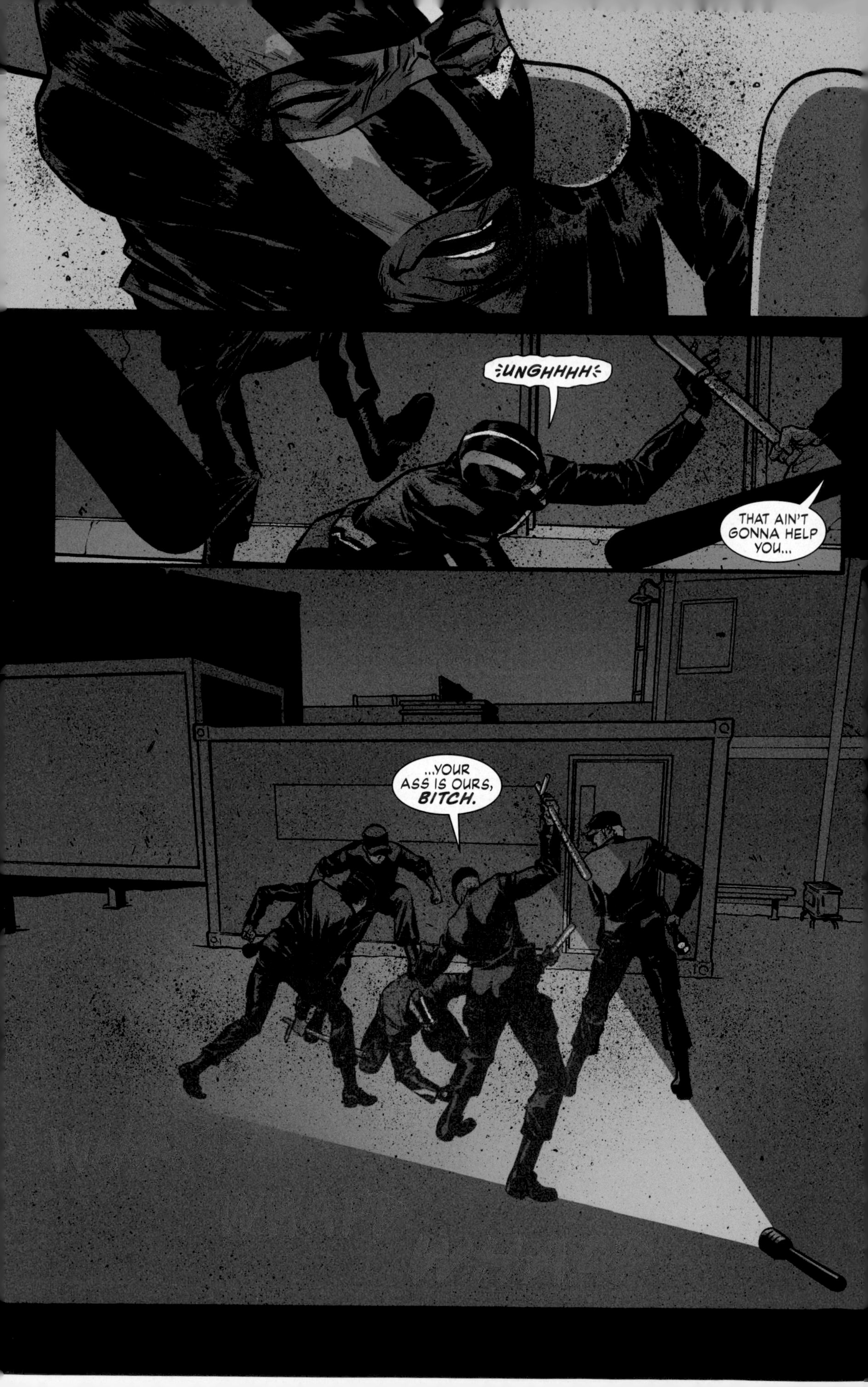
UNGHHHH
THAT AIN'T GONNA HELP YOU...
...YOUR ASS IS OURS, BITCH.

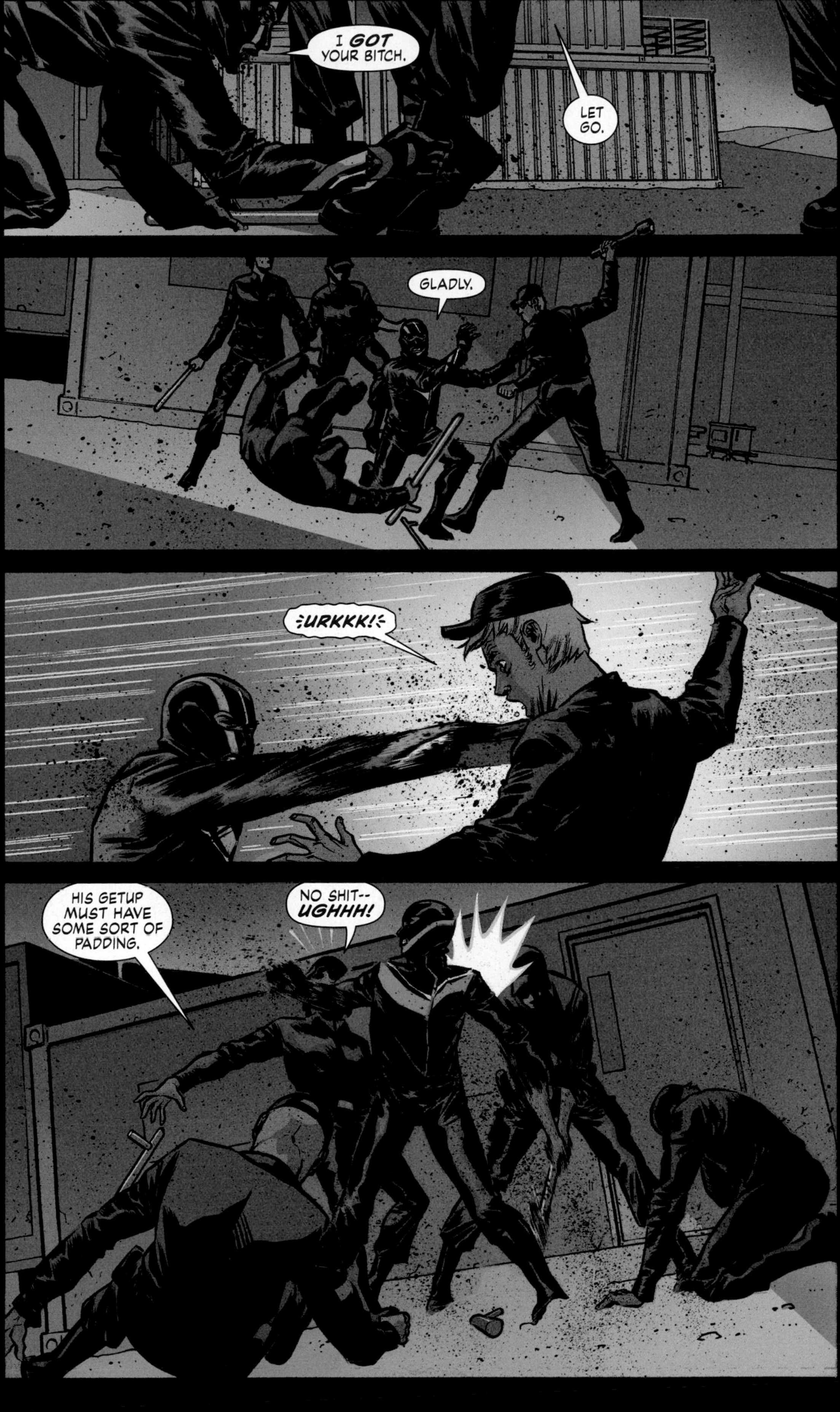
I GOT YOUR BITCH.
LET GO.
GLADLY.
URKKK!
HIS GETUP MUST HAVE SOME SORT OF PADDING.
NO SHIT-- UGHHH!

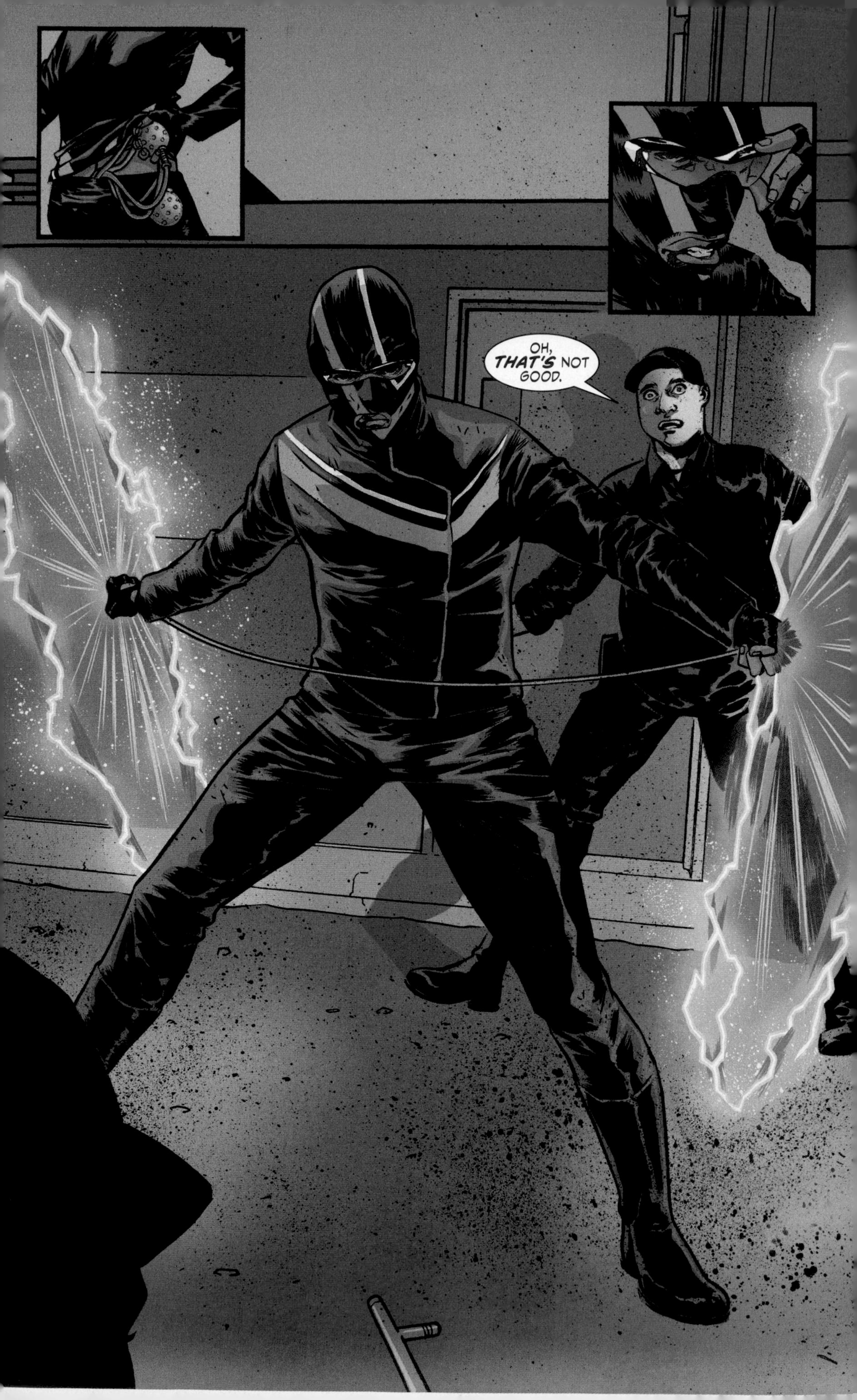
OH, THAT'S NOT GOOD.

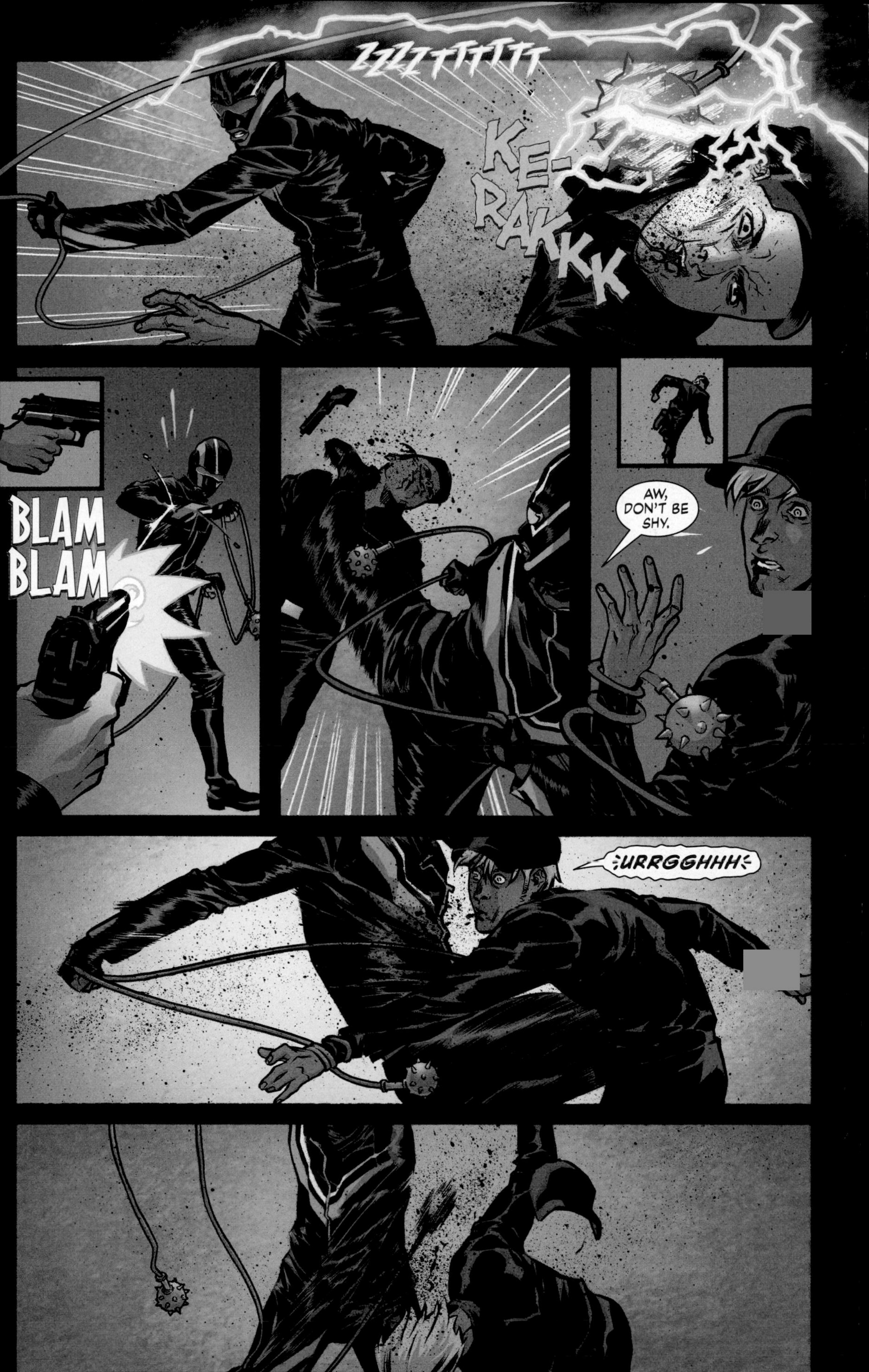
ZZZZTTTTTTT
KE-RAKKK
BLAM
BLAM
AW, DON'T BE SHY.
URRGGHHH

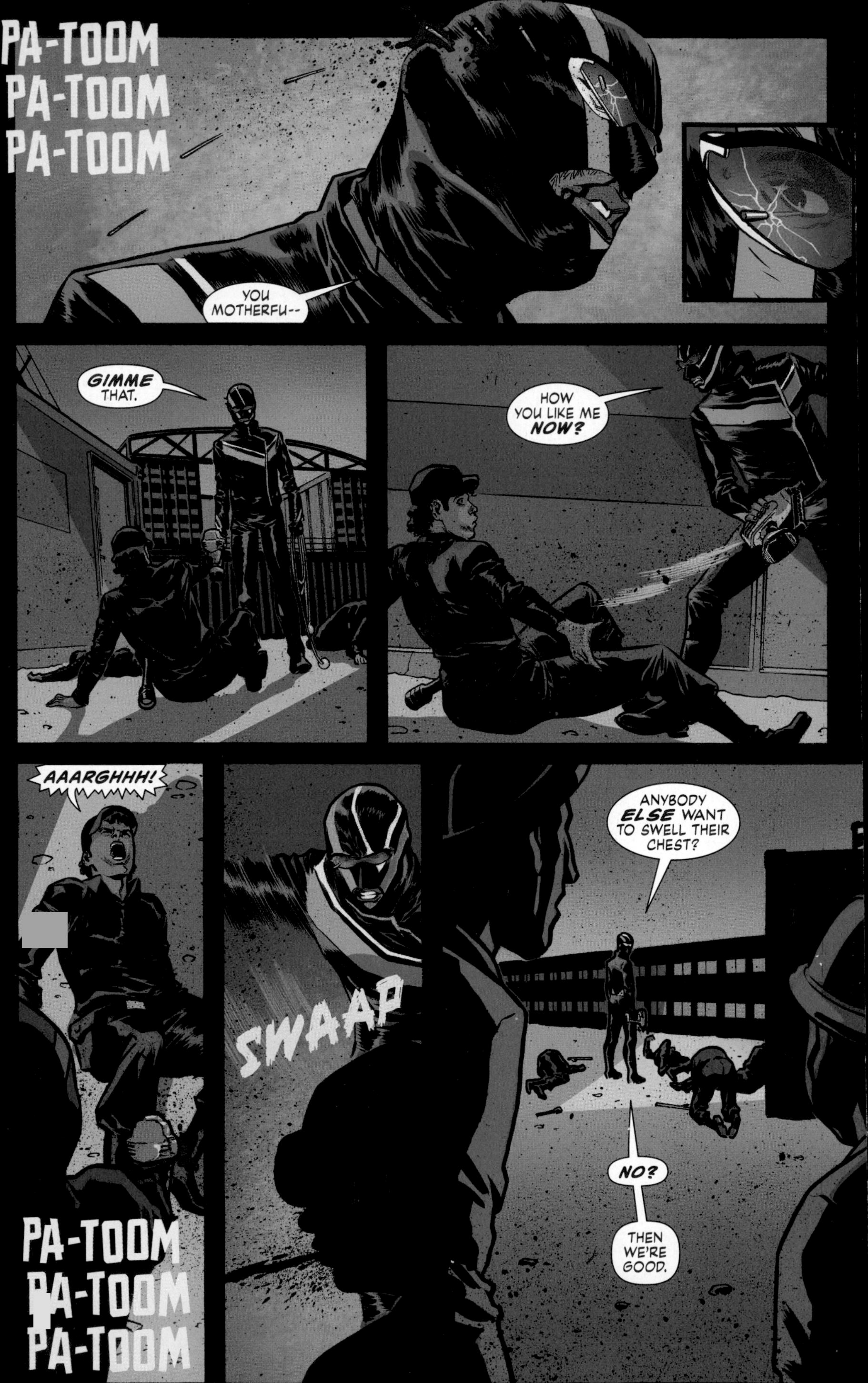
PA-TOOM
PA-TOOM
PA-TOOM
YOU MOTHERFU--
GIMME THAT.
HOW YOU LIKE ME NOW?
AAARGHHH!
SWAAP
ANYBODY ELSE WANT TO SWELL THEIR CHEST?
NO?
THEN WE'RE GOOD.
PA-TOOM
PA-TOOM
PA-TOOM

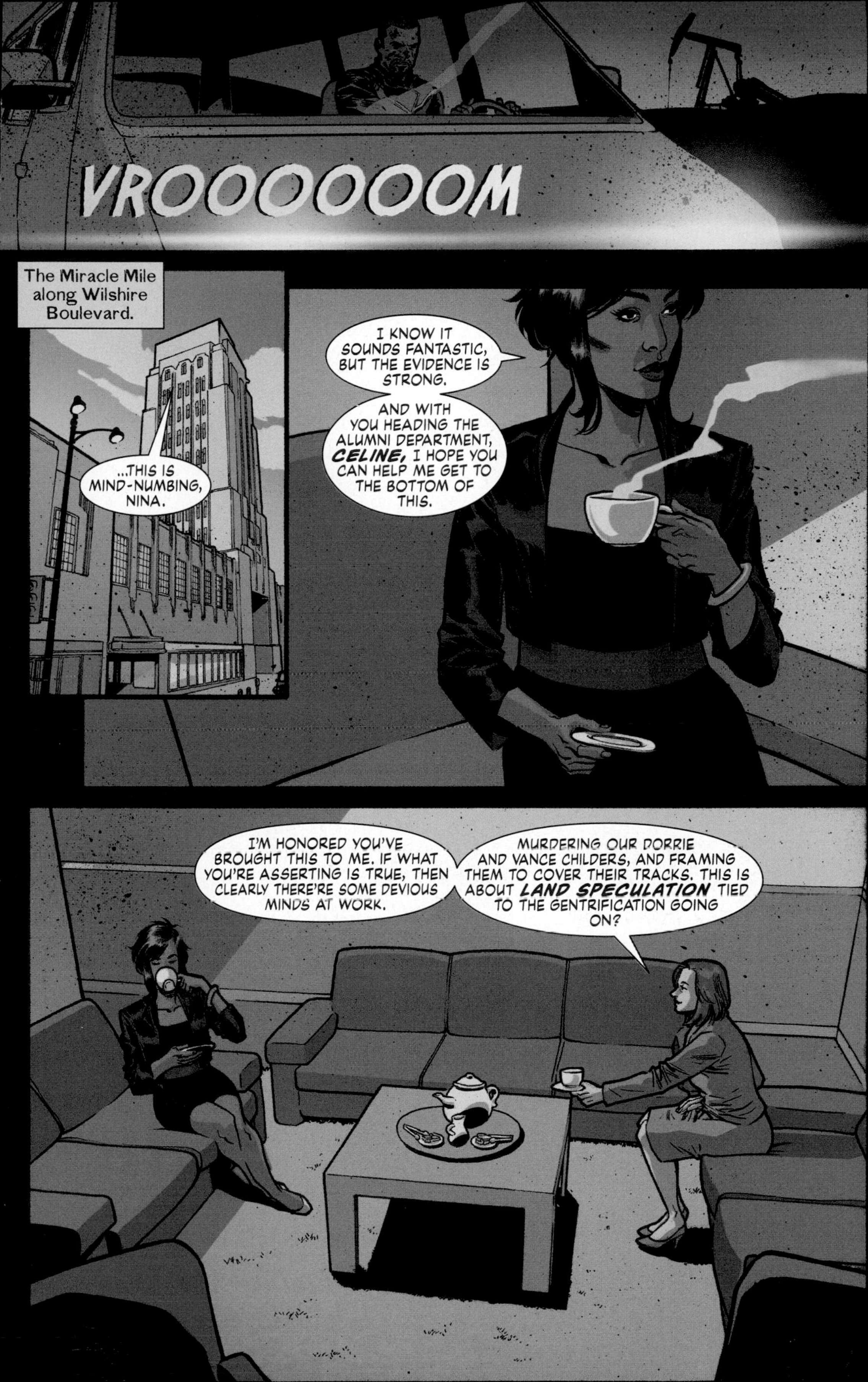
VROOOOOOM
The Miracle Mile along Wilshire Boulevard.
...THIS IS MIND-NUMBING, NINA.
I KNOW IT SOUNDS FANTASTIC, BUT THE EVIDENCE IS STRONG.
AND WITH YOU HEADING THE ALUMNI DEPARTMENT, CELINE, I HOPE YOU CAN HELP ME GET TO THE BOTTOM OF THIS.
I'M HONORED YOU'VE BROUGHT THIS TO ME. IF WHAT YOU'RE ASSERTING IS TRUE, THEN CLEARLY THERE'RE SOME DEVIOUS MINDS AT WORK.
MURDERING OUR DORRIE AND VANCE CHILDERS, AND FRAMING THEM TO COVER THEIR TRACKS. THIS IS ABOUT LAND SPECULATION TIED TO THE GENTRIFICATION GOING ON?

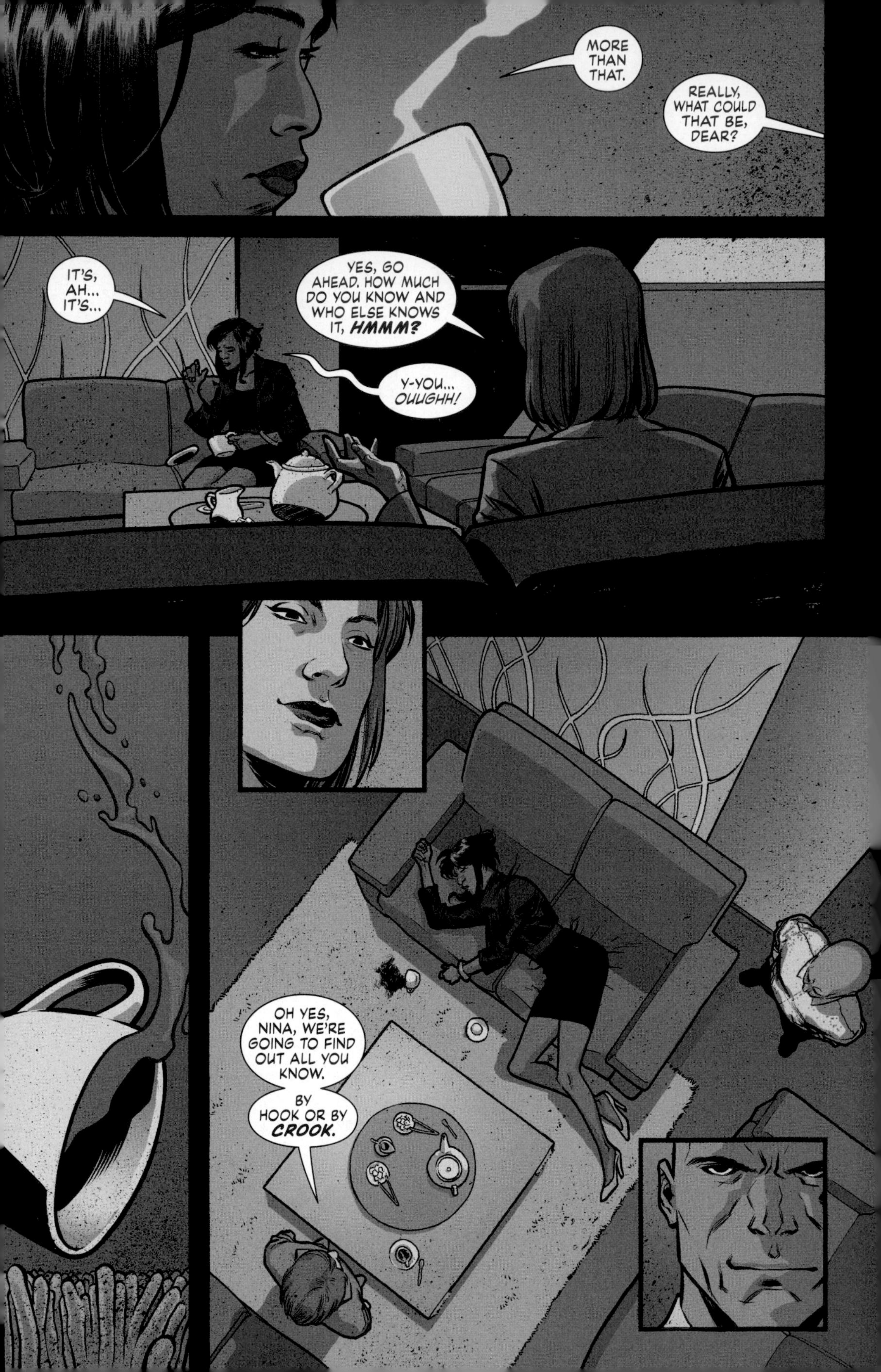

MORE THAN THAT.
REALLY, WHAT COULD THAT BE, DEAR?
IT'S, AH... IT'S...
YES, GO AHEAD. HOW MUCH DO YOU KNOW AND WHO ELSE KNOWS IT, HMMM?
Y-YOU... OUUGHH!
OH YES, NINA, WE'RE GOING TO FIND OUT ALL YOU KNOW.
BY HOOK OR BY CROOK.

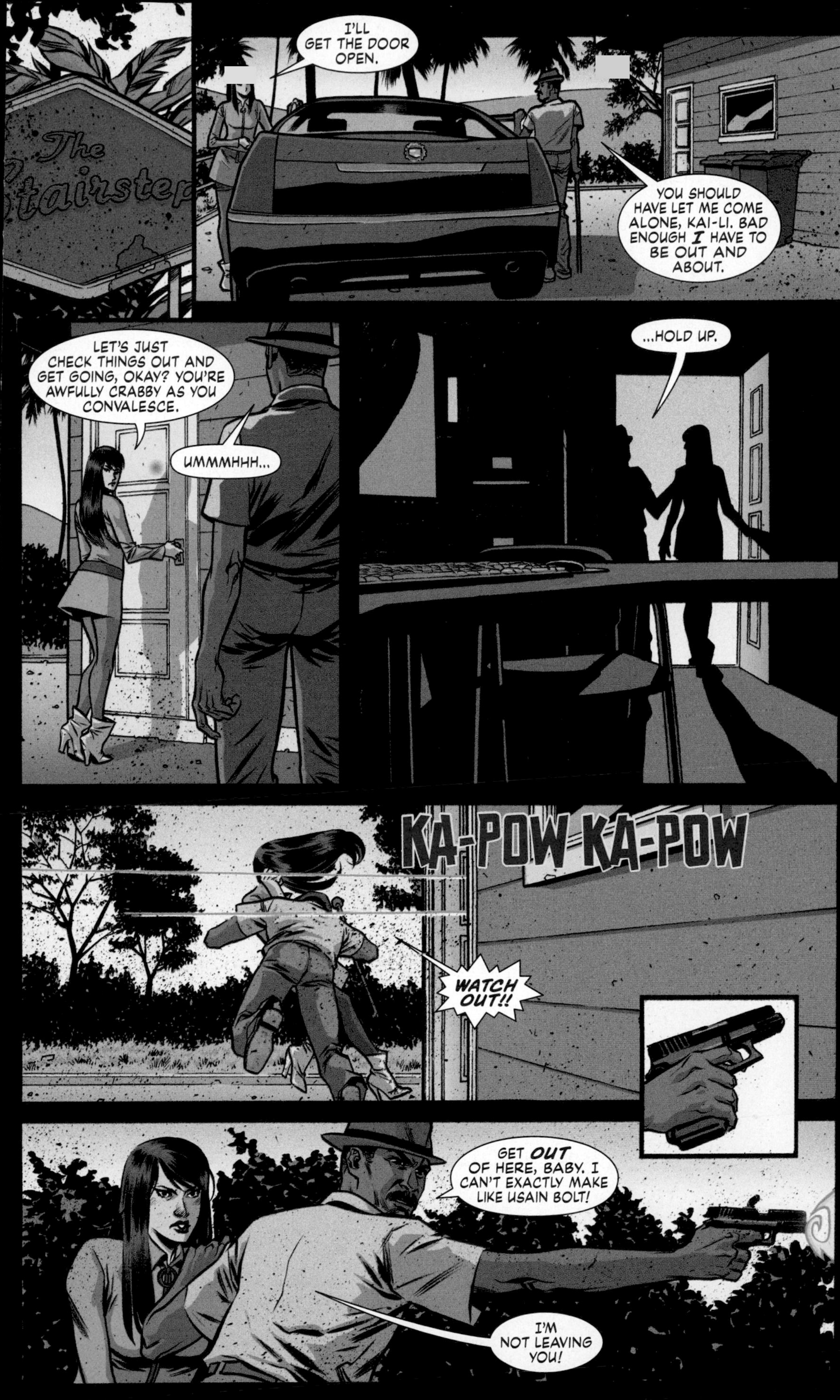
The Stairstep
I'LL GET THE DOOR OPEN.
YOU SHOULD HAVE LET ME COME ALONE, KAI-LI. BAD ENOUGH I HAVE TO BE OUT AND ABOUT.
LET'S JUST CHECK THINGS OUT AND GET GOING, OKAY? YOU'RE AWFULLY CRABBY AS YOU CONVALESCE.
UMMMHHH...
...HOLD UP.
KA-POW KA-POW
WATCH OUT!!
GET OUT OF HERE, BABY. I CAN'T EXACTLY MAKE LIKE USAIN BOLT!
I'M NOT LEAVING YOU!

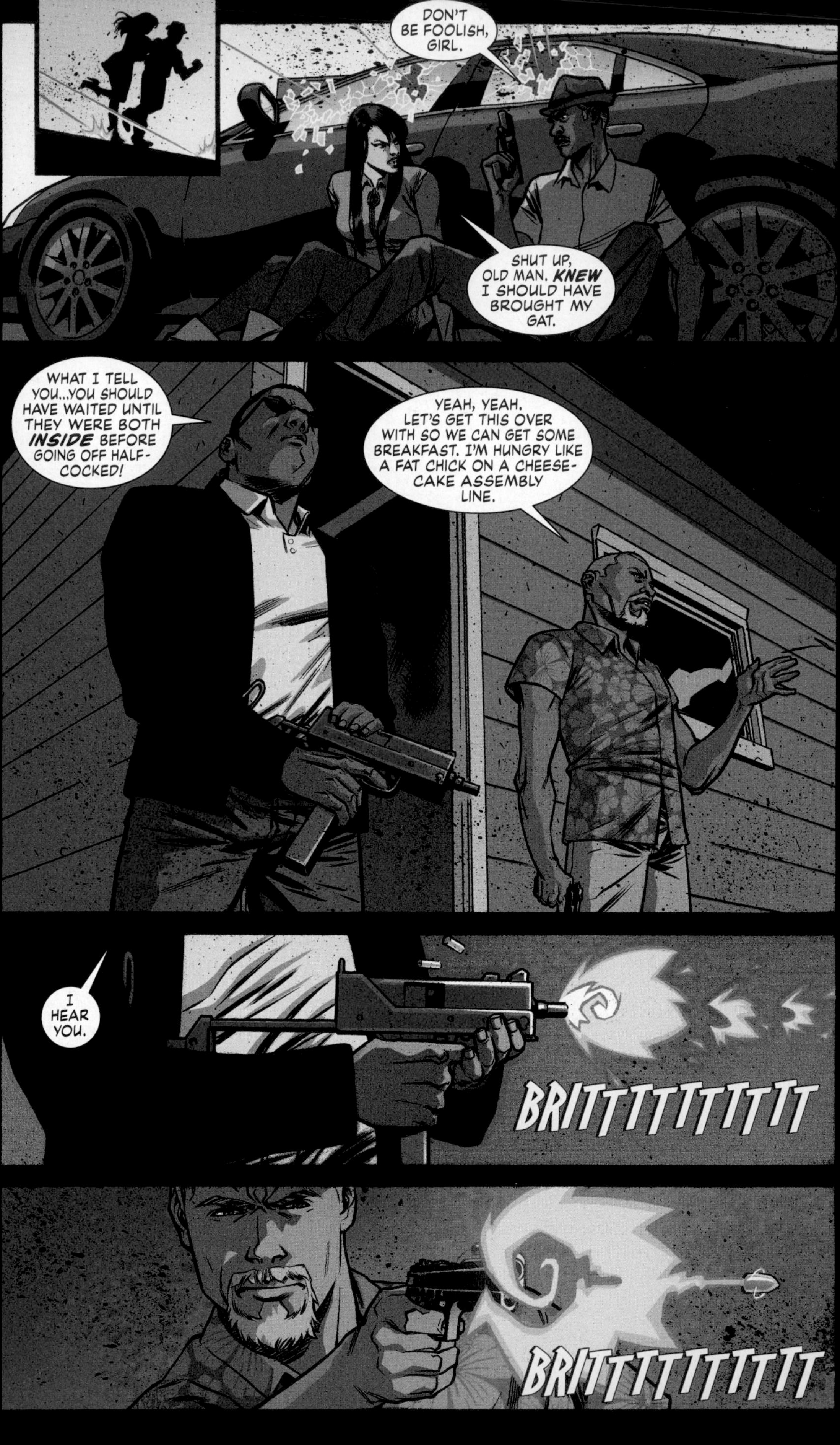
DON'T BE FOOLISH, GIRL.
SHUT UP, OLD MAN. KNEW I SHOULD HAVE BROUGHT MY GAT.
WHAT I TELL YOU...YOU SHOULD HAVE WAITED UNTIL THEY WERE BOTH INSIDE BEFORE GOING OFF HALF-COCKED!
YEAH, YEAH. LET'S GET THIS OVER WITH SO WE CAN GET SOME BREAKFAST. I'M HUNGRY LIKE A FAT CHICK ON A CHEESE-CAKE ASSEMBLY LINE.
I HEAR YOU.
BRITTTTTTTTTTT
BRITTTTTTTTTTT

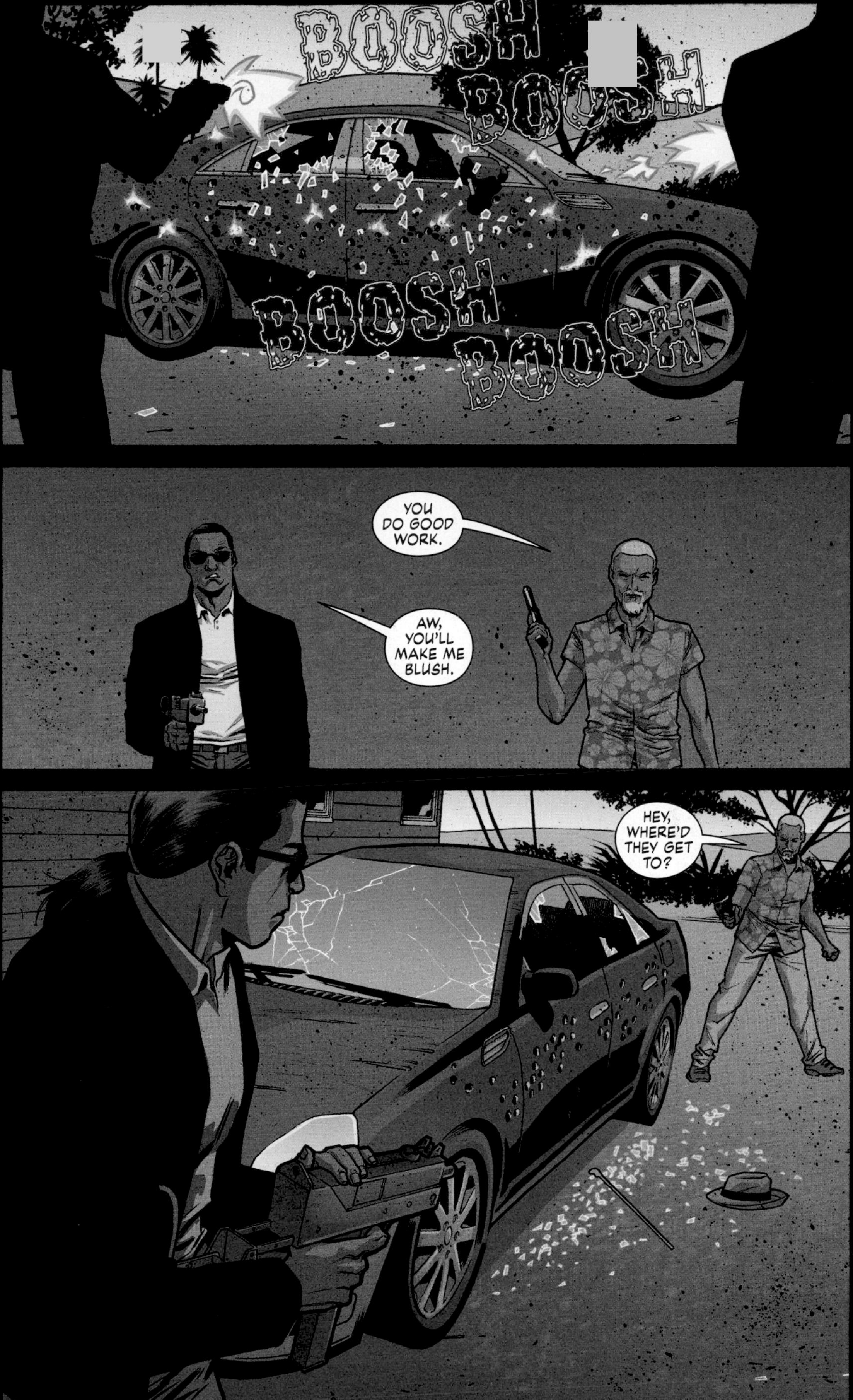
BOOSH
BOOSH
BOOSH
BOOSH
YOU DO GOOD WORK.
AW, YOU'LL MAKE ME BLUSH.
HEY, WHERE'D THEY GET TO?

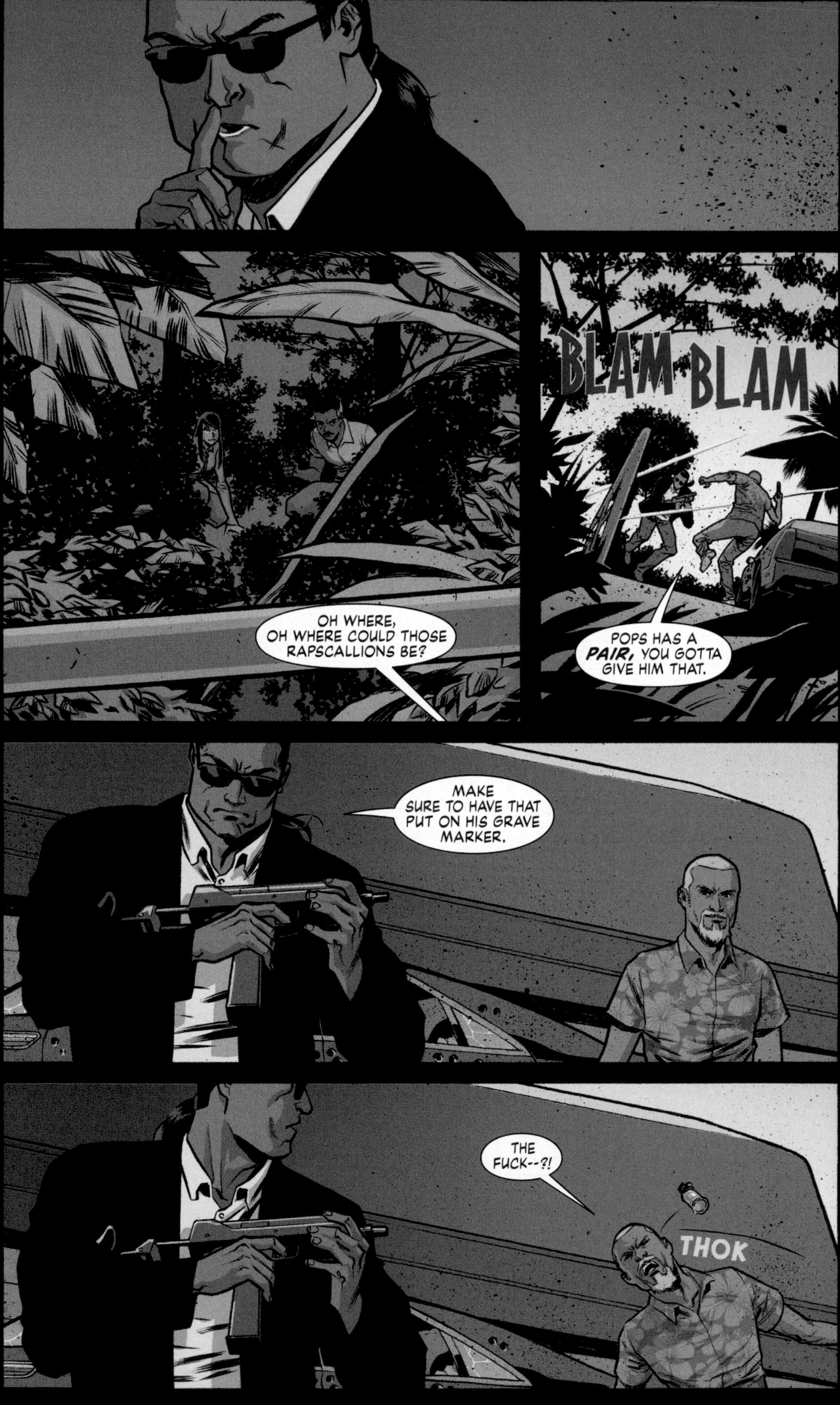
OH WHERE, OH WHERE COULD THOSE RAPSCALLIONS BE?
BLAM BLAM
POPS HAS A PAIR, YOU GOTTA GIVE HIM THAT.
MAKE SURE TO HAVE THAT PUT ON HIS GRAVE MARKER.
THE FUCK--?!
THOK

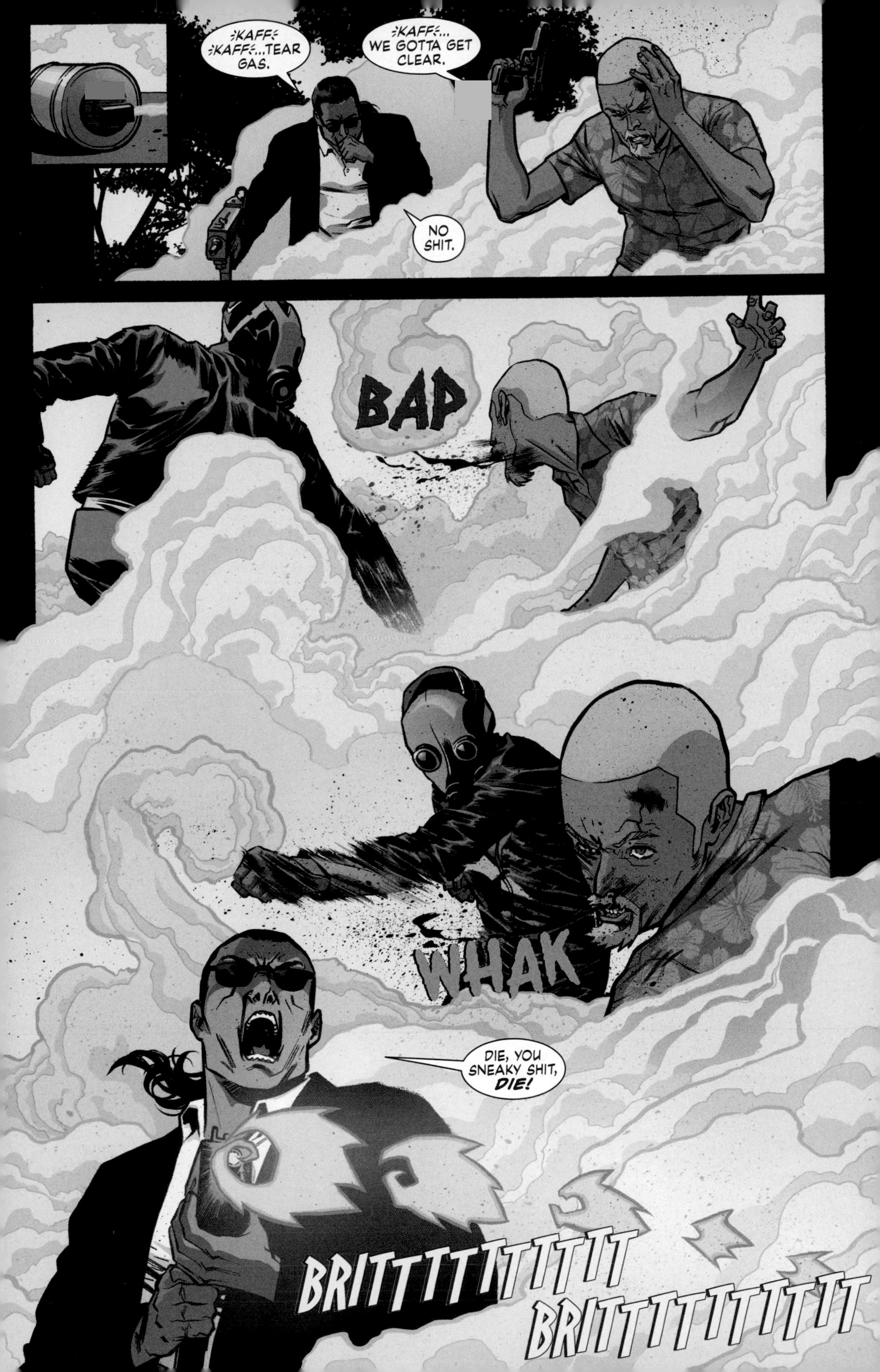
KAFF KAFF...TEAR GAS.
KAFF... WE GOTTA GET CLEAR.
NO SHIT.
BAP
WHAK
DIE, YOU SNEAKY SHIT, DIE!
BRITTTTTTTTTT
BRITTTTTTTTTTT

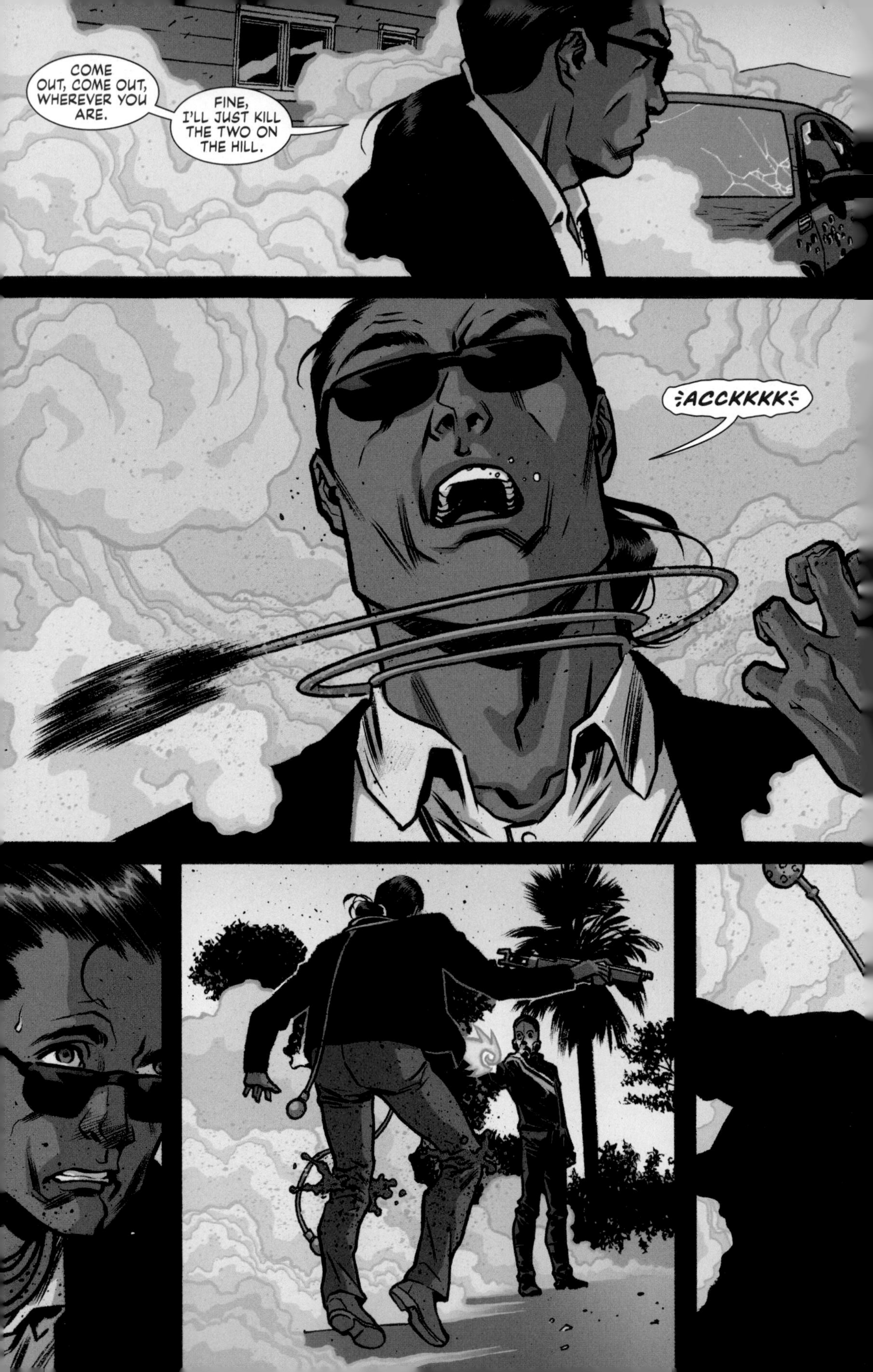
COME OUT, COME OUT, WHEREVER YOU ARE.
FINE, I'LL JUST KILL THE TWO ON THE HILL.
ACCKKKK

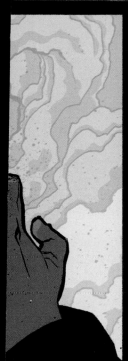

STAY THE HELL DOWN.

KER-WHACK

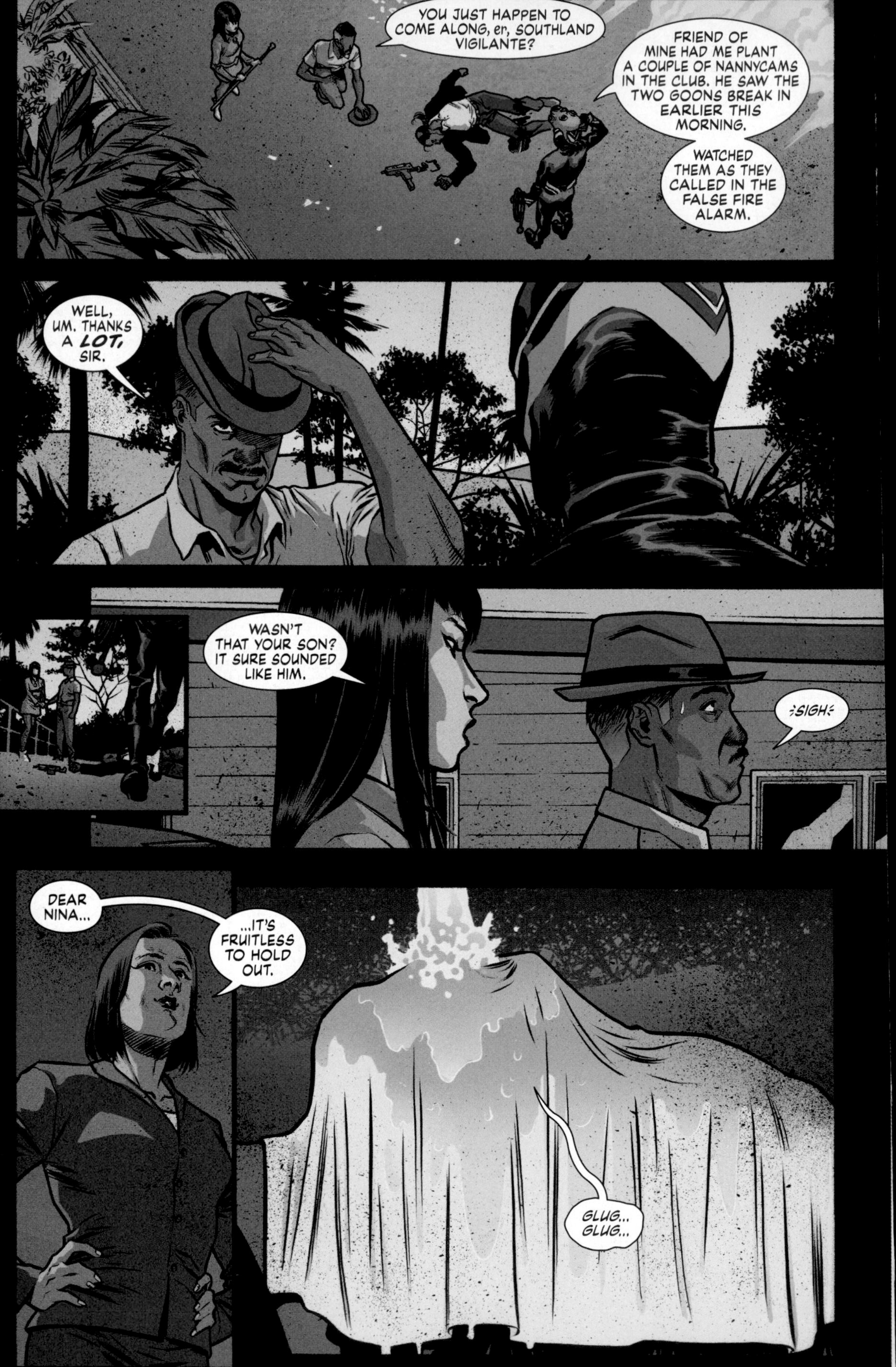
YOU JUST HAPPEN TO COME ALONG, er, SOUTHLAND VIGILANTE?
FRIEND OF MINE HAD ME PLANT A COUPLE OF NANNYCAMS IN THE CLUB. HE SAW THE TWO GOONS BREAK IN EARLIER THIS MORNING.
WATCHED THEM AS THEY CALLED IN THE FALSE FIRE ALARM.
WELL, UM. THANKS A LOT, SIR.
WASN'T THAT YOUR SON? IT SURE SOUNDED LIKE HIM.
SIGH
DEAR NINA...
...IT'S FRUITLESS TO HOLD OUT.
GLUG... GLUG...

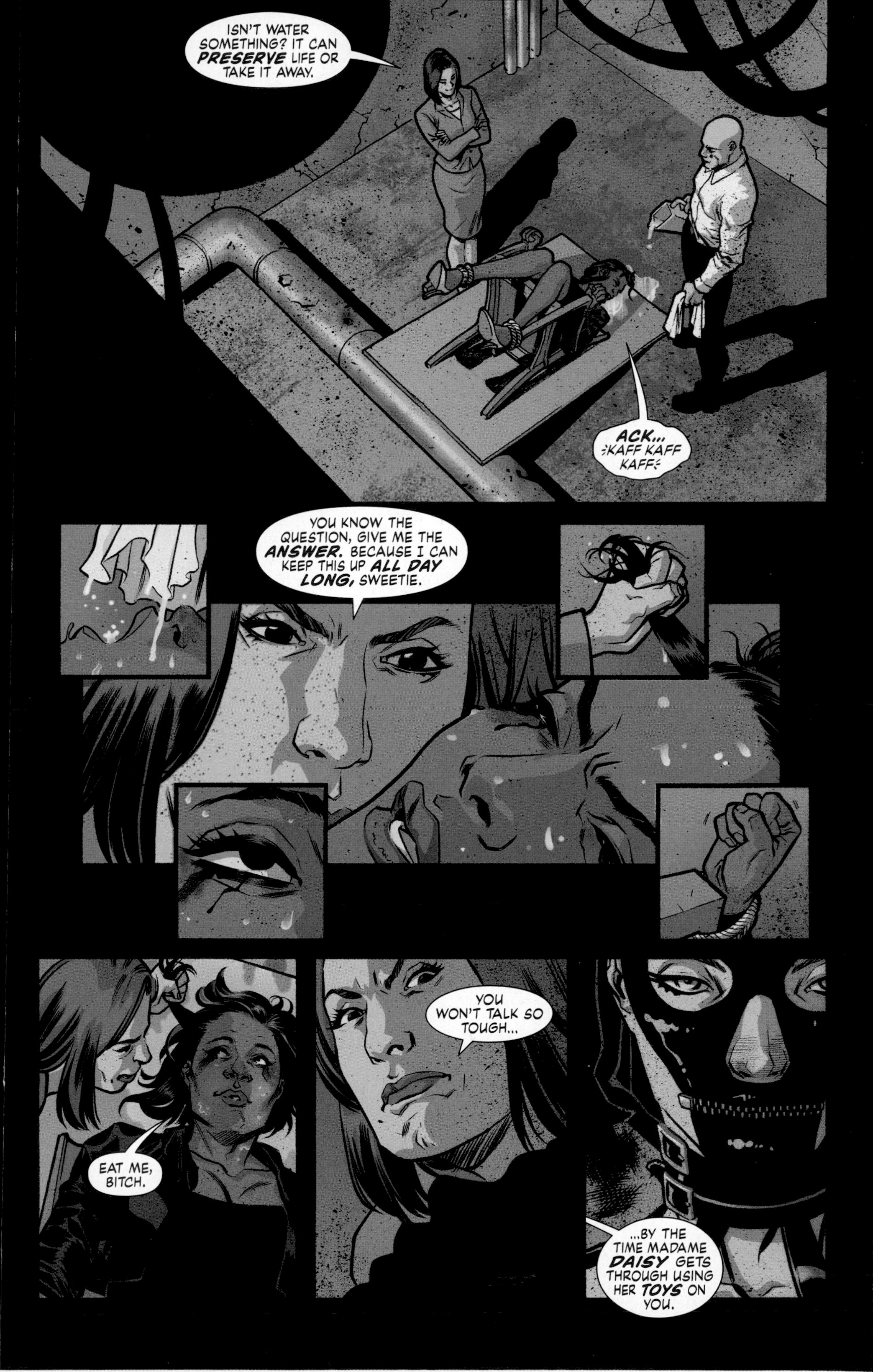
ISN'T WATER SOMETHING? IT CAN PRESERVE LIFE OR TAKE IT AWAY.
ACK... KAFF KAFF KAFF
YOU KNOW THE QUESTION, GIVE ME THE ANSWER. BECAUSE I CAN KEEP THIS UP ALL DAY LONG, SWEETIE.
EAT ME, BITCH.
YOU WON'T TALK SO TOUGH...
...BY THE TIME MADAME DAISY GETS THROUGH USING HER TOYS ON YOU.

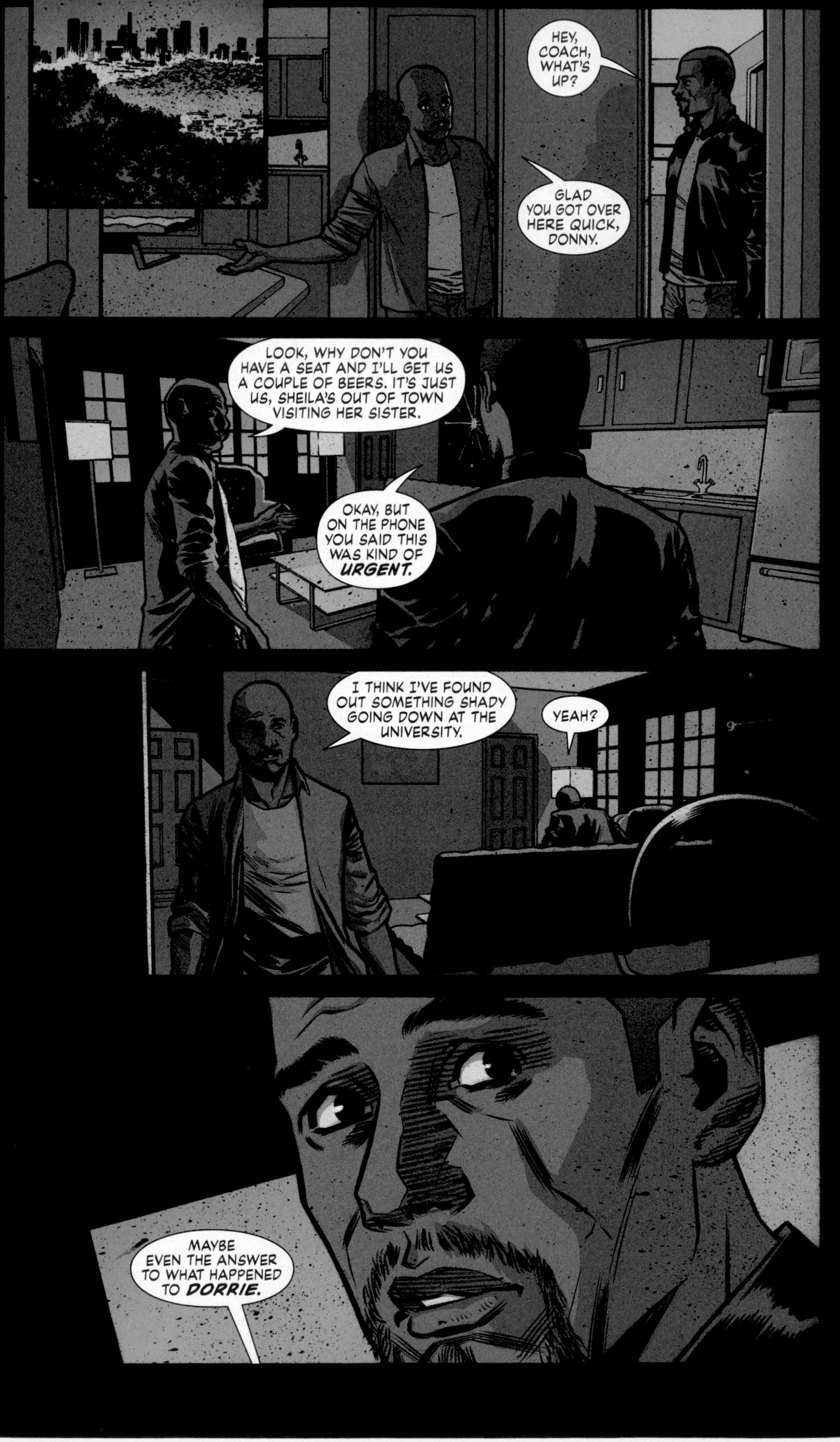
HEY, COACH, WHAT'S UP?
GLAD YOU GOT OVER HERE QUICK, DONNY.
LOOK, WHY DON'T YOU HAVE A SEAT AND I'LL GET US A COUPLE OF BEERS. IT'S JUST US, SHEILA'S OUT OF TOWN VISITING HER SISTER.
OKAY, BUT ON THE PHONE YOU SAID THIS WAS KIND OF URGENT.
I THINK I'VE FOUND OUT SOMETHING SHADY GOING DOWN AT THE UNIVERSITY.
YEAH?
MAYBE EVEN THE ANSWER TO WHAT HAPPENED TO DORRIE.

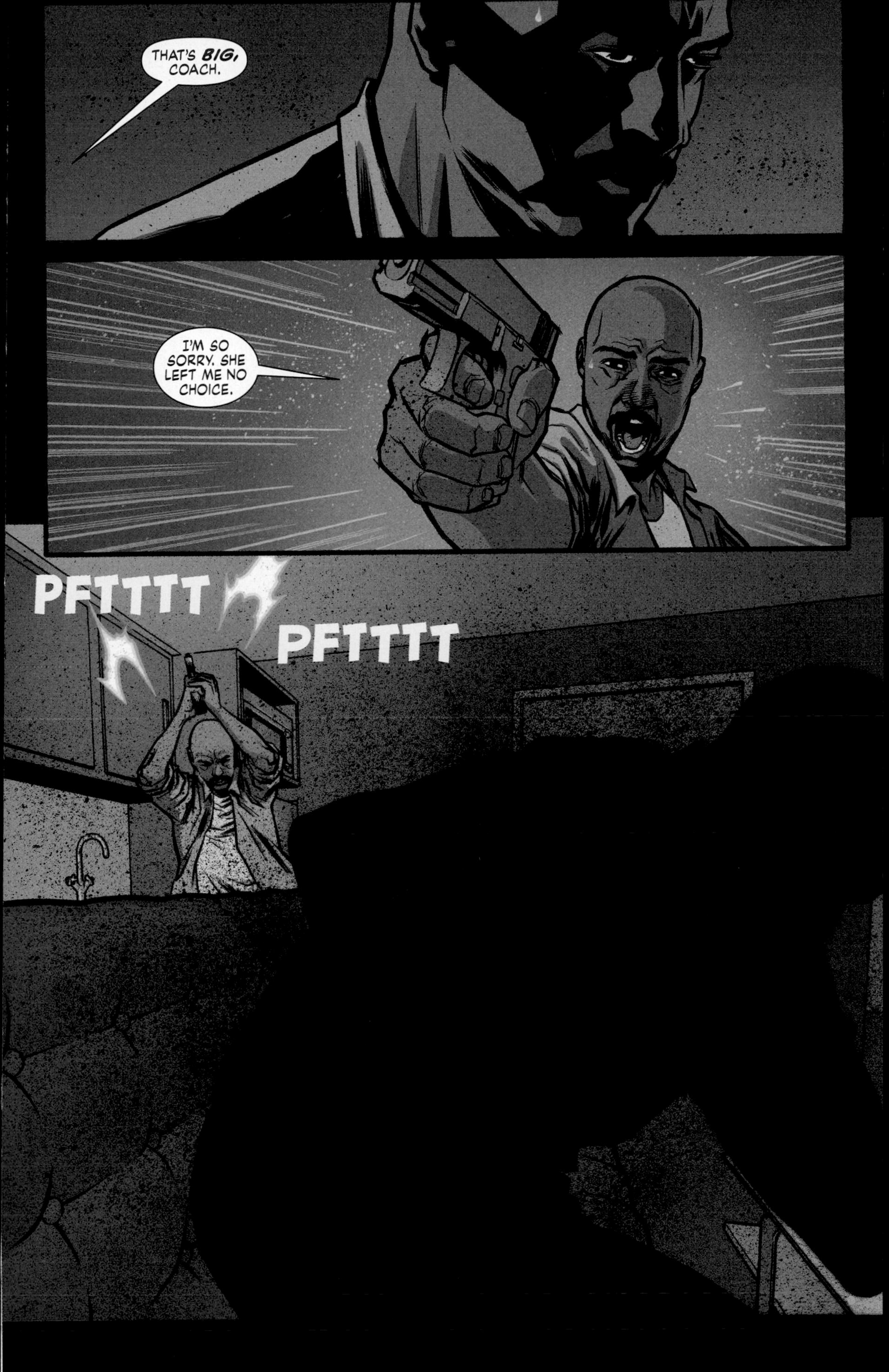
THAT'S BIG, COACH.
I'M SO SORRY. SHE LEFT ME NO CHOICE.
PFTTTT
PFTTTT

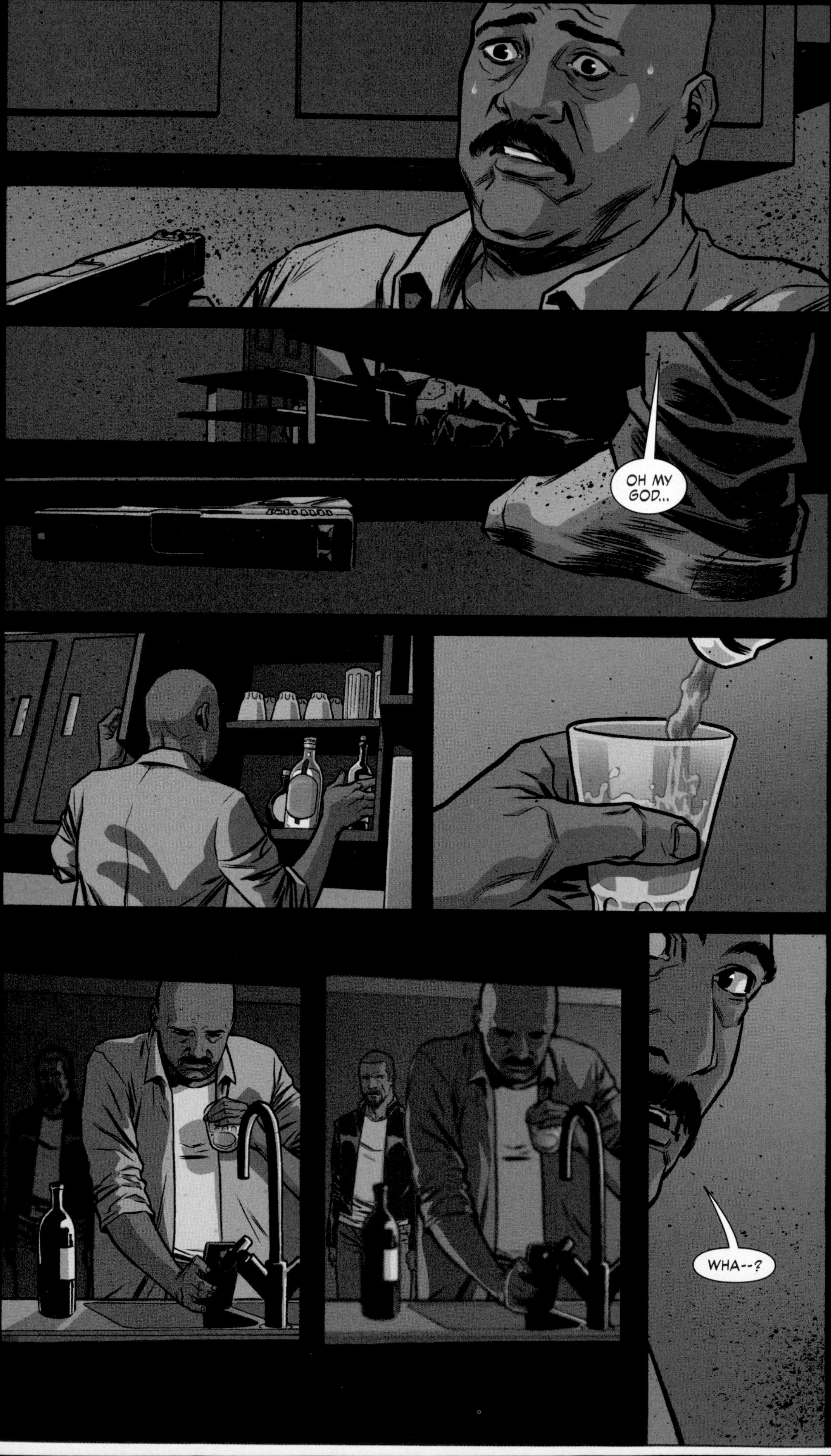
OH MY GOD...
WHA--?

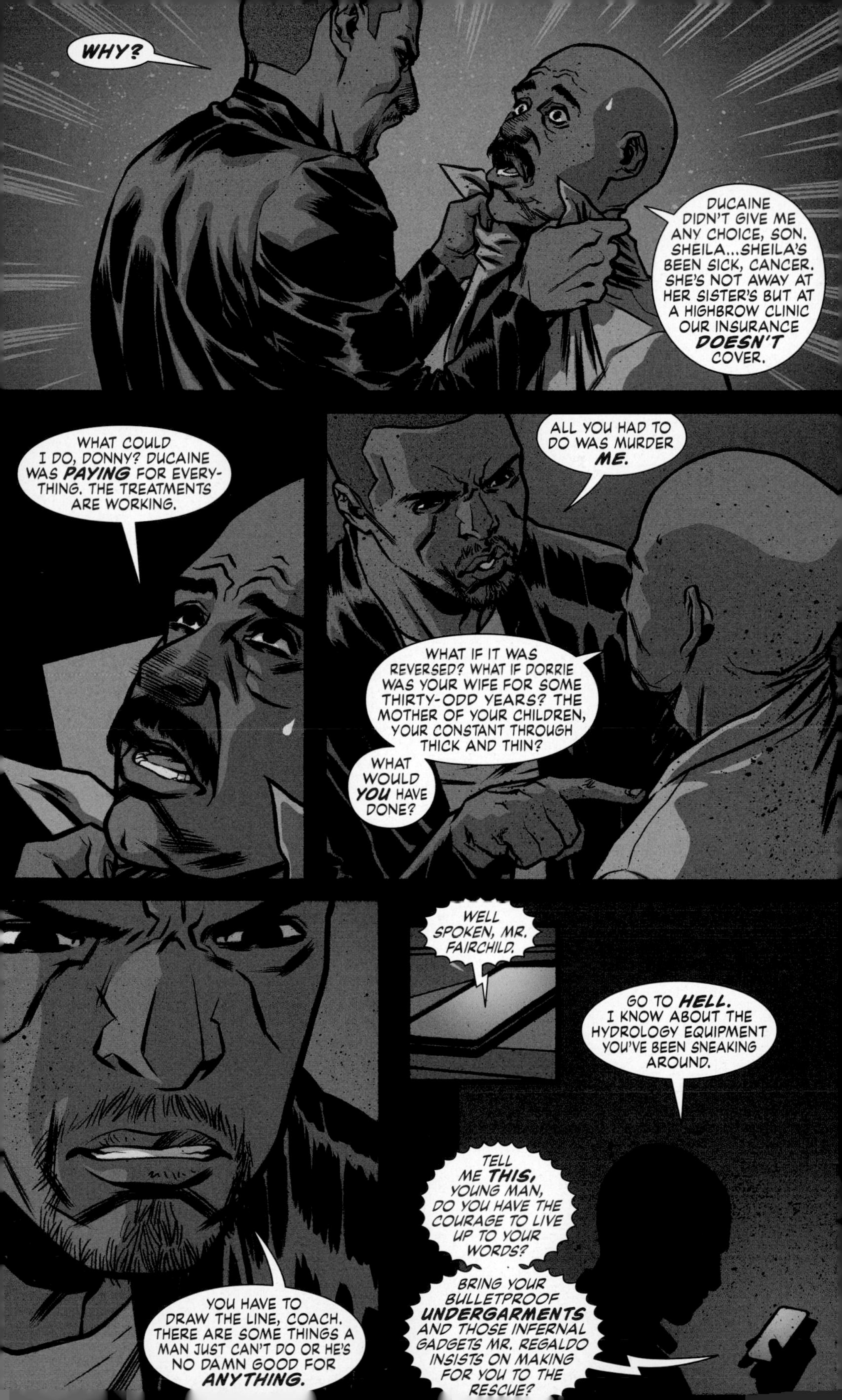
WHY?
DUCAINE DIDN'T GIVE ME ANY CHOICE, SON. SHEILA...SHEILA'S BEEN SICK, CANCER. SHE'S NOT AWAY AT HER SISTER'S BUT AT A HIGHBROW CLINIC OUR INSURANCE DOESN'T COVER.
WHAT COULD I DO, DONNY? DUCAINE WAS PAYING FOR EVERYTHING. THE TREATMENTS ARE WORKING.
ALL YOU HAD TO DO WAS MURDER ME.
WHAT IF IT WAS REVERSED? WHAT IF DORRIE WAS YOUR WIFE FOR SOME THIRTY-ODD YEARS? THE MOTHER OF YOUR CHILDREN, YOUR CONSTANT THROUGH THICK AND THIN?
WHAT WOULD YOU HAVE DONE?
YOU HAVE TO DRAW THE LINE, COACH. THERE ARE SOME THINGS A MAN JUST CAN'T DO OR HE'S NO DAMN GOOD FOR ANYTHING.
WELL SPOKEN, MR. FAIRCHILD.
GO TO HELL. I KNOW ABOUT THE HYDROLOGY EQUIPMENT YOU'VE BEEN SNEAKING AROUND.
TELL ME THIS, YOUNG MAN, DO YOU HAVE THE COURAGE TO LIVE UP TO YOUR WORDS?
BRING YOUR BULLETPROOF UNDERGARMENTS AND THOSE INFERNAL GADGETS MR. REGALDO INSISTS ON MAKING FOR YOU TO THE RESCUE?

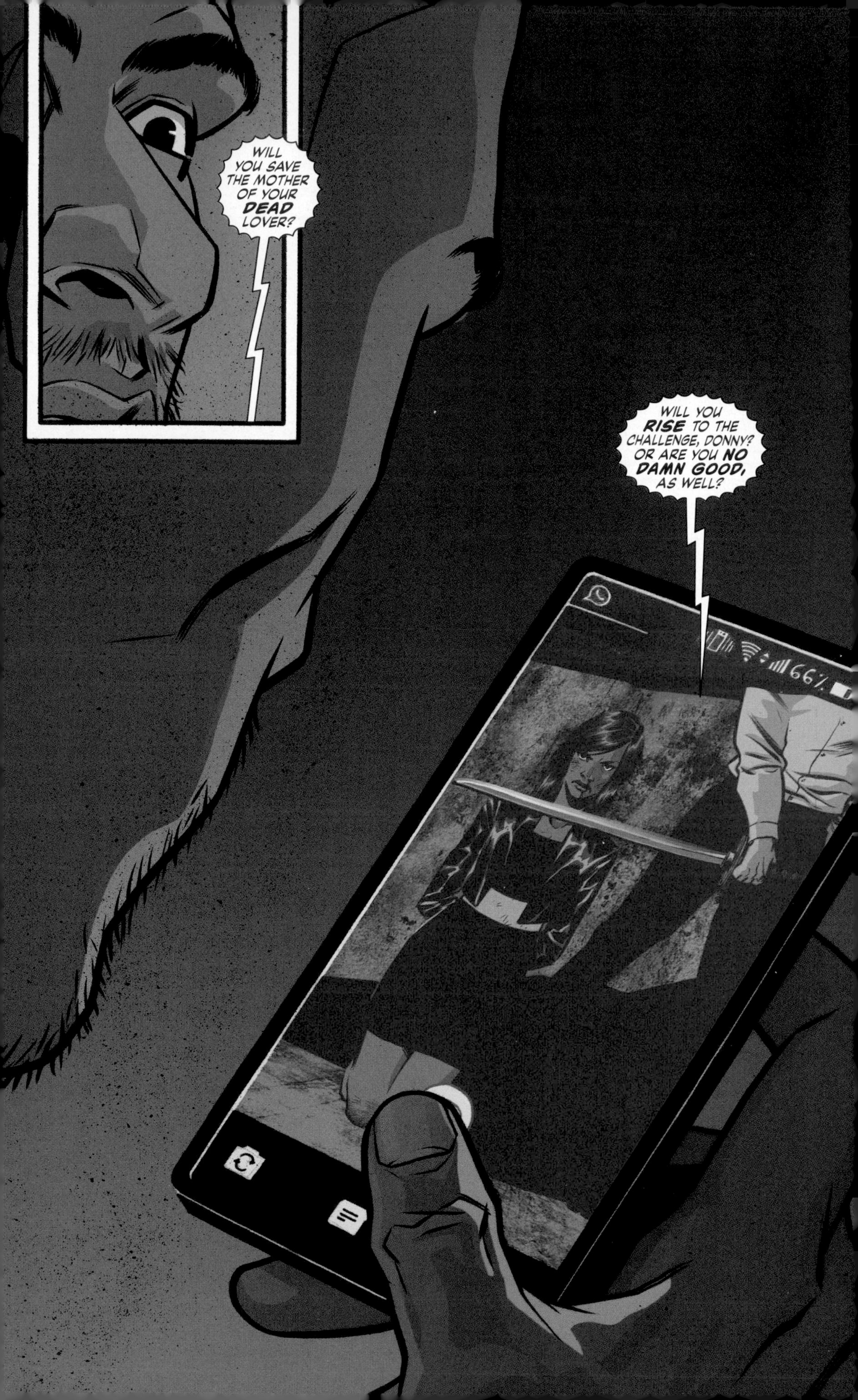
WILL YOU SAVE THE MOTHER OF YOUR **DEAD** LOVER?
WILL YOU **RISE** TO THE CHALLENGE, DONNY? OR ARE YOU **NO DAMN GOOD,** AS WELL?
66%

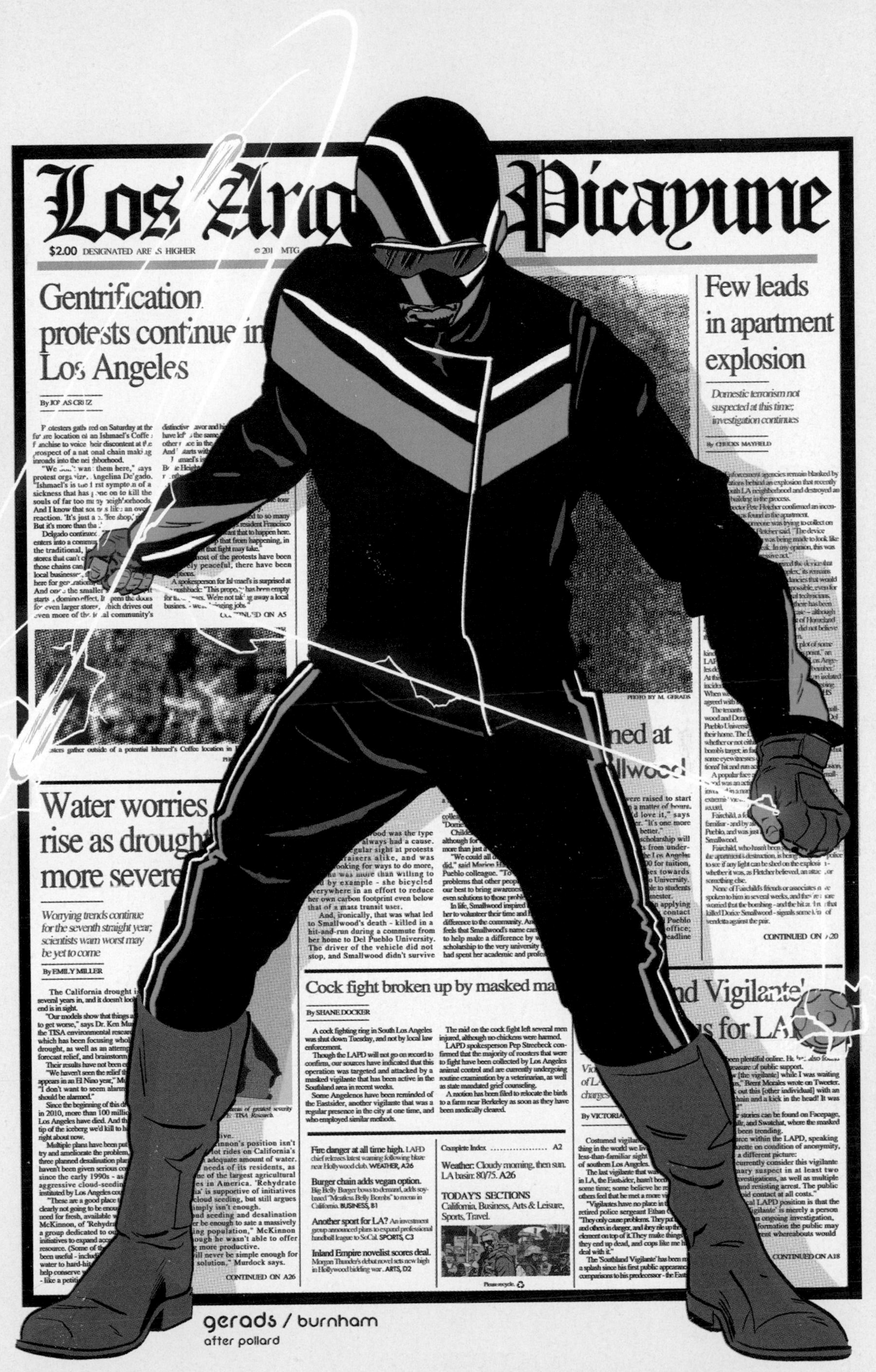
Picayune
$2.00 DESIGNATED ARE S HIGHER
Gentrification protests continue in Los Angeles
Few leads in apartment explosion
Domestic terrorism not suspected at this time; investigation continues
By CHUCKS MAYFIELD
PHOTO BY M. GERADS
Water worries rise as drought more severe
Worrying trends continue for the seventh straight year; scientists warn worst may be yet to come
By EMILY MILLER
Cock fight broken up by masked ma
By SHANE DOCKER
CONTINUED ON A26
CONTINUED ON A18
Fire danger at all time high. LAFD chief releases latest warning following blaze near Hollywood club. WEATHER, A26
Burger chain adds vegan option. Big Belly Burger bows to demand, adds soy-based "Meatless Belly Bombs" to menu in California. BUSINESS, B1
Another sport for LA? An investment group announced plans to expand professional handball league to SoCal. SPORTS, C3
Inland Empire novelist scores deal. Morgan Thunder's debut novel sets new high in Hollywood bidding war. ARTS, D2
Complete Index A2
Weather: Cloudy morning, then sun. LA basin: 80/75. A26
TODAY'S SECTIONS
California, Business, Arts & Leisure, Sports, Travel.
Please recycle.
gerads / burnham
after pollard

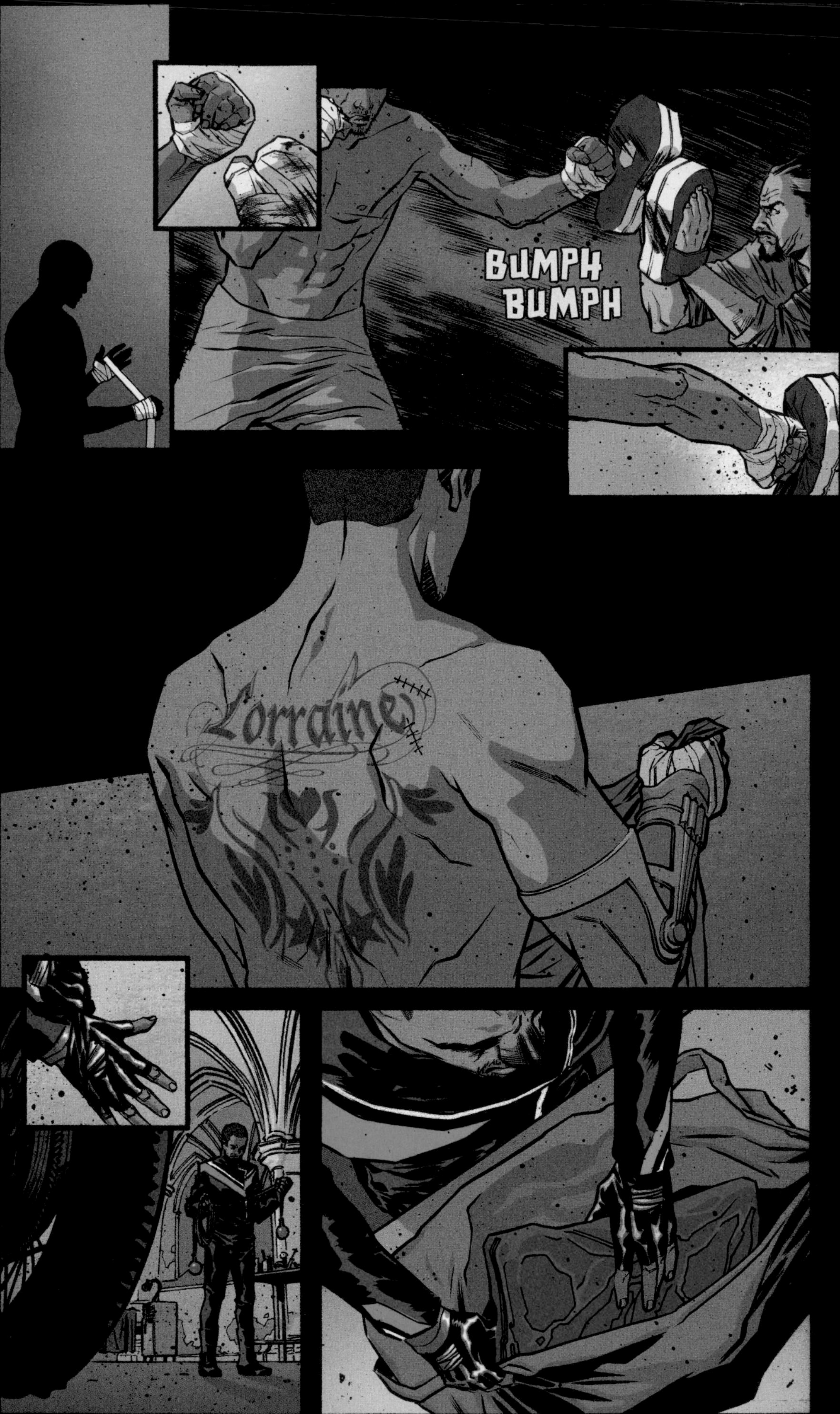
BUMPH
BUMPH
Lorraine

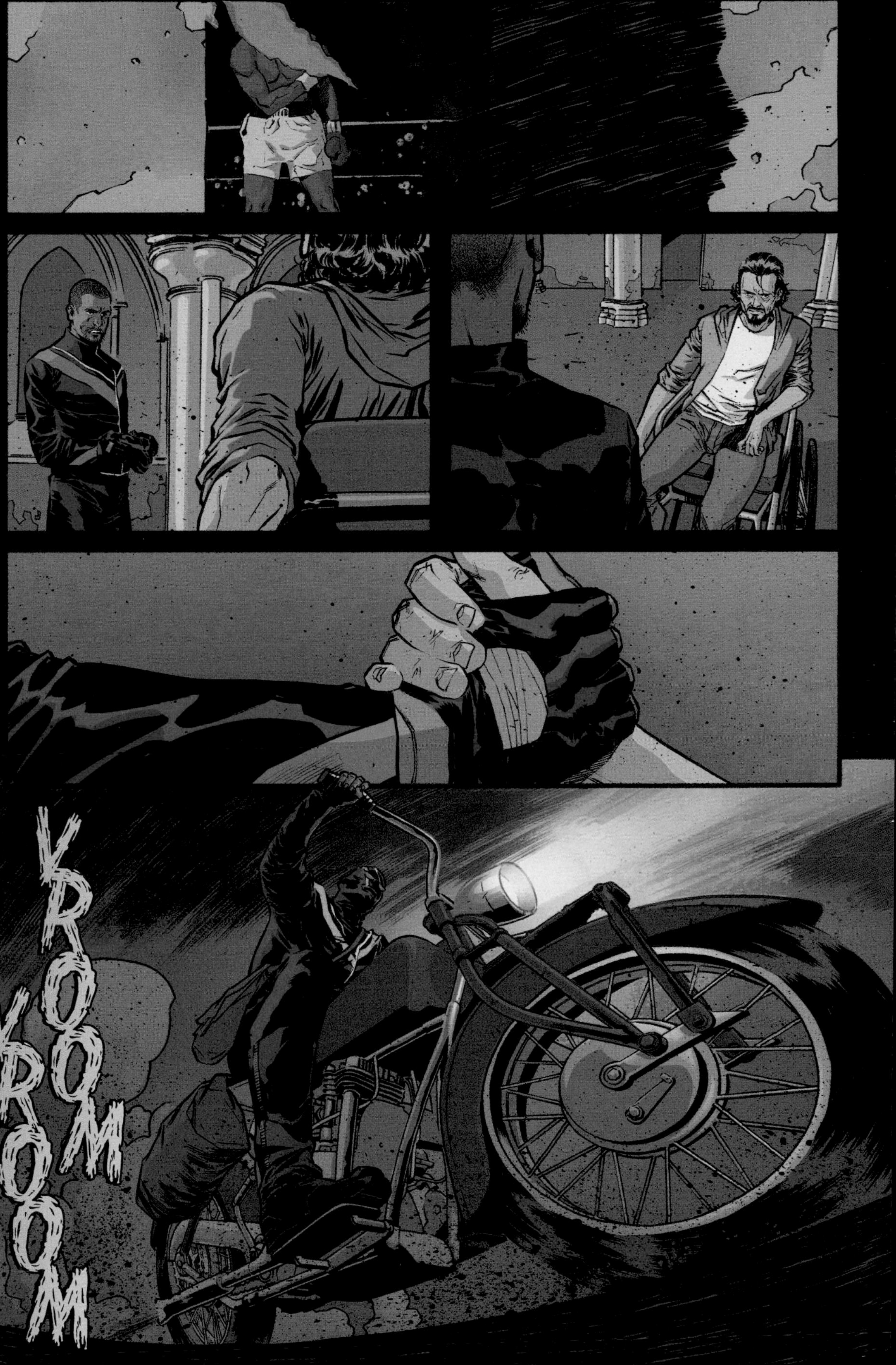
VROOM
VROOM

SHOW 'EM HOW IT'S DONE, KID.

BRROOOM

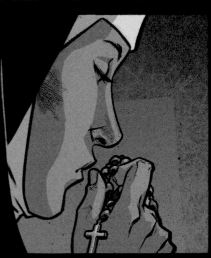

DIOS TE BENIJA, EAST-SIDER.

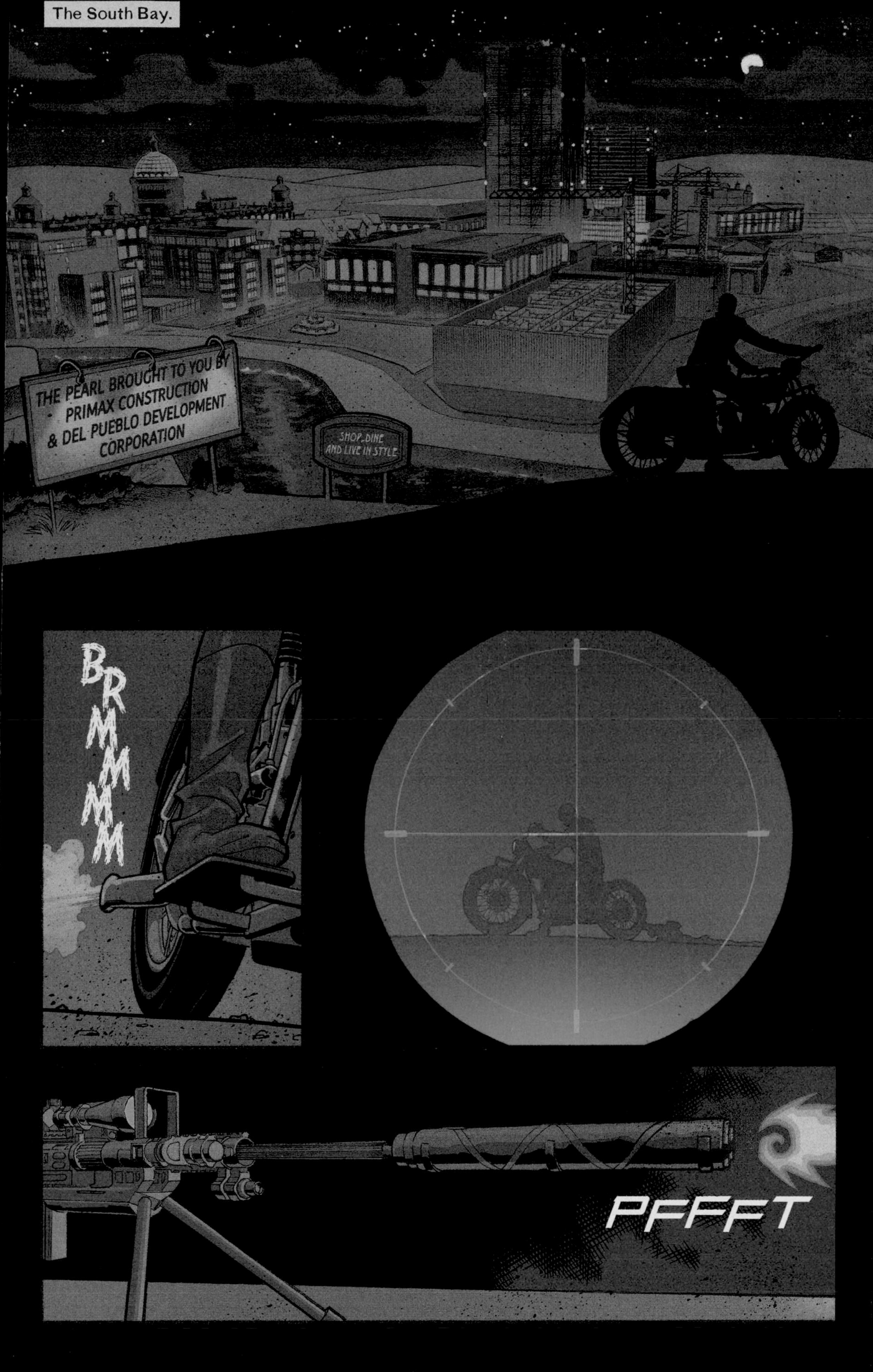
The South Bay.
THE PEARL BROUGHT TO YOU BY
PRIMAX CONSTRUCTION
& DEL PUEBLO DEVELOPMENT
CORPORATION
SHOP, DINE
AND LIVE IN STYLE
BRMMMM
PFFFT

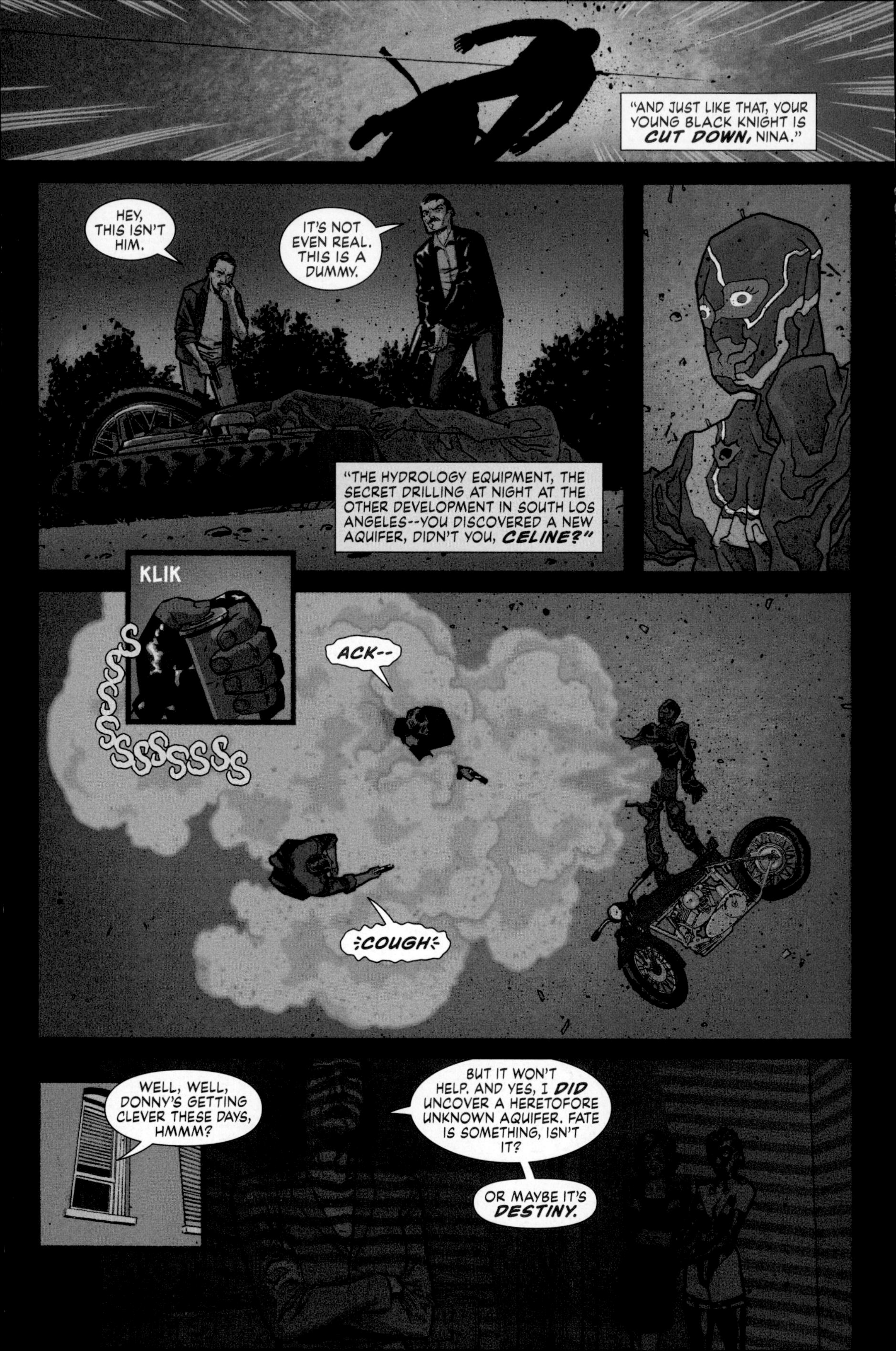
"AND JUST LIKE THAT, YOUR YOUNG BLACK KNIGHT IS CUT DOWN, NINA."
HEY, THIS ISN'T HIM.
IT'S NOT EVEN REAL. THIS IS A DUMMY.
"THE HYDROLOGY EQUIPMENT, THE SECRET DRILLING AT NIGHT AT THE OTHER DEVELOPMENT IN SOUTH LOS ANGELES--YOU DISCOVERED A NEW AQUIFER, DIDN'T YOU, CELINE?"
KLIK
SSSSSSSSSSSSSS
ACK--
COUGH
WELL, WELL, DONNY'S GETTING CLEVER THESE DAYS, HMMM?
BUT IT WON'T HELP. AND YES, I DID UNCOVER A HERETOFORE UNKNOWN AQUIFER. FATE IS SOMETHING, ISN'T IT?
OR MAYBE IT'S DESTINY.

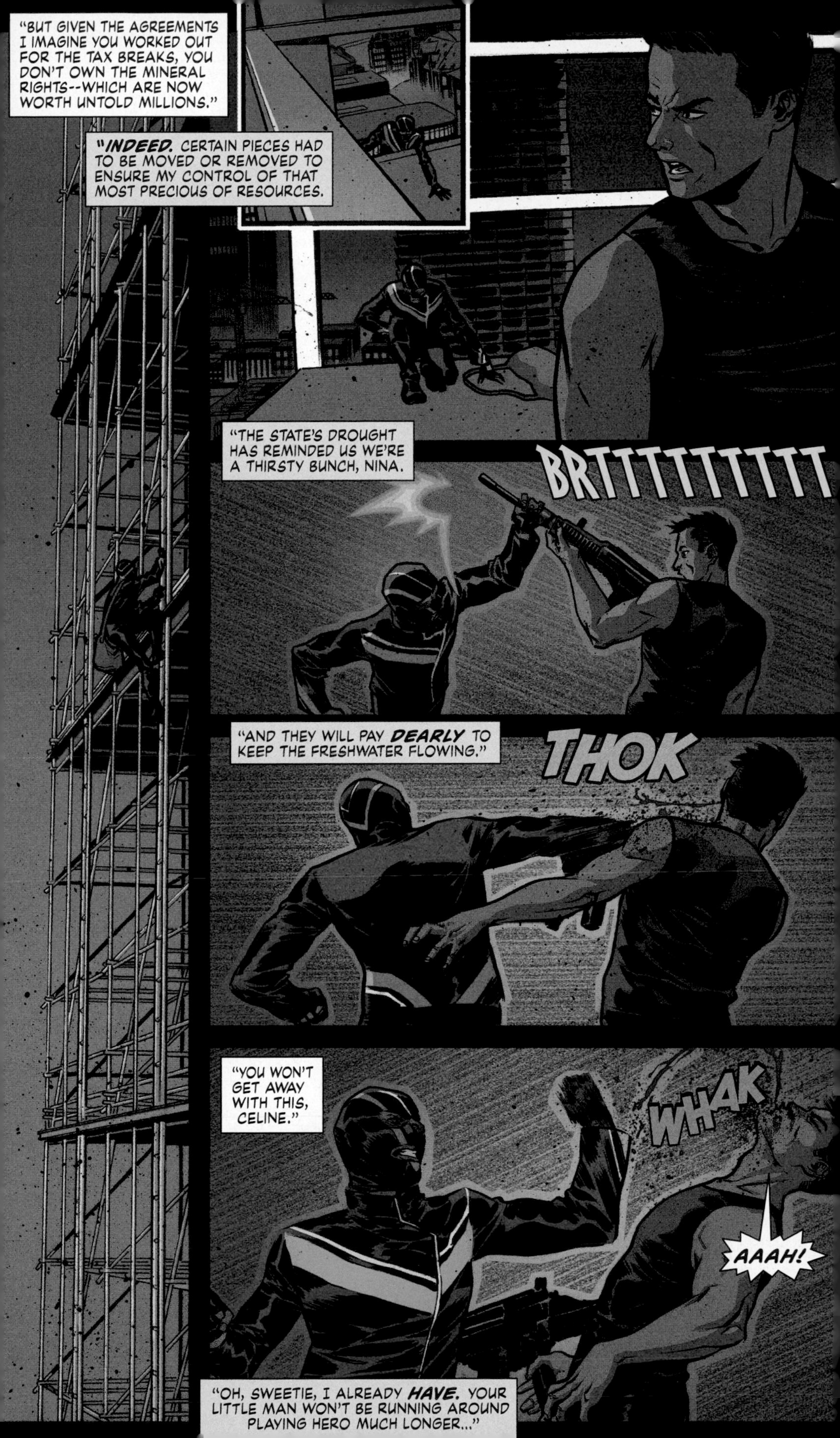
"BUT GIVEN THE AGREEMENTS I IMAGINE YOU WORKED OUT FOR THE TAX BREAKS, YOU DON'T OWN THE MINERAL RIGHTS--WHICH ARE NOW WORTH UNTOLD MILLIONS."
"INDEED. CERTAIN PIECES HAD TO BE MOVED OR REMOVED TO ENSURE MY CONTROL OF THAT MOST PRECIOUS OF RESOURCES.
"THE STATE'S DROUGHT HAS REMINDED US WE'RE A THIRSTY BUNCH, NINA.
BRTTTTTTTTT
"AND THEY WILL PAY DEARLY TO KEEP THE FRESHWATER FLOWING."
THOK
"YOU WON'T GET AWAY WITH THIS, CELINE."
WHAK
AAAH!
"OH, SWEETIE, I ALREADY HAVE. YOUR LITTLE MAN WON'T BE RUNNING AROUND PLAYING HERO MUCH LONGER..."

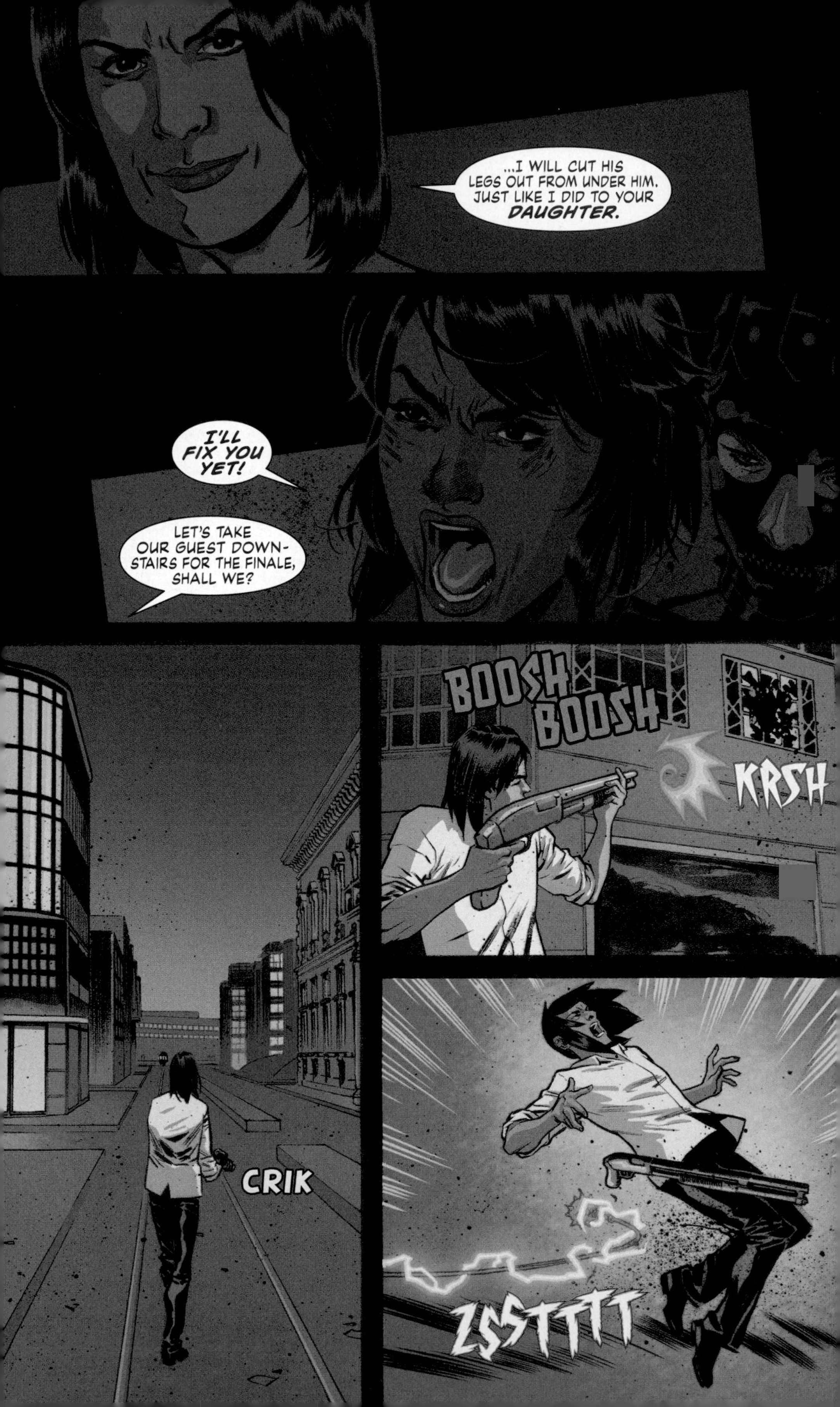
...I WILL CUT HIS LEGS OUT FROM UNDER HIM. JUST LIKE I DID TO YOUR DAUGHTER.
I'LL FIX YOU YET!
LET'S TAKE OUR GUEST DOWN-STAIRS FOR THE FINALE, SHALL WE?
CRIK
BOOSH
BOOSH
KRSH
ZSSTTTT

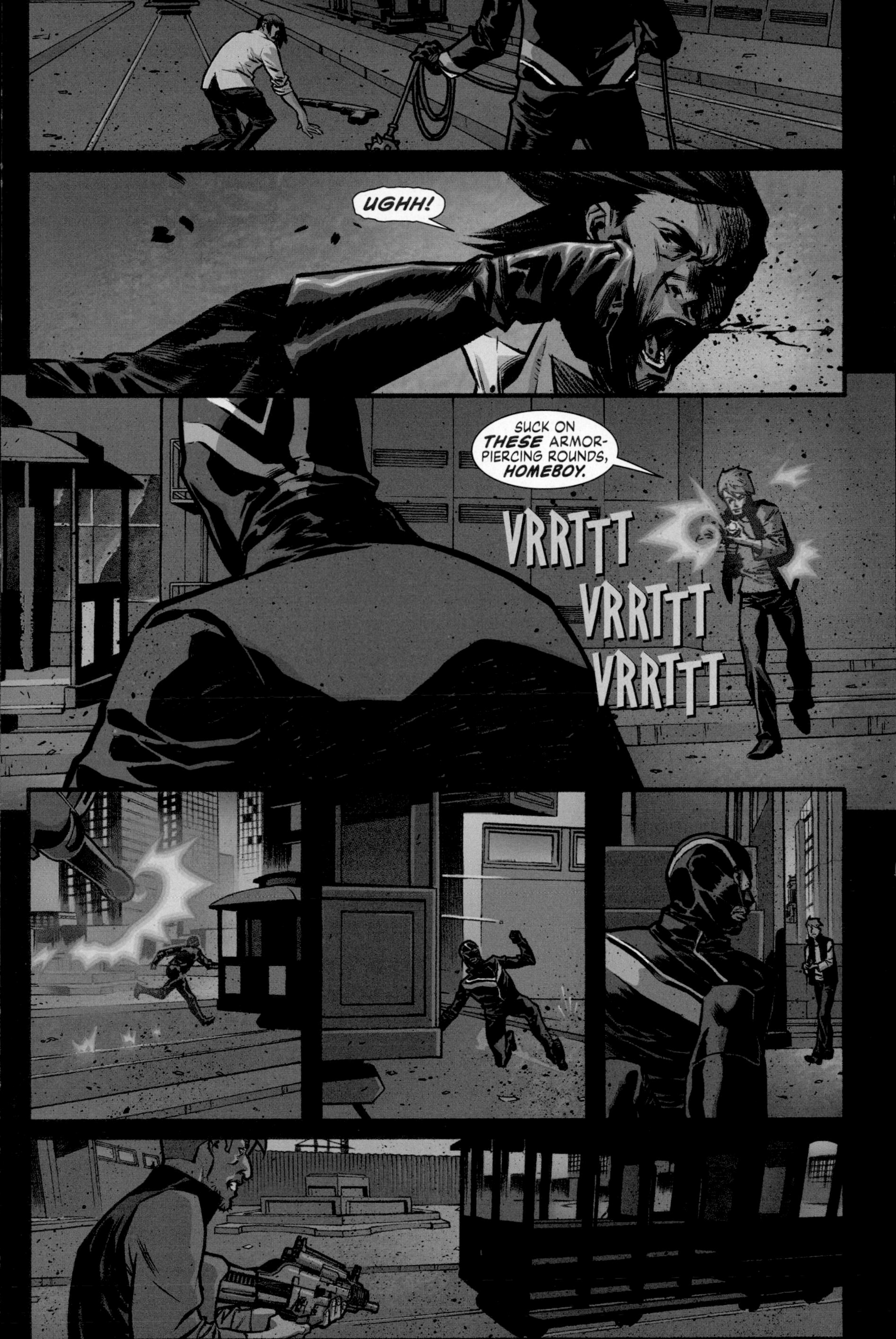

UGHH!
SUCK ON THESE ARMOR-PIERCING ROUNDS, HOMEBOY.
VRRTTT
VRRTTT
VRRTTT

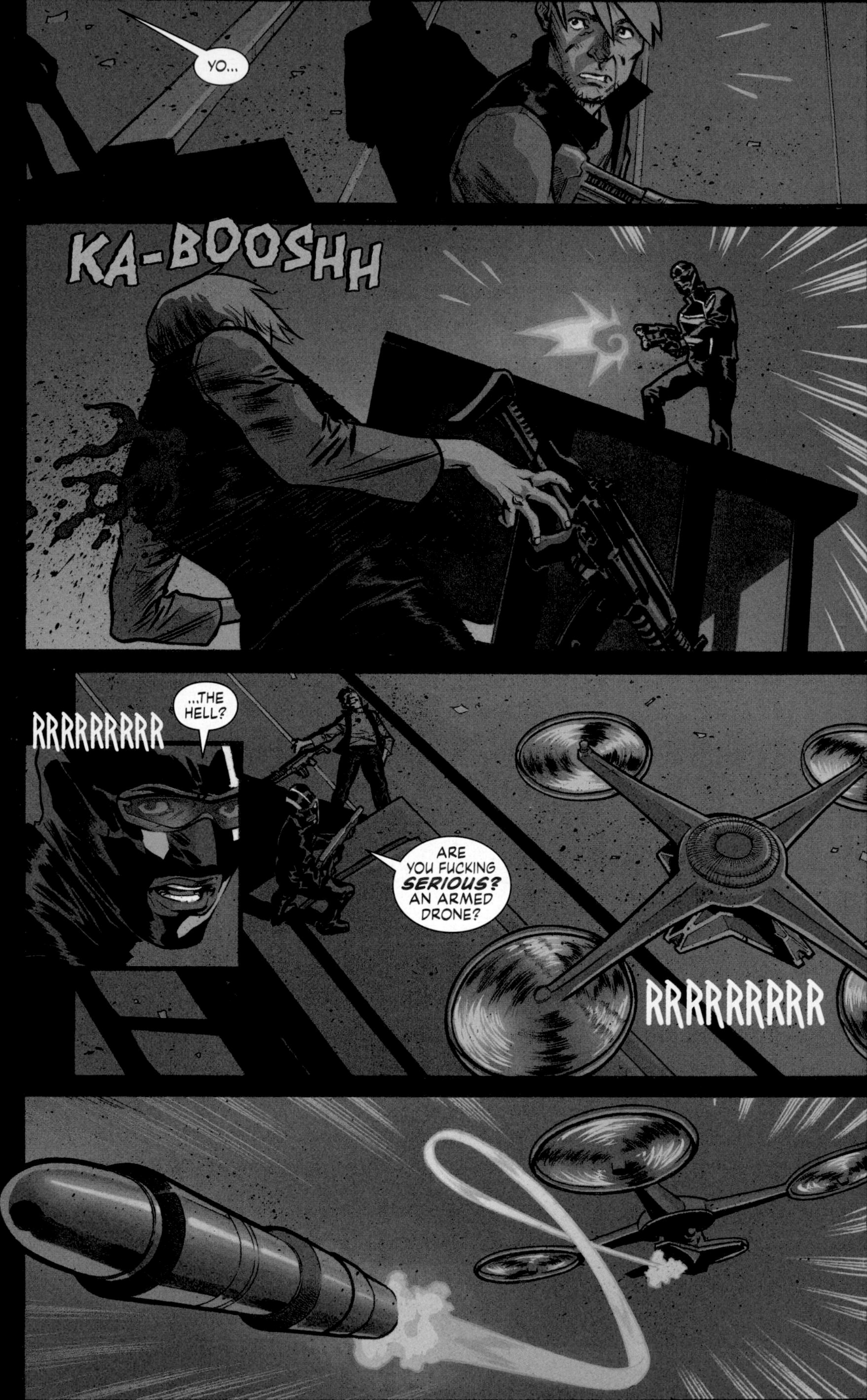
YO...
KA-BOOSHH
RRRRRRRRR
...THE HELL?
ARE YOU FUCKING SERIOUS? AN ARMED DRONE?
RRRRRRRRR

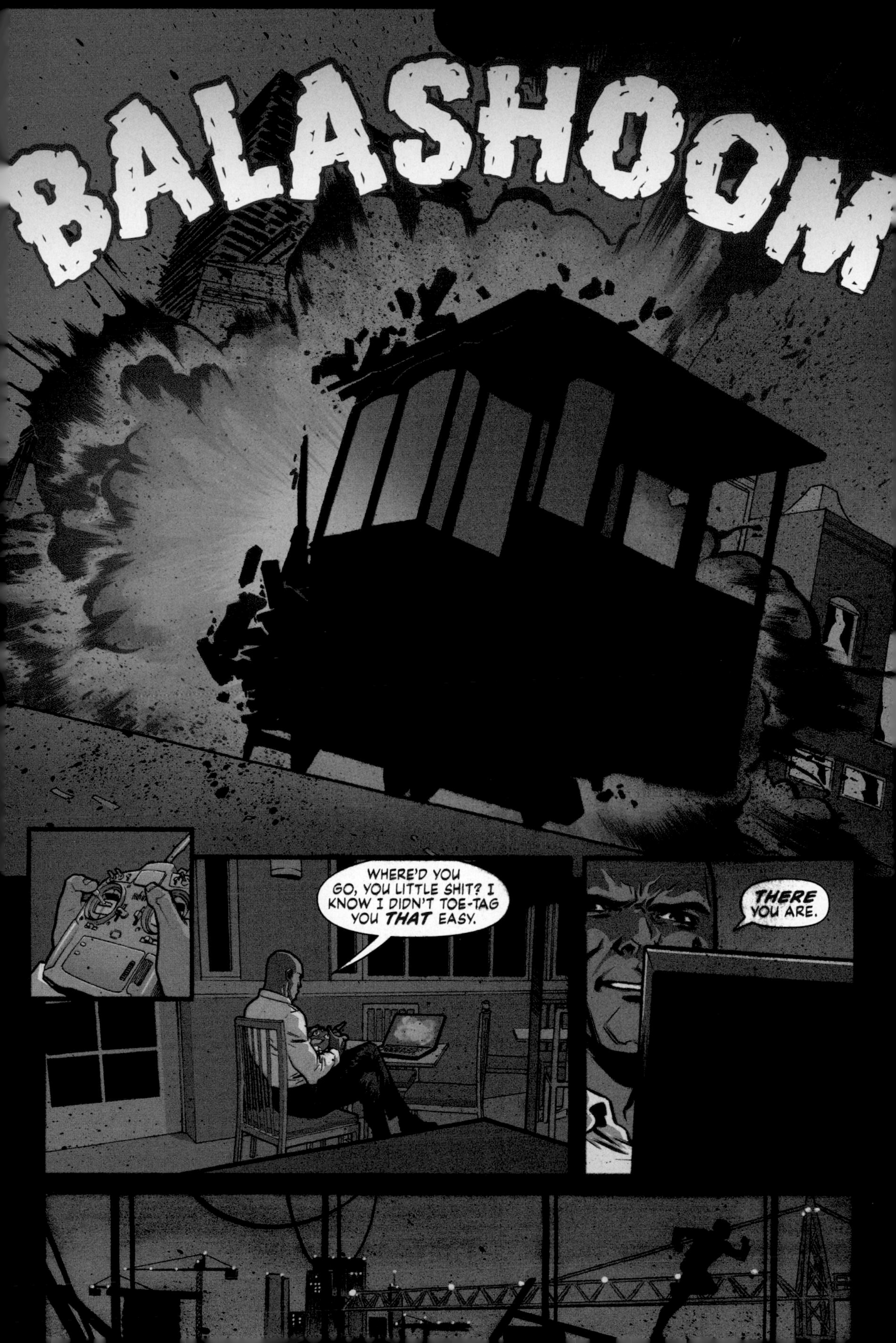
BALASHOOM
WHERE'D YOU GO, YOU LITTLE SHIT? I KNOW I DIDN'T TOE-TAG YOU THAT EASY.
THERE YOU ARE.

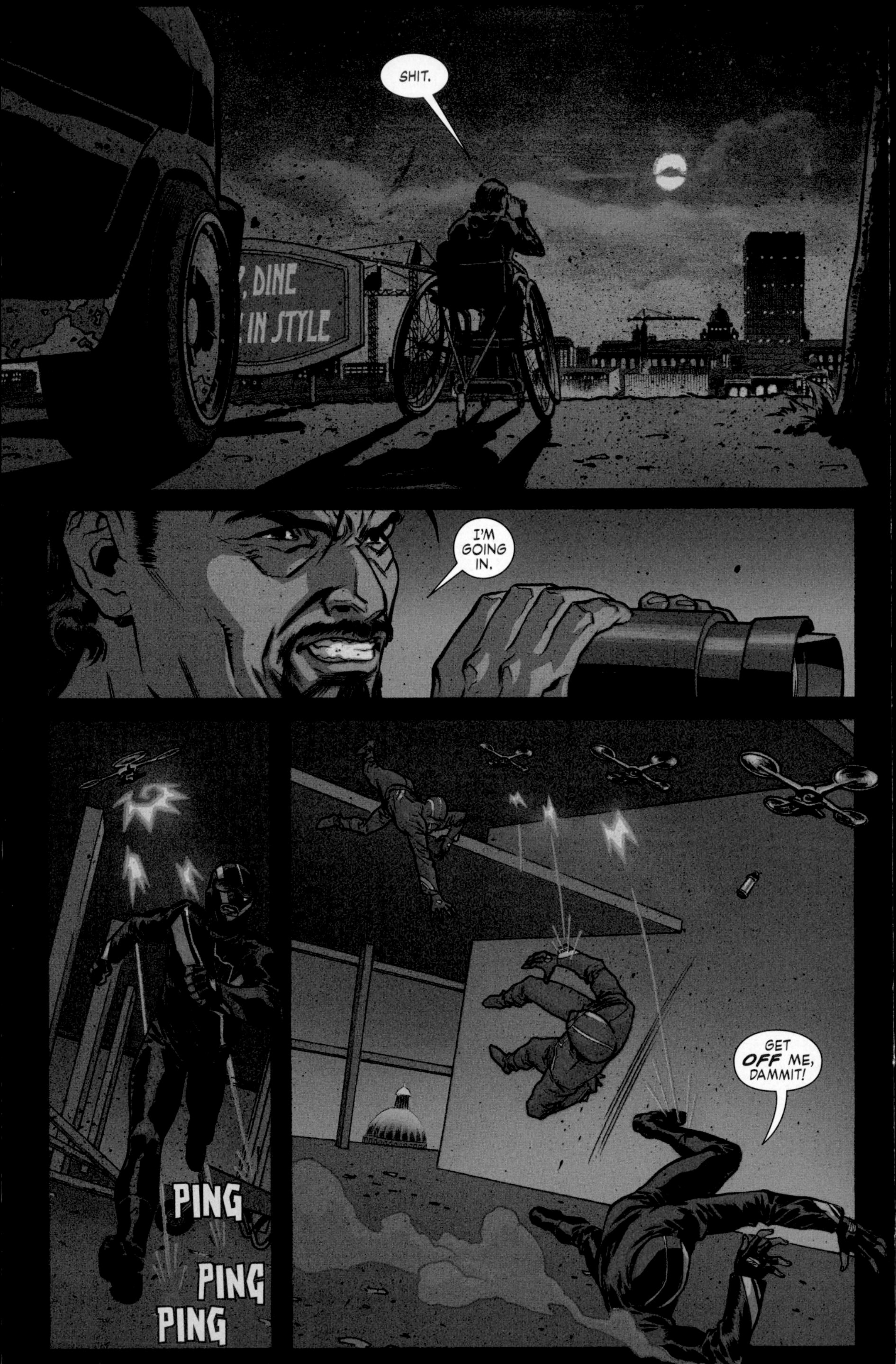
SHIT.
, DINE
IN STYLE
I'M GOING IN.
PING
PING
PING
GET OFF ME, DAMMIT!

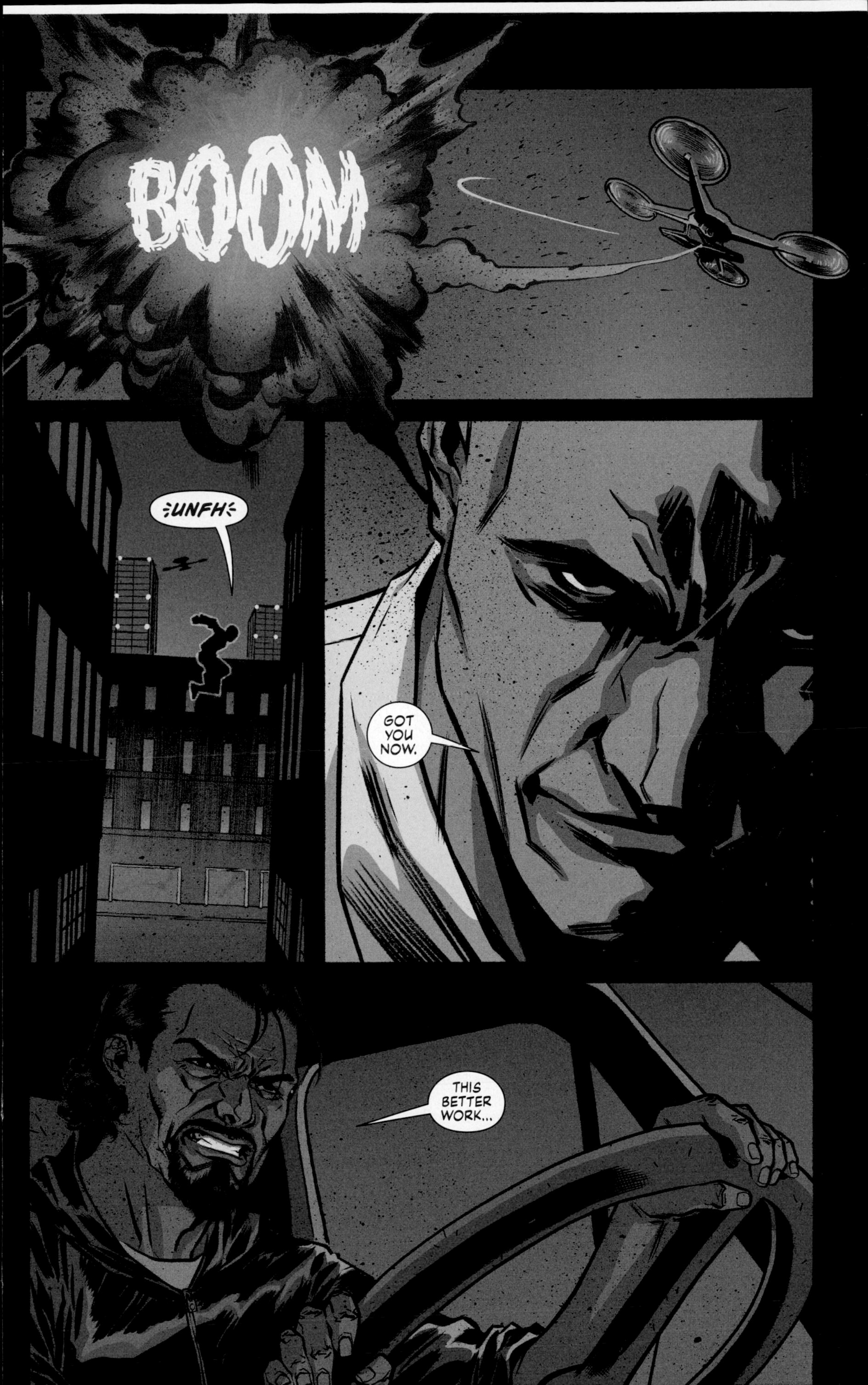
BOOM
UNFH
GOT YOU NOW.
THIS BETTER WORK...

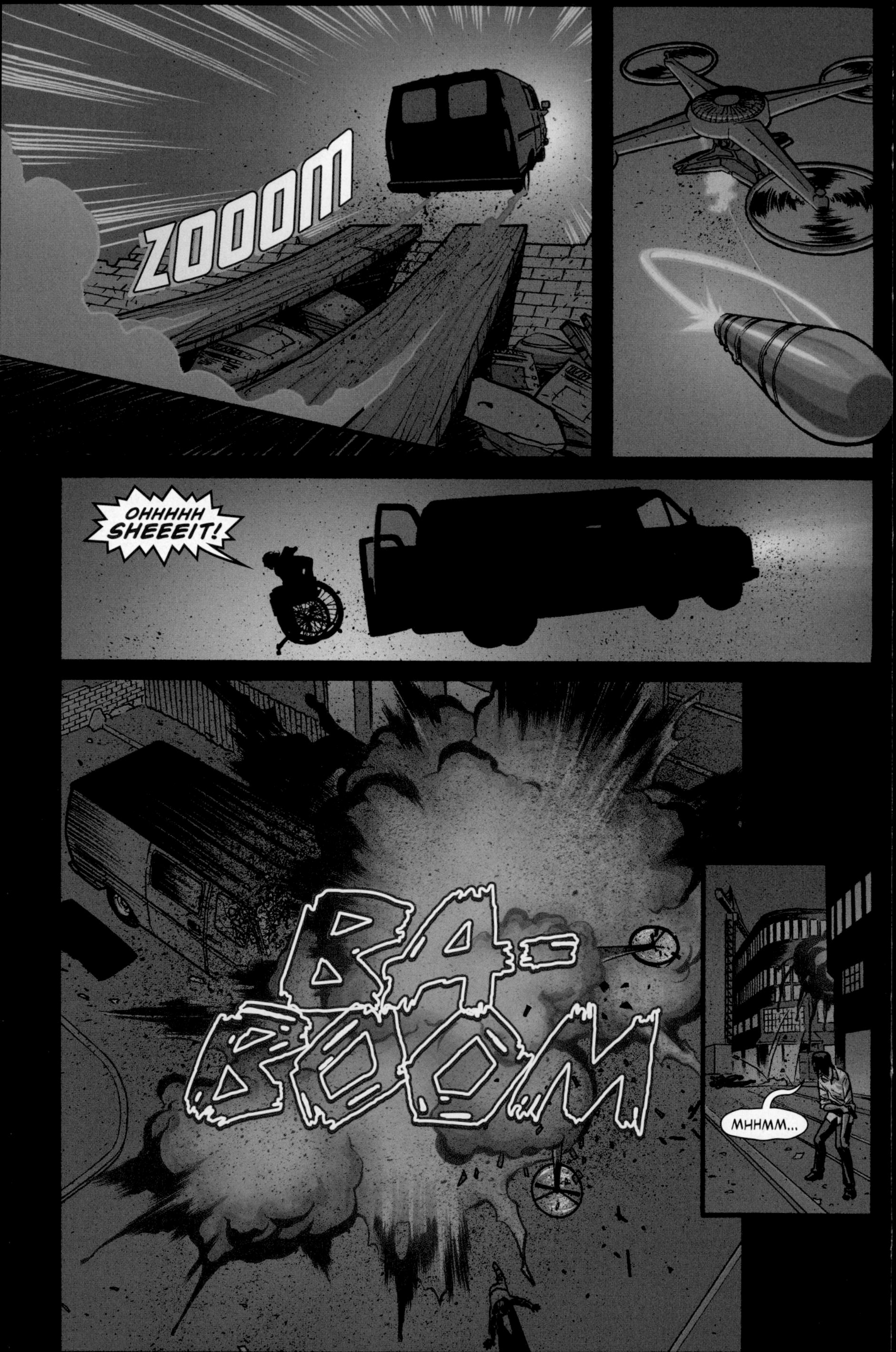
ZOOOM
OHHHHH SHEEEIT!
BA-BOOM
MHHMM...

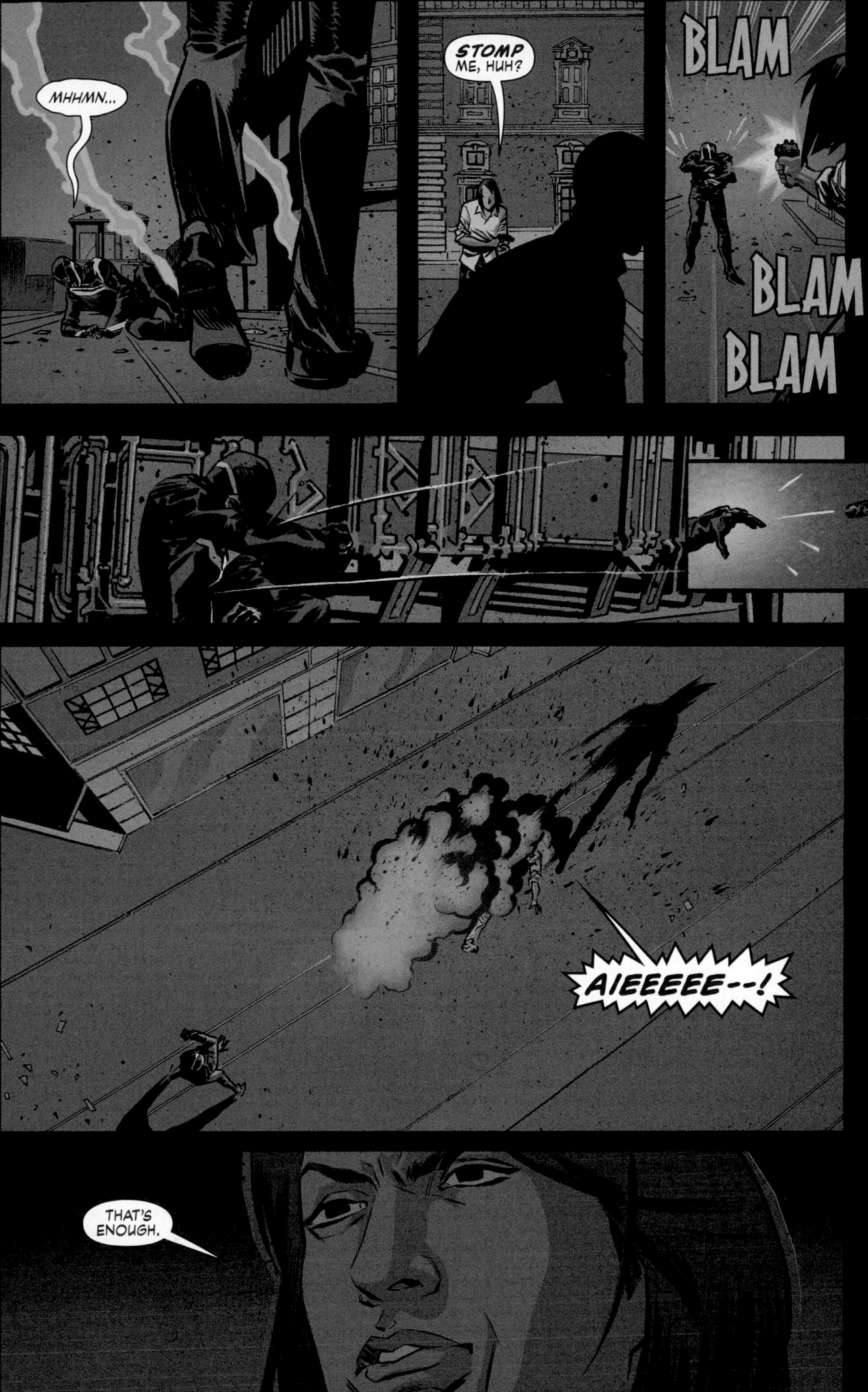
MHHMN...
STOMP ME, HUH?
BLAM
BLAM
BLAM
AIEEEEE--!
THAT'S ENOUGH.

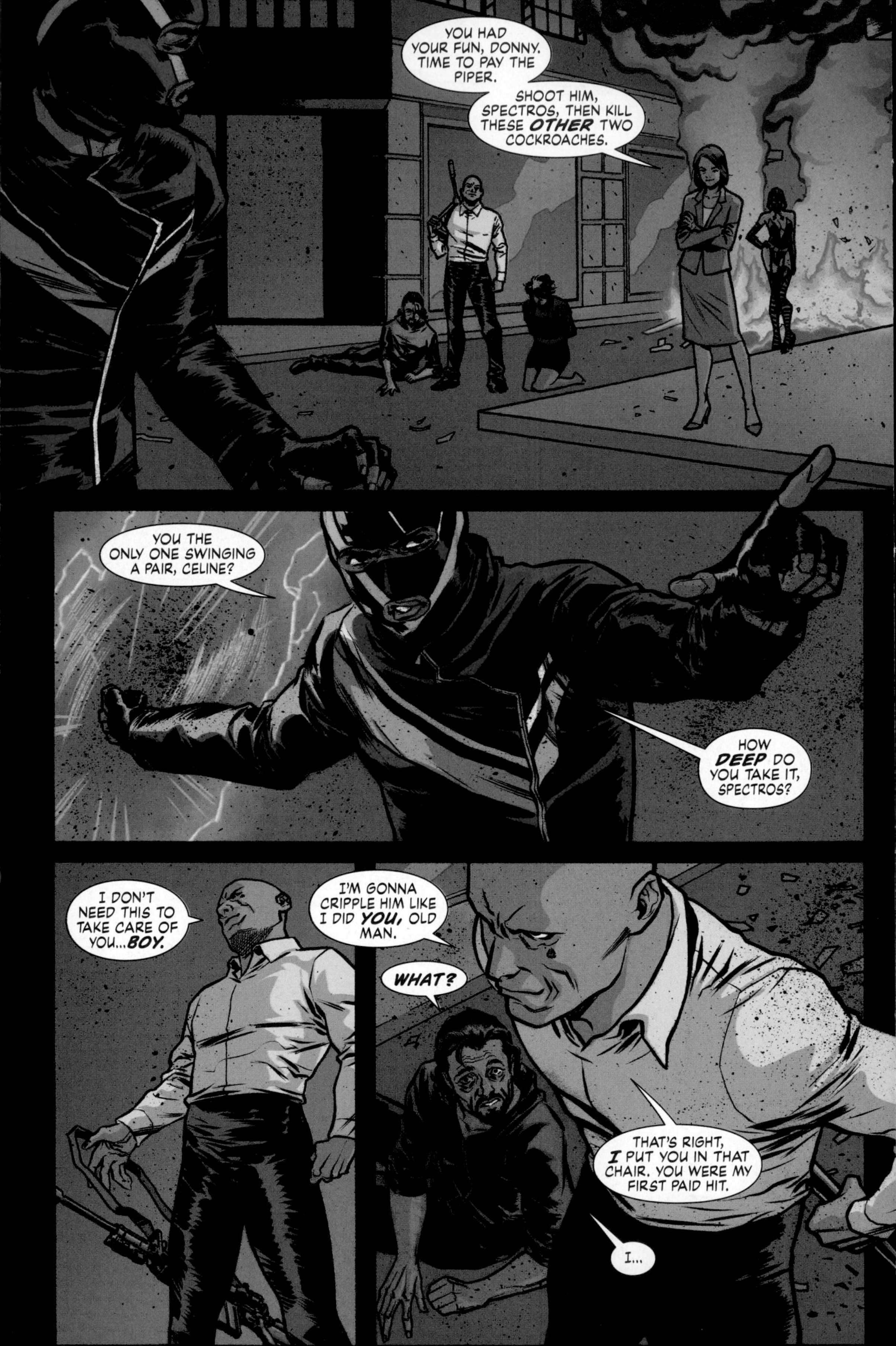
YOU HAD YOUR FUN, DONNY. TIME TO PAY THE PIPER.
SHOOT HIM, SPECTROS, THEN KILL THESE **OTHER** TWO COCKROACHES.
YOU THE ONLY ONE SWINGING A PAIR, CELINE?
HOW **DEEP** DO YOU TAKE IT, SPECTROS?
I DON'T NEED THIS TO TAKE CARE OF YOU...**BOY.**
I'M GONNA CRIPPLE HIM LIKE I DID **YOU,** OLD MAN.
WHAT?
THAT'S RIGHT, **I** PUT YOU IN THAT CHAIR. YOU WERE MY FIRST PAID HIT.
I...

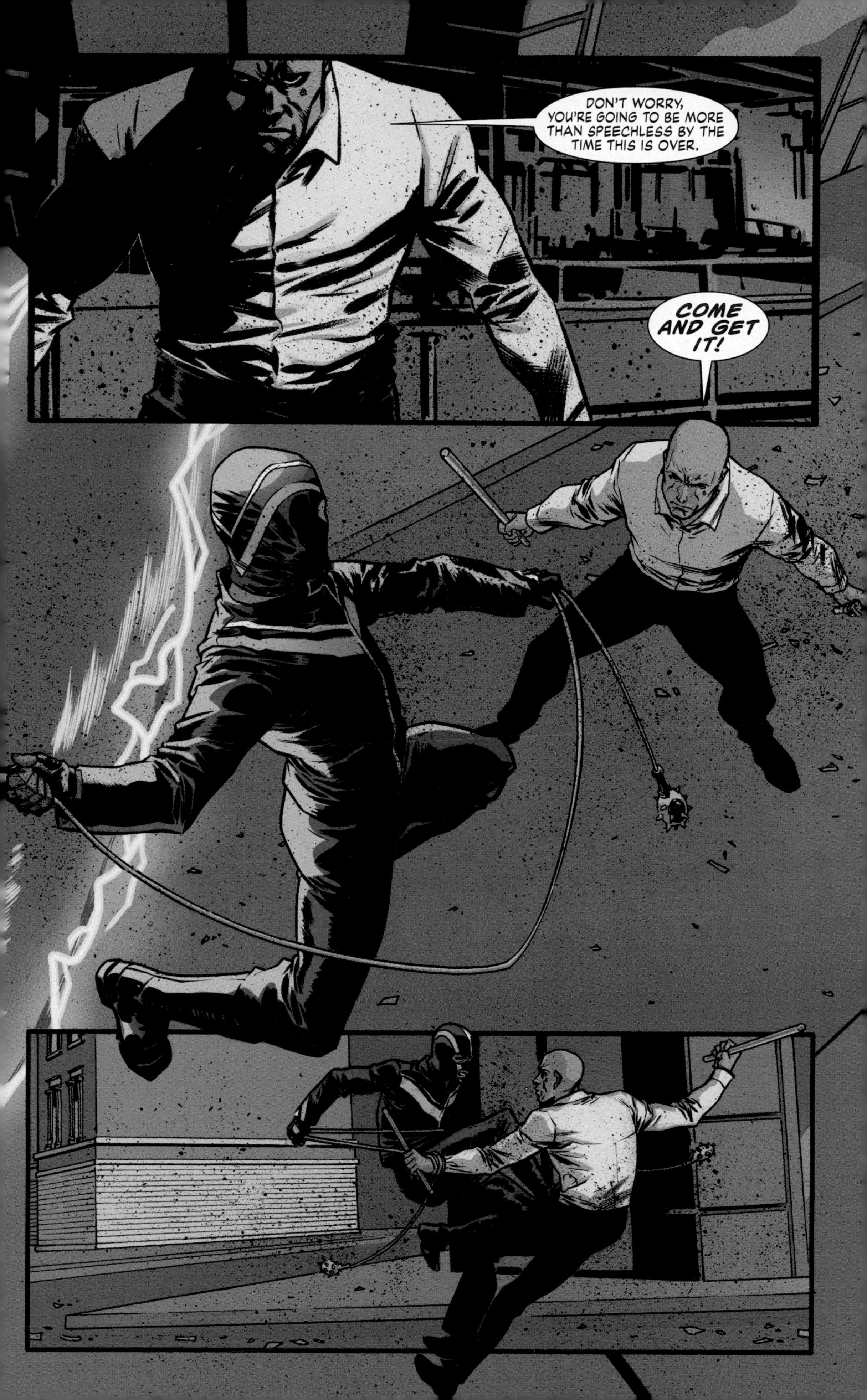
DON'T WORRY, YOU'RE GOING TO BE MORE THAN SPEECHLESS BY THE TIME THIS IS OVER.
COME AND GET IT!

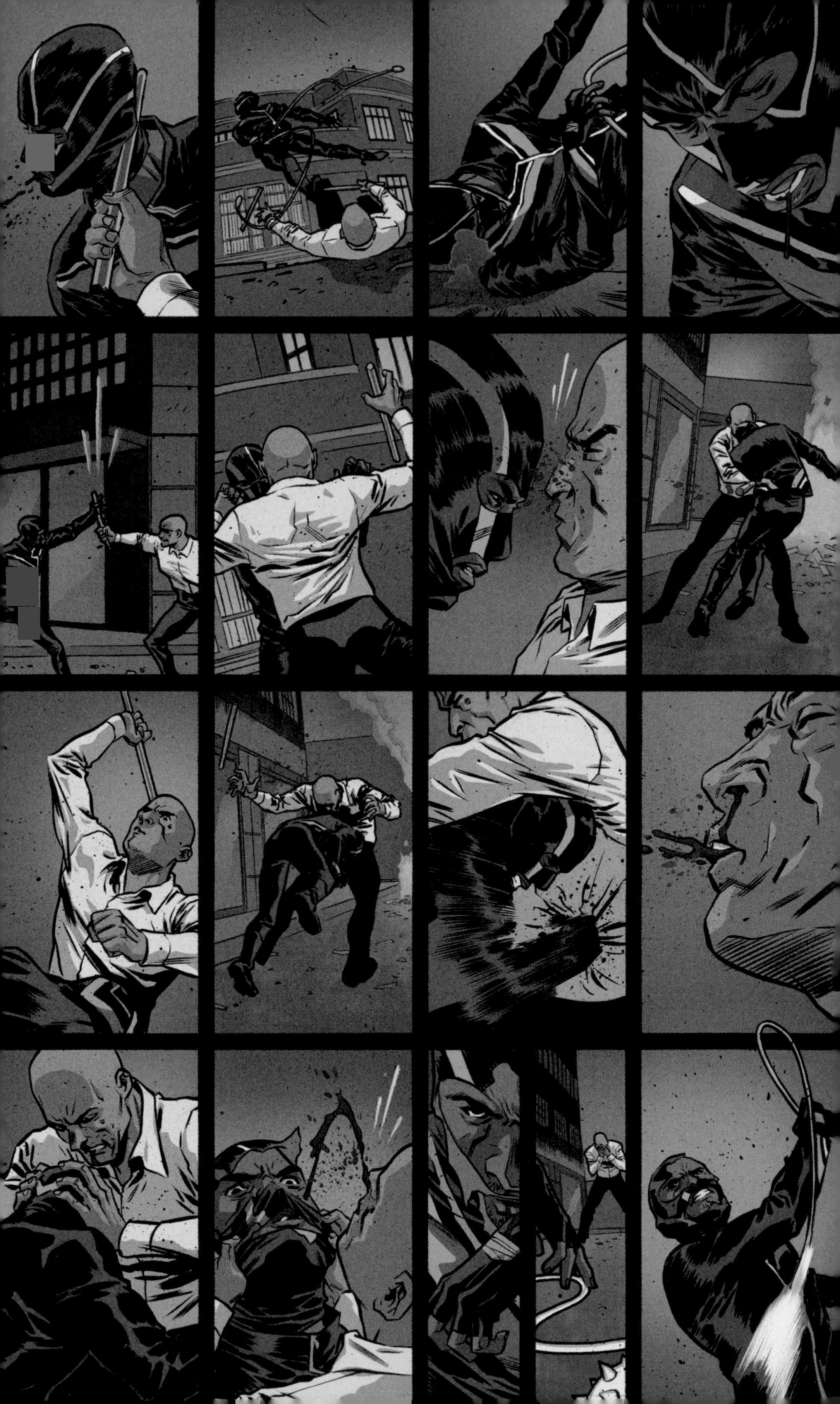

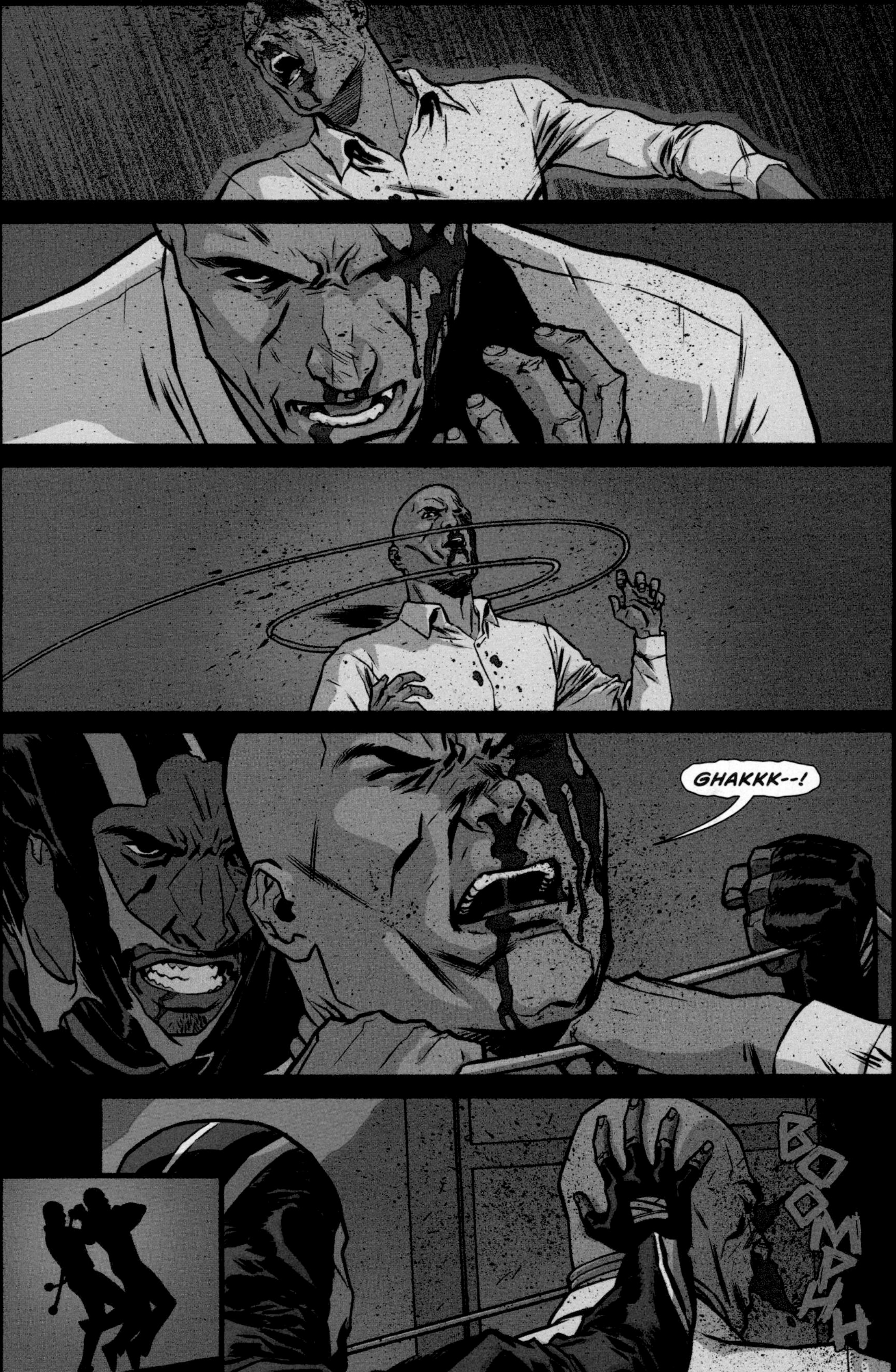
GHAKKK--!
BOOMPHH

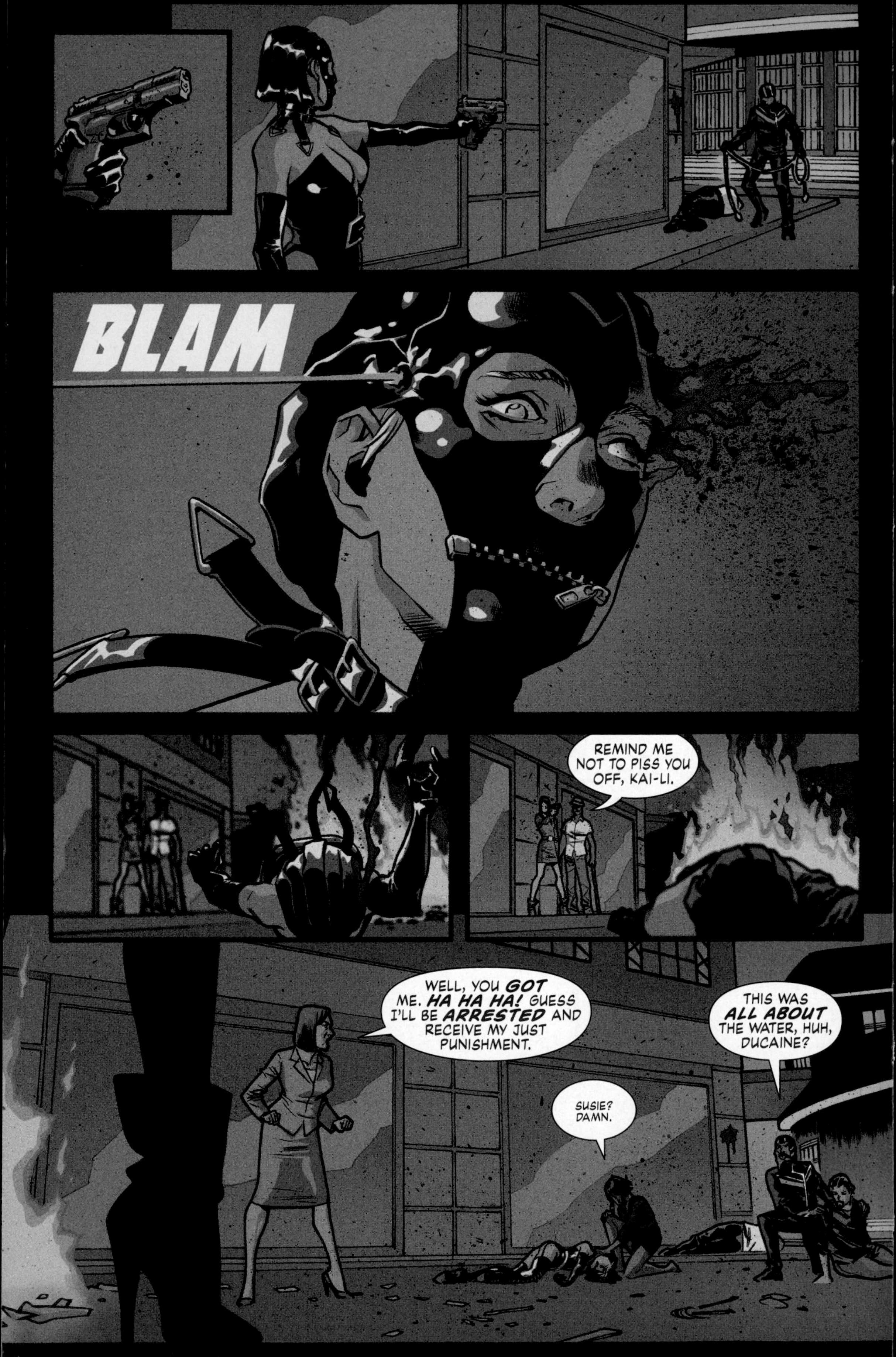
BLAM
REMIND ME NOT TO PISS YOU OFF, KAI-LI.
WELL, YOU GOT ME. HA HA HA! GUESS I'LL BE ARRESTED AND RECEIVE MY JUST PUNISHMENT.
THIS WAS ALL ABOUT THE WATER, HUH, DUCAINE?
SUSIE? DAMN.

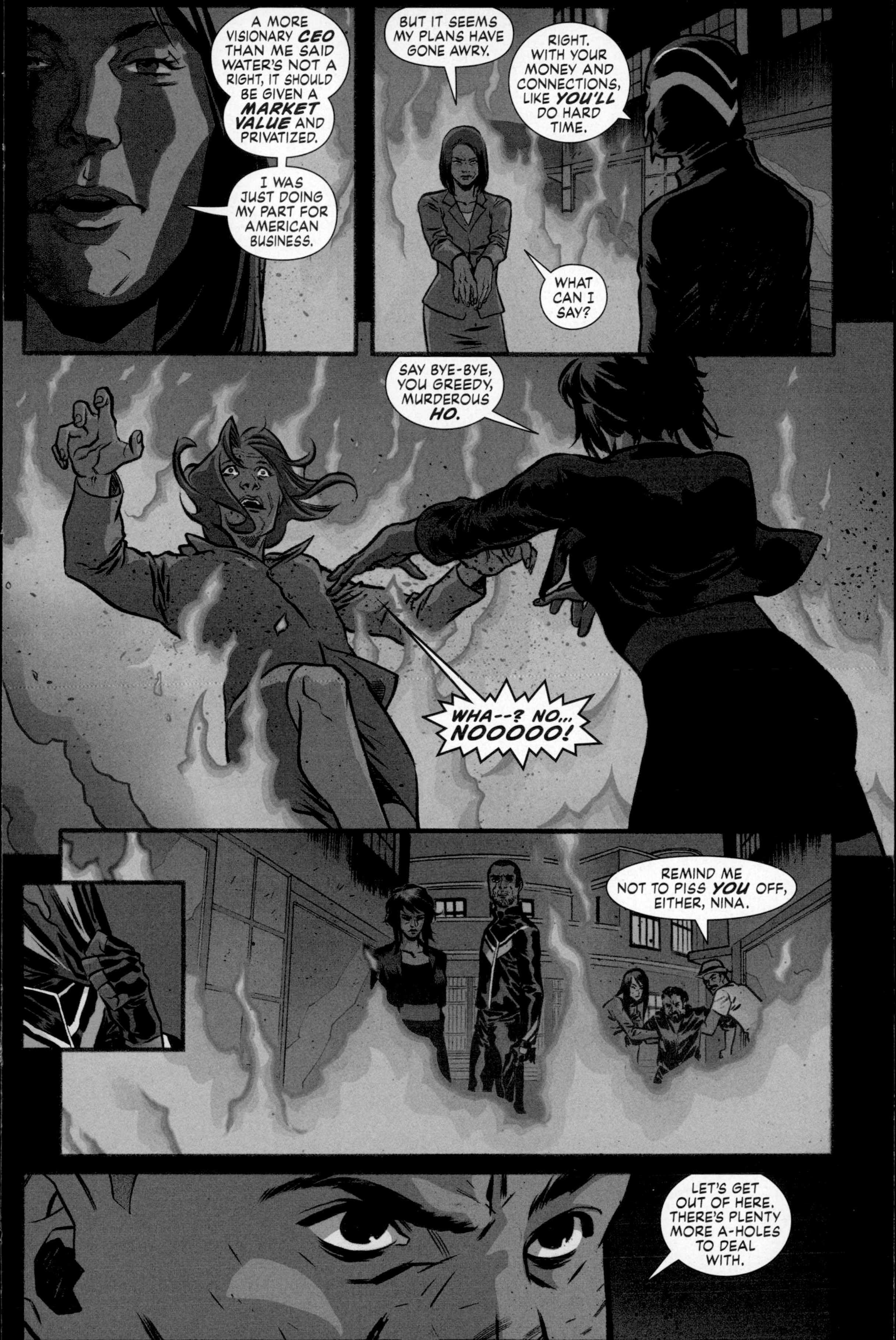
A MORE VISIONARY CEO THAN ME SAID WATER'S NOT A RIGHT, IT SHOULD BE GIVEN A MARKET VALUE AND PRIVATIZED.
I WAS JUST DOING MY PART FOR AMERICAN BUSINESS.
BUT IT SEEMS MY PLANS HAVE GONE AWRY.
RIGHT. WITH YOUR MONEY AND CONNECTIONS, LIKE YOU'LL DO HARD TIME.
WHAT CAN I SAY?
SAY BYE-BYE, YOU GREEDY, MURDEROUS HO.
WHA--? NO... NOOOOO!
REMIND ME NOT TO PISS YOU OFF, EITHER, NINA.
LET'S GET OUT OF HERE. THERE'S PLENTY MORE A-HOLES TO DEAL WITH.

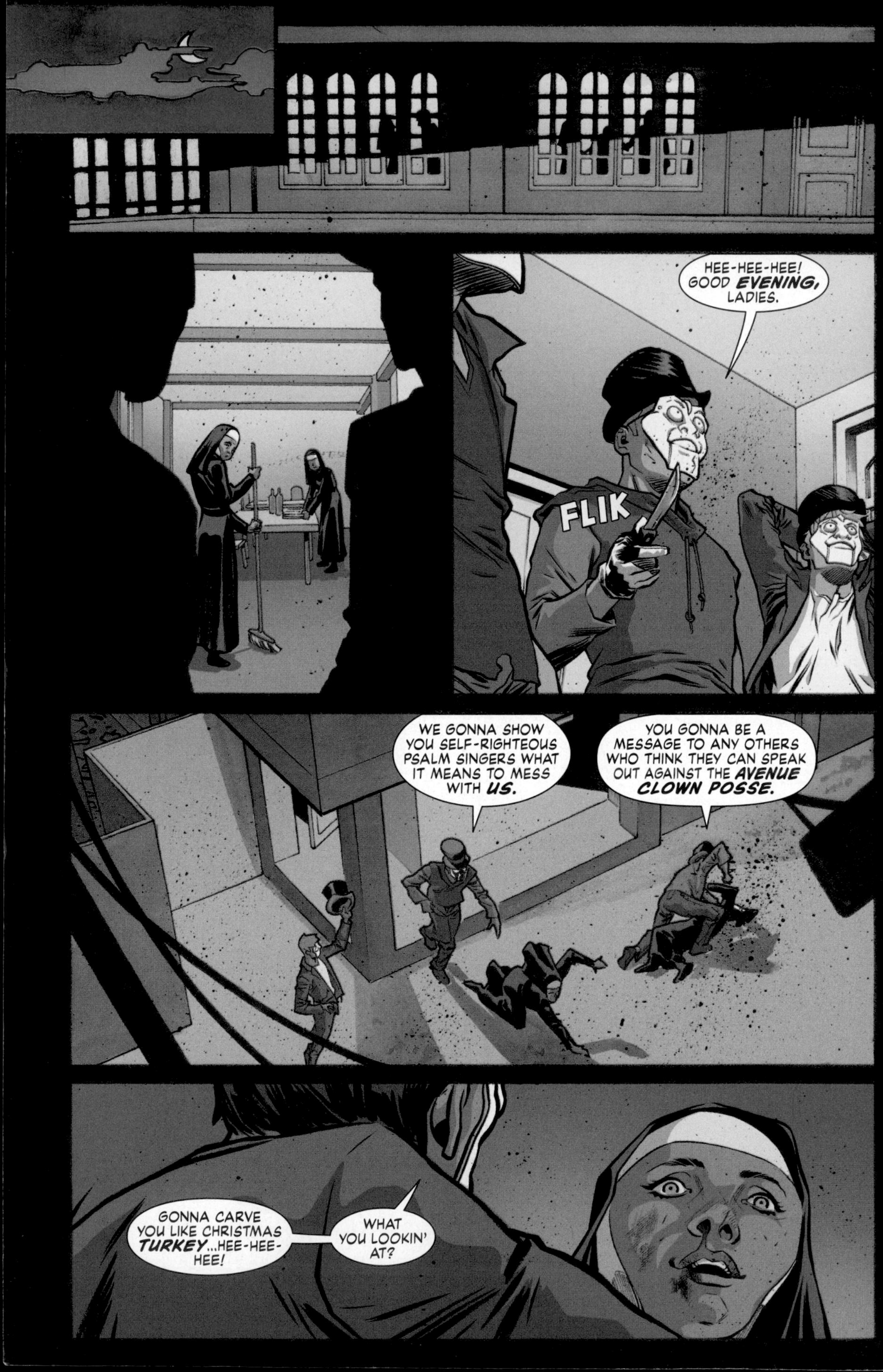
HEE-HEE-HEE! GOOD EVENING, LADIES.
FLIK
WE GONNA SHOW YOU SELF-RIGHTEOUS PSALM SINGERS WHAT IT MEANS TO MESS WITH US.
YOU GONNA BE A MESSAGE TO ANY OTHERS WHO THINK THEY CAN SPEAK OUT AGAINST THE AVENUE CLOWN POSSE.
WHAT YOU LOOKIN' AT?
GONNA CARVE YOU LIKE CHRISTMAS TURKEY...HEE-HEE-HEE!

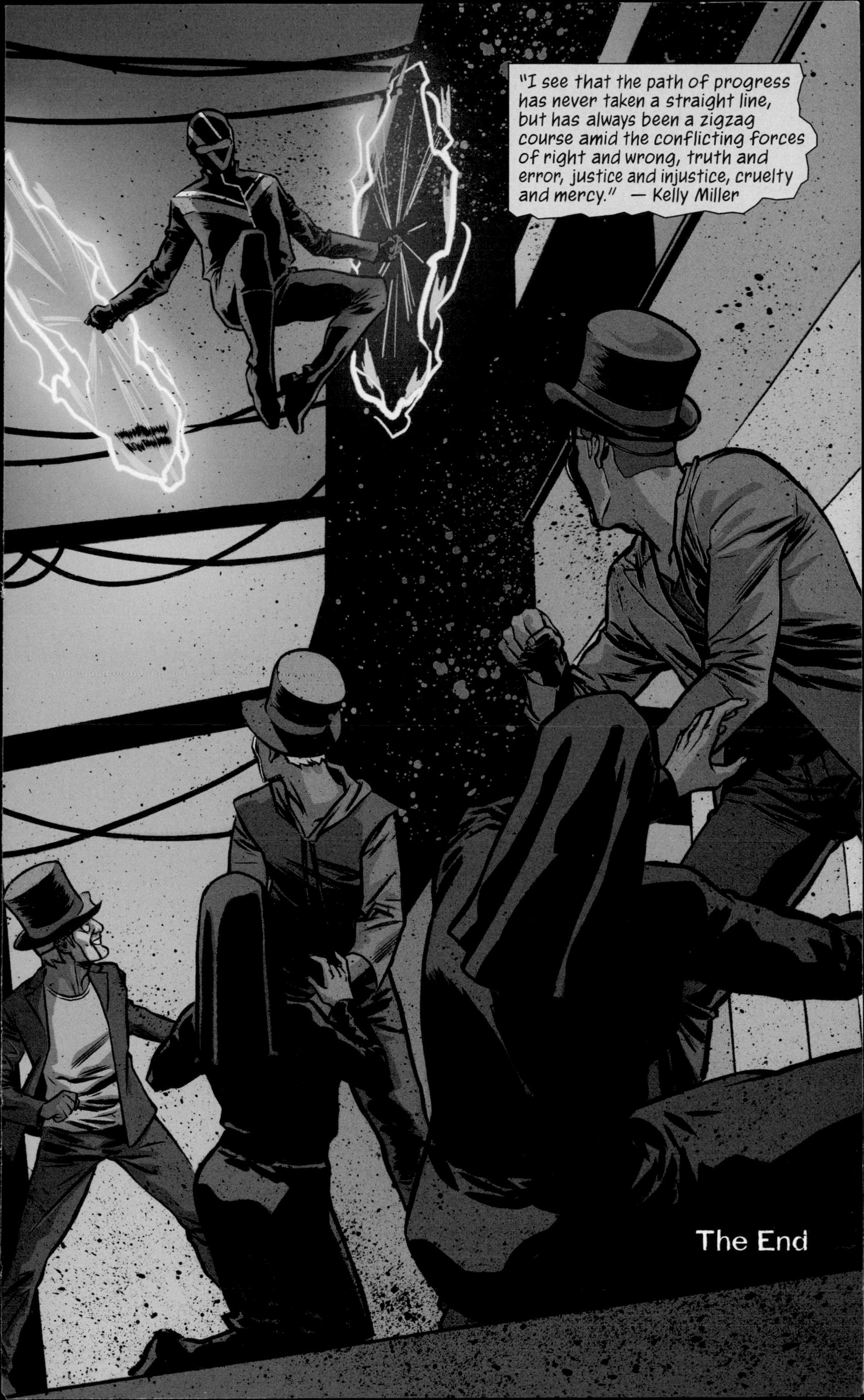
"I see that the path of progress has never taken a straight line, but has always been a zigzag course amid the conflicting forces of right and wrong, truth and error, justice and injustice, cruelty and mercy." — Kelly Miller
The End

VIGILANTE: SOUTHLAND #1 variant cover
by **Tony S. Daniel**, **Sandu Florea** and **Tomeu Morey**

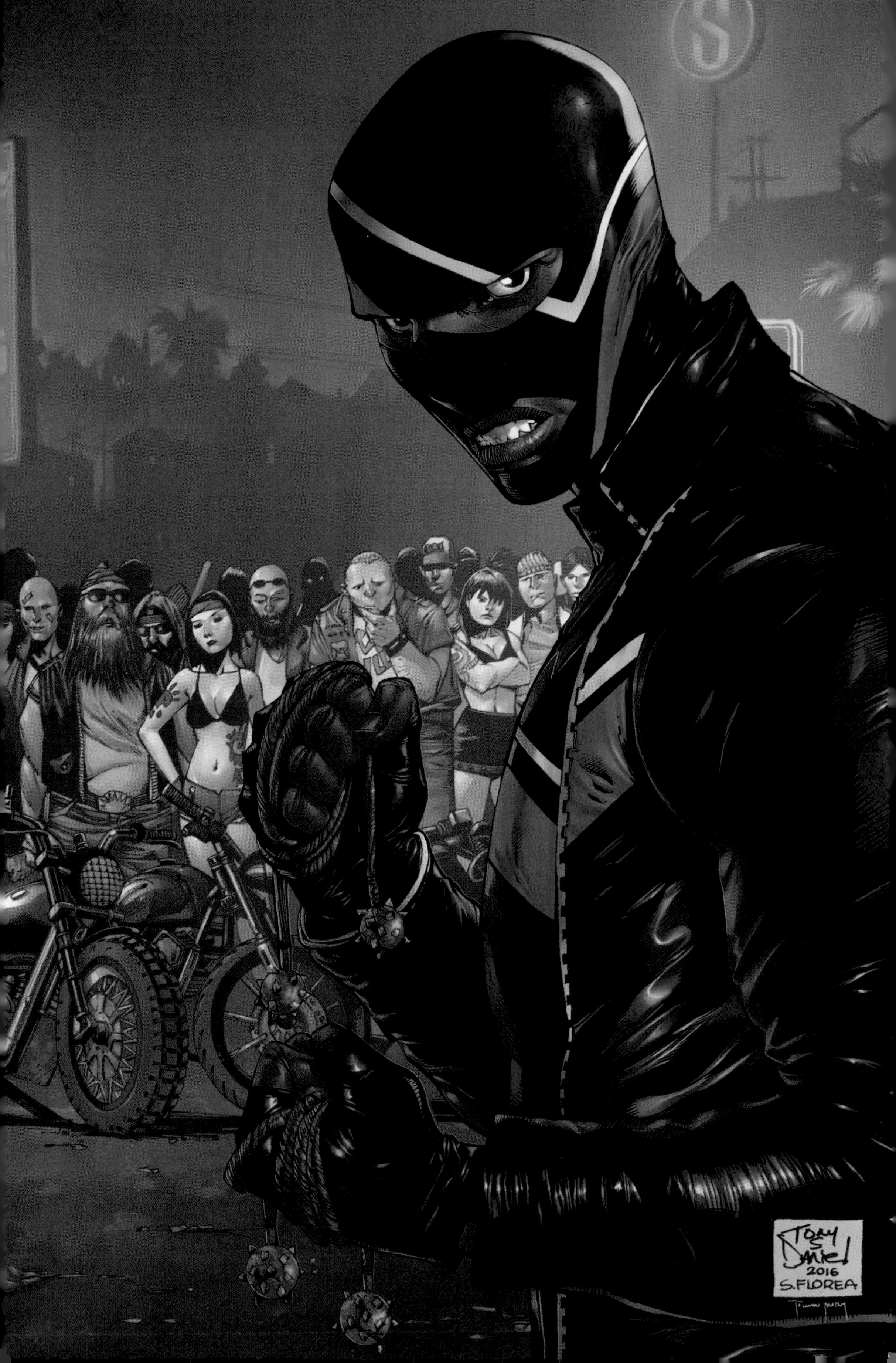
TONY S DANIEL 2016
S.FLOREA